STUDY GUIDE for

Ralph, Lerner, Meacham, Wood, Hull, and Burns
World Civilizations

Volume 1

D1412093

NINTH EDITION

by J. Michael Allen

 W • W • NORTON & COMPANY • NEW YORK • LONDON

Printed in the United States of America

ISBN 0-393-96882-0 (pbk.)

W. W. Norton & Company, Inc., 500 Fifth Avenue, New York, N.Y. 10110

http://www.wwnorton.com

W. W. Norton & Company Ltd., 10 Coptic Street, London WC1A 1PU

1 2 3 4 5 6 7 8 9 0

Contents

VOL. 1 PREFACE | To the Teacher and the Student

This edition of the *Study Guide* is designed specifically to accompany the ninth edition of *World Civilizations*. Though it incorporates material from earlier editions, it has been completely revised and updated. Every chapter has been carefully tailored to correspond to the material as it now stands in the ninth edition, including material that is new to that edition. This applies to the exercises as well as to the readings.

The purpose of this *Study Guide* is to help students master the material in *World Civilizations* and to assist teachers in initiating discussions that will both review and extend the topics covered in the textbook. The guide may also be convenient as the basis for tests. In order to approach the material in a variety of ways to pursue these objectives, each chapter of the guide is divided into several sections. Not every chapter contains every type of section, nor is every chapter the same length. This reflects both the varying lengths of chapters in the textbook, and the author's belief that the most valuable kinds of review and evaluation may vary from topic to topic. The sections into which a chapter may be divided are as follows:

Chronology. Chronological reviews are provided for many, but not all, chapters. These reviews are designed to put the information in the chapter into a broad, chronological perspective. Their value as study aids is to help students remember both specific and relative chronology; that is, in some cases dates are emphasized, whereas in other cases the order of events is more important than specific dates. In no case, however, does the chronology section include every date mentioned in the textbook chapter.

Identifications. Again, the choice of items for the identifications is selective. Identification sections might involve matching, multiple-choice questions, short answers, fill-in-the-blank questions, or a combination. Identifications may cover events, ideas, works of literature and art, people, or all four. This section is designed not only to allow rapid evalu-

ation (by either teachers or the students themselves) of students' grasp of specific information, but also to assess students' ability to understand the broader historical significance of specific items.

Study Questions. These are found in every chapter. Some of them take the form of multiple-choice questions, but generally they are the type that can be answered by an essay or in a class discussion. They can thus serve either as the basis for essay examinations or as the starting point for class discussions, in addition to providing the student with a way of assessing his or her grasp of material in the textbook. The primary distinction between the study questions and the problems that follow is that the study questions can be answered from the material in the textbook alone. Therefore, if students answer all of the study questions thoroughly, they will have a convenient, point-by-point summary of the textbook.

Problems. These are also included in all chapters. Unlike the study questions, however, they require students to move beyond the material in the textbook. Designed to stimulate students' curiosity and provoke discussion and inquiry, they must be answered on the basis of additional reading and study. In some cases, specific books (both fiction and nonfiction) are recommended. The problems can be used in a variety of ways: as the basis for class discussions, as topics for papers, or as extra reading assignments. They can also, of course, be modified to meet the needs and preferences of particular classes and individual teachers.

Map Exercises. These are included for each of the textbook's major divisions, and are taken from the maps in the textbook itself. The map exercises are based on the belief that a certain amount of geographic knowledge is essential for an understanding of the development of human societies. In the map exercises students will identify the stages on which the drama of human history has been enacted. Ideally, students will be able to visualize changes over time more easily by reference to concrete locations and features on maps. The exercises are not comprehensive: unlike the study questions, they do not provide a thorough review of all the important geographic information mentioned in the textbook. But they do require students to familiarize themselves with a certain minimal amount of information about cities, rivers, regions, empires, oceans, and other details that will enhance their understanding of the course of human history.

Readings. The readings accompanying each chapter were selected with two primary purposes in mind: to illustrate material discussed in the textbook chapter, and to provide students with the opportunity to "roll up their sleeves" and plunge directly into the stuff of historical research. It is one thing to read *about* Confucius, or the Crusades, or the framing of the American constitution; it is quite another thing to actually read from the *Analects*, or follow a speech of Pope Urban II, or delve into the *Federalist* papers. An attempt has been made to include readings that are both relevant and interesting. To further enhance the value of the readings, a few questions are provided to help tie the readings to the other material in the textbook and the guide.

In every way, this *Study Guide* is designed to enhance students' use of the textbook and their understanding of the topics presented there. This guide is not intended to limit the creativity of teachers or the inquisitiveness of students. On the contrary, it is meant to be a resource for both teachers and students, to be used in a variety of ways and incorporated into the structure of the class as appropriate.

ACKNOWLEDGMENTS

I would like to thank Jon Durbin of W. W. Norton, the point man for this project. His suggestions, patience, and insight were greatly appreciated. Steve Forman and Kate Nash, also at Norton, were most helpful with their timely responses to inquiries. My wife and children, as usual, gave up time with me so that I could spend it with maps and questions, documents and dates. My thanks to them.

CHAPTER 1 | The Earliest Beginnings

IDENTIFICATIONS

You should be able to identify the following:

paleoanthropology
the Leakey family
"Nutcracker Man"
Homo habilis
"bipedality"

Homo erectus
Homo sapiens
Neanderthal man
sympathetic magic

CHRONOLOGY

Match the development in column A with the approximate date in column B:

A	B
Bronze manufacture perfected	125,000–40,000 years ago
Emergence of modern *Homo sapiens*	4.4 million years ago
Emergence of cities in western Asia	5–7 million years ago
Earliest ancestors of humans lived in Ethiopia	1.8 million years ago
"Nutcracker Man"	6000 B.C.E.
Humans and apes separated from each other	3500–3000 B.C.E.
Stone toolmaking appears	2.5 million years ago
Homo erectus migrates from Africa	100,000 years ago
"Neanderthal man"	3500–3200 B.C.E.
Cave paintings in France and Spain	6500–3000 B.C.E.

Agriculture adopted in western Asia	30,000–12,000 years ago
Food production begins in southwestern Asia	1 million years ago
Villages are the most advanced form of human organization in western Asia	9000 B.C.E.

STUDY QUESTIONS

1. Why is a definition of history as "past politics" inadequate? What other kinds of activities can (and should) historians consider?
2. What effect have migration and racial adaptation had on the development of humans and the pattern of human habitation?
3. How have recent fossil discoveries altered our conception of human origins? According to the most recent scientific evidence, how long ago did modern humans appear?
4. Explain the evolutionary anatomical changes that led to the emergence of *Homo habilis*. What are the essential differences between the "apelike" and "manlike" categories?
5. Approximately how much time elapsed between the emergence of *Homo habilis* and the emergence of *Homo erectus*?
6. In what ways was *Homo erectus* superior to *Homo habilis*?
7. Why can the ability to use tools for food gathering be regarded as the first step toward civilization?
8. During what period, approximately, was Neanderthal man dominant in much of Europe and neighboring countries?

9. Summarize the technical and cultural advances made by Neanderthal man.
10. Between 40,000 and 30,000 years ago a significant transition occurred in the earth's human population. What was it?
11. How do you account for the magnificent cave paintings found in parts of southern France and northern Spain? What can we learn from them?
12. What impact did the vanishing of large herds (beginning about 12,000 years ago) have on the development of human civilization?
13. Identify the "momentous revolution" that occurred about 4,000–3,000 years after the end of the Ice Age, and explain why it was revolutionary.
14. What is the difference between "prehistory" and "history," and why can the latter be said to begin with the birth of civilization?
15. Trace the stages in the transition from a nomadic to an agricultural society. What role did cereals play in this transition, and in the later development of civilization?
16. Identify the most important differences between a wandering band and a village, and between a village and a city.
17. What new handicrafts arose during the age of villages?
18. Explain the following two assertions: "Settled life would have inspired ongoing warfare." "Cities existed to exploit villages."
19. What was the significance or the effect of the emergence of a priestly class in society?
20. What is the basis for claiming that by around 3200 B.C.E. Mesopotamia was "civilized"?

PROBLEMS

1. If much of the past is irrecoverable, how can an attempt to reconstruct the past help us to better understand the present?
2. On the basis of reading in such books as Christopher Dawson, *The Age of the Gods*, B. Malinowski, *Magic, Science, and Religion*, and Edward Norbeck, *Religion in Primitive Society*, describe what you consider to be the essential characteristics of primitive religion and explain its appeal for early human communities.
3. Explore further the origin of the state. Make use of such books as R. H. Lowie, *Primitive Society*, M. J. Herskovits, *Man and His Works*, and C. C. Lamberg-Karlovsky and J. Sabloff, *Ancient Civilizations*.
4. Study and explain the importance of each of the following to the rise of civilizations:
   a. The development of agriculture
   b. The development of organized religion
   c. The origin of the city
5. Read Ruth Benedict, *Patterns of Culture*, and see how many ancient peoples you can fit into her system of classification.
6. Analyze the impact of technology on the development of human civilizations. In particular, examine the difference between the adjustment of details of life and genuine technological change. Explore the impetus for each, and the effects of each.

AIDS TO AN UNDERSTANDING OF THE EARLIEST BEGINNINGS

THE SUBJECTIVE ELEMENT IN HISTORY
Bernard Lewis

There are many ways of defining and subdividing history; traditionally, by who, and when, and where; then, in a more sophisticated age, by topic—by what; and how, and, for the intellectually ambitious, why; methodologically, by types of sources and the manner of their use; ideologically, by function and purpose—of the historian more than of the history, and many others. The classification used here, as will have emerged from the above remarks, is into three types, as follows:

(1) Remembered history. This consists of statements about the past, rather than history in the strict sense, and ranges from the personal recollections claimed by the elders to the living traditions of a civilization, as embodied in its scriptures, its classics, and its inherited historiography. It may be described as the collective memory of a community or nation or other entity—what it, or its rulers and leaders, poets, and sages, choose to remember as significant, both as reality and symbol.

(2) Recovered history. This is the history of events and movements, of persons and ideas, that have been forgotten, that is to say, at some stage and for some reason rejected by the communal memory, and then, after a longer or shorter interval, recovered by academic scholarship—by the study of records, the excavation of buried cities, the decipherment of forgotten scripts and languages, and the consequent reconstruction of a forgotten past. But reconstruction begs the basic question, and disguises what would be better described as construction. The word itself indicates the dangers of the process, and leads us to the third type of history.

(3) Invented history. This is history for a purpose, a new purpose differing from previous purposes. It may be invented in ei-

ther the Latin or the English sense of the word, devised and interpreted from remembered and recovered history where feasible, and fabricated where not.

Remembered history of one kind or another is common to all human groups from the primitive tribe to the universal empire, from the tribal cult to the universal church. It embodies poetic and symbolic truth as understood by the people, even where it is inaccurate in detail, but it becomes false or is rejected as false when the desired self-image changes and the remembered past no longer corresponds to it or supports it. It is preserved in commemorative ceremonies and monuments, religious and later secular, and in the words and rituals associated with them—in pageantry and drama, song and recitation, chronicle and biography, epic and ballad and their modern equivalents, also in official celebrations, popular entertainment, and elementary education.

Recovered history is the result of the discovery and reassessment of the past by critical scholarship—basically a modern and European task. The ancients, with few exceptions, were not interested in ancient history; indeed most history, until the new curiosity of the Renaissance, was either remembered or contemporary and much of it still purposive.

The invention of history is no new invention. It is an ancient practice dating back to remote antiquity and directed to a variety of purposes. Again, it is common to all groups, ranging in type from the primitive heroic myths of nomadic tribes to Soviet official historiography or American revisionism.

Critical history begins with a dissatisfaction with memory and a desire to remedy its deficiencies. But there is more than one kind of dissatisfaction. The critical scholar may be dissatisfied with what remembered history offers him because he feels that it is inaccurate or deficient or misleading. But there are others whose dissatisfaction springs from a different cause. They would rather rewrite history not as it was, or as they have been taught that it was, but as they would prefer it to have been. For historians of this school the purpose of changing the past is not to seek some abstract truth, but to achieve a new vision of the past better suited to their needs in the present and their aspirations for the future. Their aim is to amend, to restate, to replace, or even to recreate the past in a more satisfactory form. Here we may recall two of the main purposes of remembering the past, for communities as for individuals. One is to explain and perhaps to justify the present—a present, some present—on which there may be dispute. Where there are conflicting loyalties or clashing interests, each will have its own version of the past, its own presentation of the salient events. As Dr. Plumb has remarked, "Warring authorities means warring pasts." It is such situations which lead and have led, from immemorial antiquity, to the invention of the past, that is, to the improvement of memory.

A second use of the past, from very early times, has been to predict and even to control the future. This is manifested in the oracle-bones of ancient China, the omen tablets of Babylon, the messianic tracts of the Jews, Christians, and Muslims, Nostradamus, Old Moore's Almanac, and the Marxist-Leninist classics of modern Communism. They are all equally reliable.

Invention is of several types, and has several functions. Broadly, its aim is to embellish—to correct or remove what is distasteful in the past, and replace it with something more acceptable, more encouraging, and more conducive to the purpose in hand. It may be spontaneous, as in the heroic sagas, romantic, as in a good deal of 19th- and 20th-century writing, or officially sponsored and even imposed.

Much of it is literary, and continues or imitates the tradition of the old heroic poems. The famous Portuguese epic, the Lusiads of Camoens, though derivative and neo-classical in form, deals with contemporary events and presents an idealized version of the great Portuguese discoveries and conquests, in which the poet himself was a proud participant. The events in Palestine in 1929 and in Kashmir in 1947 have been described in Arabic and Pathan war-songs, in the true heroic style; in a different key, the American opening of the West and conquest of the Indian have been similarly celebrated in legend and balladry, in the whole neo-epical and pseudo-epical cycles of cowboy and Indian stories, in song and verse, fiction and film. Through these, as well as through schoolbooks and children's literature, they occupy a place in American corporate self-awareness comparable with the heroic memories of Greece and the imperial consciousness of Rome. Of late there has been some revulsion from the traditional self-congratulatory view of the conquest of the American West, but it still falls far short of the change which took place in the Mexican view of the past, when, as part of their revolution, they began to distinguish between their Hispanic and Indian heritages and to identify themselves more and more with the latter. The European visitor to the United States and to Mexico cannot but be struck by the contrast between the attitudes of the two to the Indians. While Americans speak, with guilt or otherwise, of "what we did to the Indians," Mexicans, even of pure European descent, speak of "what the Spaniards did to us." The contrast is driven home in the vast historical murals painted by Diego Rivera for the Palacio Nacional in Mexico City.

It is not for nothing that a Soviet historian once remarked that the most difficult of a historian's tasks is to predict the past.

From Bernard Lewis, *History Remembered, Recovered, Invented*, pp. 11–69. Copyright © 1975 by Princeton University Press. Reprinted by permission of the publisher.

THE MIND OF PRELITERATE MAN
Franz Boas

The difference in the mode of thought of primitive man and that of civilized man seems to consist largely in the difference of character of the traditional material with which the new perception associates itself. The instruction given to the child of primitive man is not based on centuries of experimentation, but consists of the crude experience of generations. When a new experience enters the mind of primitive man, the same process which we observe among civilized man brings about an entirely different series of associations, and therefore results in a different type of explanation. A sudden explosion will associate itself in his mind, perhaps, with tales which he has heard in regard to the mythical history of the world, and consequently will be accompanied by superstitious fear. The new, unknown epidemic may be explained by the belief in demons that persecute mankind; and the existing world may be explained as the result of transformations, or by objectivation of the thoughts of a creator.

When we recognize that neither among civilized nor among primitive men the average individual carries to completion the attempt at causal explanation of phenomena, but only so far as to amalgamate it with other previous knowledge, we recognize that the result of the whole process depends entirely upon the character of the traditional material. Herein lies the immense importance of folk-lore in determining the mode of thought. Herein lies particularly the enormous influence of current philosophic opinion upon the masses of the people, and the influence of the dominant scientific theory upon the character of scientific work.

It would be vain to try to understand the development of modern science without an intelligent understanding of modern philosophy; it would be vain to try to understand the history of medieval science without a knowledge of medieval theology; and so it is vain to try to understand primitive science without an intelligent knowledge of primitive mythology. "Mythology," "theology" and "philosophy" are different terms for the same influences which shape the current of human thought, and which determine the character of the attempts of man to explain the phenomena of nature. To primitive man—who has been taught to consider the heavenly orbs as animate beings; who sees in every animal a being more powerful than man; to whom the mountains, trees and stones are endowed with life or with special virtues—explanations of phenomena will suggest themselves entirely different from those to which we are accustomed, since we still base our conclusions upon the existence of matter and force as bringing about the observed results.

From Franz Boas, *The Mind of Primitive Man*, The Macmillan Company, 1938. Selection reprinted by permission of the publisher.

HUMAN SOCIETY AND HUMAN NATURE
Eli Sagan

When we look closely at primitive societies, there seems to be nothing in their economic, political, or social (kinship) systems that produces the kind of "internal contradictions," as Marx would have it, that demand radical changes. In regard to economic viability, recent research has demonstrated the remarkable capacity of primitive cultures to provide themselves with daily necessities. True, there were periods of extreme drought or severe damage to herds by disease but all societies have suffered from such disruptions in nature. The myth of primitive man's fighting a daily battle against the constant threat of starvation and losing that struggle with great frequency no longer has any validity. We have even discovered that the Bushmen of the Kalahari Desert in Africa, the most hostile of environments, who were supposedly living the most marginal of existences, spend at most 60 percent of their days in the hunting and gathering of food. They can even afford the luxury of having the men spend all their productive time in hunting, which provides no more than 25 percent of the total

caloric intake of the band. Such, and similar, information has led Marshall Sahlins to declare half-ironically that hunters and gatherers were "the original affluent society." It seems clear that the threat of starvation did not launch human society on the path that eventually led to complex monarchies.

Similarly, in regard to matters touching on the social system and politics, the unmistakable impression one gains from acquaintanceship with the data on primitive societies is the profound *stability* of the systems. Nothing, for instance, that we know of the Nuer or of Australian tribes indicates that, left alone, they would not stay essentially as they are for a million years. No writer on the origins of the state that I know of has suggested any irreconcilable contradictions in the politics or social life of primitive society that would force a developmental advance. The most that is offered theoretically is that the possibilities of economic surplus are seized upon by a few people who produce political oppression and the state. What in the nature of primitive society makes this last development possible, how an egalitarian society provides the beginnings of tyranny, no one, to my knowledge, has truly explained. No one has answered the great question of what there is in the nature of the kinship system that could make the kinship system untenable.

Primitive society maintains itself only by repressing a profound human drive to separate and individuate. It becomes thereby to a significant extent alien to the human condition. That this alienation can maintain itself in a more or less permanent state cannot be denied, but there is nevertheless a profound contradiction within the kinship system produced by its denial of a basic drive. The situation is potentially explosive, though the explosion in most primitive societies never came. Why it occurred when it did, why certain primitive cultures began the transformation into complex society and others did not—such questions cannot as yet be answered.

What seems plausible is that the great contradiction, the severe tension, in primitive society was not economic, political, or social, but psychological. The energy that drives the whole history of the world is the force of the psyche struggling to fulfill its developmental destiny. That struggle is essentially an internal one against the energy of repression. The two great elements of developmental drive and repression, at eternal war with each other, dominate political life now as much as in the days when the first lonely chief emerged out of the kinship-system world. Our understanding of our present situation could be greatly enhanced if we would consider two questions about our society: What human drives and needs does it satisfy? And what needs and drives does it repress? We live at the intersection of those two questions.

From Eli Sagan, *At the Dawn of Tyranny*, pp. 381–83. © 1985 by Alfred A. Knopf.

HISTORY, HISTORIOGRAPHY, AND FABLE
Baruch Halpern

The word *history* is like a secret set of homonyms. Distinguishing them through different spellings, such as pear and pair, might help. But the lack of differentiation in the term actually reflects a lack of differentiation in popular reflection on the subject. The average schoolchild, once taxed, recognizes a difference between history as event and history as a description of event. But the finer distinctions among the types of history—and among their functions (mythic charter, and so on)—are not so self-evident.

Except insofar as they trench on the critiques of the confessionalists, negative fundamentalists, Pyrrhonists, and social scientists, the varieties of history are not material here. It must be remembered, however, that history as a program or endeavor (for simplicity's sake, we may exclude history as human events past) involves three stages, the first two dialectically related: the identification of evidence, the interpretation of evidence, and the presentation of a reconstruction from the evidence. One must take care not to apply arguments concerning one stage to the others. The literary critics, for example, focus primarily on the presentation, implying that reconstruction and presentation are identical. But reconstruction is a stage unto itself, entailing various operations, from the most local to the most general levels of problem-solving.

History produces histories, from broad, not too detailed textbooks (for example, *The History of Modern Europe*) to short notes in obscure journals about the date of a battle or of a battle-ax. In common parlance, however, history is the undertaking of rendering an account of a particular, significant, and coherent sequence of past human events. This delimits the genres of historiography—or history-writing—fairly narrowly. Thus an accounts book is not a history, in that it involves neither research into the past nor an attempt to make the past coherent. Similarly, a chronicle, or a list of events without any necessary connections among them, does not constitute a history as the term is conventionally understood: the sequence lacks coherence and particularity by definition. Nevertheless, in common with such texts, histories purport to be true, or probable, representations of events and relationships in the past. They make this claim as to particular allegations: the people they describe, the significant actions they describe, are historical, authentic.

This definition of historiography means that it always has a subject: it can be about one thing, and ignore other things; but it must always be *about something* (some sequence of events or set of relationships). In the ancient Near East, Assyrian royal inscriptions are historiography about the king's building and military accomplishments—they are concatenations of snippets about individual campaigns and public works projects. Often found in works of dedication, they never expose royal political or strategic programs, or the real politics of a governor's appointment here, a priesthood's there, and so on. Yet these texts contain historiography. Their subject is the king's service to nation and god, or the divine blessings for which the king is grateful, or the events to which the dedication is in theory a response (such as the completion of a temple).

This limitation is not crucial. Historiography cannot—and should not—be infinitely detailed. All history is at best an abridgment—better or worse—of an originally fuller reality. Can one write a history of the American Revolution that follows every individual affected through a period even of twenty years? That traces crop yields and profits on every farm and in every firm in the New World and in Britain? That relates the tortured politics, economics, and logistics of French and Spanish involvement in the New World? Who would have the time or zeal to read the result? Does a textbook cover the history of the United States, or only selected economic, or social, or political aspects of it? What this textbook suppresses from the most detailed professional studies is nothing to the omissions that they all share. History is always the study of one thing, or of several things, and the exclusion of many others. Until history is brought down to the level of physical particles, until it reduces the past to beta particles and midget misuns, "as it really was," it can represent nothing more than a selective approximation. History, in sum, is a literally false but scientifically more or less useful coherence imposed by reason on reality. An infinity of sculptures lurk inside the ghostly marble of the past; only the unfashioned stone will ever be complete.

It follows that historiography need not be comprehensively accurate in order to be historiography: much can be omitted; indeed, most events must be. History is not how things happened, but an incomplete account, written toward a specific end, of selected developments. Yet normally we would say that if the author does not *mean* to be accurate in representing the past ("as it really was"), if the author does not try to get the events right and to arrange them in the right proportion, the result cannot be history.

This is an important point, ignored in the survey of Near Eastern historiography previously mentioned. It is most easily illuminated through concrete illustration. Imagine the extreme case of a history of England in which there is no Tudor accession, no break with the Roman church, no rise of a middle class, no exploration on the seas, and no war with Spain: England continues Plantagenet, Catholic, medieval, and insular until the Long Parliament.

From our vantage point, such a work would share much in common with those novels, produced in the first decades of this century, that portray a world after a German victory in World War I. But under what circumstance would our book be historiography? Only if the author knew no better—if the author had no evidence of the Tudors. If this condition does not obtain, our book on England is plainly not historiography. If the author, for example, attempts knowingly to perpetrate on the reader a fraudulent reconstruction contradicted or unsupported by evidence, then the author is not engaged in writing history. Quite the opposite: the author is attempting to fob off as history a text known to be something else.

Whether a text is a history, then, depends on what its author meant to do. Consider this: when Edgar Rice Burroughs writes a book, such as *A Princess of Mars*, about inhabitants of another planet, we entertain no doubt as to its character. Yet it is as possible, historically, as the story of a known person, say Talleyrand, in a populated city in a real epoch. When Alan Grant, Josephine Tey's fictional detective, assembles the revisionist case for rehabilitating Richard III, never for a moment does the reader hesitate to distinguish the historical, evidential claims from the fictional. As readers, we identify what is historiography and what is not based on our perception of the author's *relationship to the evidence*.

It is a function of this relationship to the evidence that an untutored reader may, like the author ignorant of Henry VII, fall into confusion. In 1985, the governor of New York titillated the American press by celebrating publicly a "great American," Miss Jane Pittman. The governor had "misread" a television movie about this fictional character as a (fictionalized) biography of a historical character. Lacking an adequate acquaintance with the personalities of American social history, he was incapable of assessing what parts of the film dramatized reconstructed events, and what parts dramatized the scriptwriters' fancy: he could not draw the line between the movie and historiography. The line, then, falls not between history and fiction—all history is fictional, imaginative, as the literary critics say. The distinction is between history and romance, or fable; it is a distinction in authorial intention, in the author's adherence to sources.

From Baruch Halpern, *The First Historians*, pp. 6–8. © 1988 by Harper & Row Publishers, Inc.

ANALYSIS AND INTERPRETATION OF THE READINGS

1. What uses are made of the past in each of the three types of history identified by Bernard Lewis? Is there any way in which any one of these types of history is more legitimate than the others? Why or why not?
2. According to Franz Boas, what is the relationship between experience and explanation? How does this help us understand the "mythology" of early societies, and the "theology" or "philosophy" of later societies?
3. According to Eli Sagan, what basic aspect of human nature is contradicted by the development of primitive society?
4. How does Baruch Halpern account for, and justify, the fact that the writing of history is never "comprehensively accurate"?

| # Mesopotamian Civilization

CHRONOLOGY

Write in the blank next to each epoch or item the correct dates (or approximations) selected from the list below. All dates are B.C.E.

1792–1750	c. 3200
3200–2000	c. 2000–c. 1600
705–681	539
1450–1300	1300–612

Sumerian era _____

Period of Assyrian ascendancy _____

Fall of Babylon to the Persians _____

Reign of Sennacherib _____

Old Babylonian era _____

Reign of Hammurabi _____

Height of Hittite power _____

Beginning of wheeled transportation _____

IDENTIFICATIONS

Below are a number of items with which you should be familiar after reading Chapter 2. In each blank write the term described. It may be an individual, a people, a place, or a thing.

1. Akkadian warrior, called "the Great," who conquered Sumeria

_____

2. Most advanced in astronomy of all ancient Mesopotamian peoples

_____

3. Southernmost part of Mesopotamia, and for centuries its most advanced region

_____

4. Most militaristic people of ancient Mesopotamia

_____

5. First people to learn the processes of multiplication and division and the extraction of square and cube roots

_____

6. New Babylonian king who conquered Jerusalem

_____

7. Assyrian king memorable for his large library at Nineveh

_____

8. People who invented the lunar calendar

_____

9. Major Babylonian contribution to world literature

_____

10. Sumerian terraced tower surmounted by a shrine

_____

11. Wedge-shaped writing on clay tablets

_____

12. Babylonian promulgator of a famous ancient legal code

_____

You should also be able to identify the following:

salinization	Indo-European language group
Semitic language group	Kassites
Amorites	Medes
"King of Justice"	"Hanging Gardens"
duodecimal system	

STUDY QUESTIONS

1. What is the justification for the assertion that "history begins at Sumer"?
2. What is the basis for the claim that Mesopotamia was the first civilized territory on earth?
3. Identify the three major Sumerian contributions to the course of civilization.
4. Why was the development of a calendar essential to the flourishing of civilization in Mesopotamia?
5. Trace the steps in the development of writing by the Sumerians.
6. Show how religious concepts evolved from the Sumerians through the Old Babylonians to the Chaldeans.
7. Describe the characteristics of Sumerian temple architecture. What purposes other than religious did the temple serve?
8. What classes comprised Sumerian society? How free were the "free farmers"?
9. What were the causes of the Sumerian economic decline around 2000 B.C.E.?
10. What were the two chief differences between the cultures of the Sumerian and the Old Babylonian eras?
11. Describe the character of justice embodied in the Code of Hammurabi. To whom did the term "man" apply in the code?
12. How do you account for the seemingly unfair provisions of Hammurabi's Code? What is the lasting importance of this ancient document?
13. What philosophical or dictatorial principles are embodied in the Gilgamesh epic?
14. What changes in religion came under the Old Babylonians? Explain the difference between "political gods" and "personal gods."
15. Explain the following statement: "The Old Babylonians were the most accomplished arithmeticians in antiquity."
16. What superior military techniques were used by the Kassites and the Hittites?
17. Why was the discovery of ancient Hittite civilization important? What early misjudgments were made about it?
18. How important was the use of iron for the Hittites?
19. Point out the distinctive features of Assyrian civilization at its height. To what extent were the Assyrians indebted to earlier Mesopotamian cultures?
20. What part did "frightfulness" play in Assyrian society and government policy? How did this affect the Assyrians' ultimate fate?
21. Describe the city of Babylon under the New Babylonians.
22. How do you account for the development of astrology by the New Babylonians? What were some of the valuable by-products of the development of this pseudoscience?
23. Why were the Hebrews heavily indebted to Mesopotamian civilization?

PROBLEMS

1. Read the first five chapters of the Book of Daniel in the Old Testament and comment on the picture you derive of Nebuchadnezzar and the Chaldeans. Why were Daniel's gifts so peculiarly appealing to his captors?
2. Ancient Mesopotamian civilization produced a number of remarkable contributions to civilization. Explore the reasons why so many groundbreaking advancements came from one civilization, and trace the effects of those contributions.
3. What lessons do you think modern nations might draw from the history of the Mesopotamian peoples?
4. Compare the premises underlying the Code of Hammurabi with those underlying law codes from several countries today. Consider both differences and similarities.
5. Trace the growth of Assyria from a small independent state to a great empire.
6. Study the forms of Assyrian art and evaluate its quality.
7. Compare the mathematical achievements of the Mesopotamians with those of the ancient Greeks.
8. Read the epic of *Gilgamesh* to discover what light it throws upon Babylonian culture and value judgments. What are the major themes found in this work of literature?
9. What can we learn about the process of historical discovery and interpretation from the early misconceptions about ancient Hittite and other early civilizations? Examine the ways in which our understanding of ancient civilizations has changed over time.

AIDS TO AN UNDERSTANDING OF MESOPOTAMIAN CIVILIZATION

THE CODE OF HAMMURABI: Sundry Enactments

If a son strike his father, they shall cut off his fingers.

If a man destroy the eye of another man, they shall destroy his eye.

If one break a man's bone, they shall break his bone.

If one destroy the eye of a freeman or break the bone of a freeman, he shall pay one mana of silver.

If one destroy the eye of a man's slave or break a bone of a man's slave he shall pay one-half his price.

If a man knock out a tooth of a man of his own rank, they shall knock out his tooth.

If one knock out a tooth of a freeman, he shall pay one-third mana of silver.

If a man strike the person of a man . . . who is his superior, he shall receive sixty strokes with an ox-tail whip in public.

If a man strike another man of his own rank, he shall pay one mana of silver. . . .

If a man strike another man in a quarrel and wound him, he shall swear: "I struck him without intent," and he shall be responsible for the physician. . . .

If a physician operate on a man for a severe wound . . . with a bronze lancet and save the man's life; or if he open an abscess . . . of a man with a bronze lancet and save that man's eye, he shall receive ten shekels of silver. . . .

If he be a freeman, he shall receive five shekels.

If it be a man's slave, the owner of the slave shall give two shekels of silver to the physician.

If a physician operate on a man for a severe wound with a bronze lancet and cause the man's death; or open an abscess . . . of a man with a bronze lancet and destroy the man's eye, they shall cut off his fingers.

If a physician operate on a slave of a freeman for a severe wound with a bronze lancet and cause his death, he shall restore a slave of equal value. . . .

If a builder build a house for a man and do not make its construction firm and the house which he has built collapse and cause the death of the owner of the house, that builder shall be put to death.

From R. F. Harper, *The Code of Hammurabi, King of Babylon.*

THE SOCIAL ORDER IN ASSYRIA: *As Revealed in Letters*

In the two following letters we see officials taking an oath, and can observe the hierarchical structure of official society, while the second letter stresses the importance attached to this particular ceremony.

(1) 'To the king my lord, from his servant Ishtar-shum-eresh. Health to the king my lord, and may Nabu and Marduk bless him. The scribes, the diviners, the magicians, the doctors, the observers of the flight of birds, the palace officials who dwell in the city have taken an oath to the gods on the sixteenth day of Nisan: now they can take an oath to the king.'

(2) 'To the king my master from his servant Kaptia. Health to the king my master. Regarding the matter of the oaths of Babylon about which the king wrote to me, I was not present, for the king's letter only reached me after I and my brothers had left for the country of Arashi on a tour of inspection, and I could not reach Babylon in time for the taking of the oaths. On my journey I met the great chamberlain of the palace. When he had led me to Uruk in the presence of your gods, I should have been able to receive the oaths sworn to the king my master. But I had not full confidence in these oaths sworn privately, and I thought: "Let the soldiers with their sons, and their wives as well as their gods, swear the oaths which are due to the king: but I will accept them according to the formula laid down in the letter from the king, when the Elders shall come to swear their oaths to the king my lord."

Finally, here is an astonishing letter from some high official, whose name we do not know, to King Sennacherib, who had reversed the laws governing the succession by nominating his favourite younger son Ashurbanipal to the throne of Assyria, and his elder son to the throne of Babylon.

'What had never been done even in heaven, the king, my lord, hath brought to pass on earth, and hath made us witnesses of it. Thou hast robed one of thy sons in the royal robes and hast named him as ruler of Assyria, and hast named thy elder son to succeed to the throne of Babylon. What the king my lord hath done for his son is not for the good of Assyria. Surely, O King, Ashur hath granted thee power, from the rising to the setting of the sun, and, as touches thy dear children, thy heart may well be content. None the less, the lord my king has conceived an evil plan, and thou hast therein been weak . . .'

Compare this with the following letter from a citizen of Babylon who had come to lay his complaints before the king and had rapidly been dismissed from the royal presence.

'I am as a dead man, I am faint after the sight of the king my master. When I see the countenance of the king my master, I begin again to live, and, though I am still hungered. I am as though refreshed. When last I was granted an audience of the king, I was overcome with fear, and I could not find words to utter . . .'

This terror of royalty is indeed far removed from the other respectful but undaunted reminder of duly established law. We may well feel baffled by the Assyrian court with its strange mixture of servility and frankness towards the person of the king, which is so marked a feature of the ancient East.

From Georges Contenau. *Everyday Life in Babylon and Assyria*, St. Martin's Press, 1954. Reprinted by permission of the publisher.

ETHICAL CONCEPTS IN THE SUMERIAN RELIGION
S. N. Kramer

The gods preferred the ethical and moral to the unethical and immoral, according to the Sumerian sages, and practically all the major deities of the Sumerian pantheon are extolled in their hymns as lovers of the good and the just, of truth and righteousness. Indeed, there were several deities who had the supervision of the moral order as their main functions: for example, the sun-god, Utu. Another deity, the Lagashite goddess named Nanshe, also played a significant role in the sphere of man's ethical and moral conduct. She is described in one of her hymns as the goddess.

> Who knows the orphan, who knows the widow,
> Knows the oppression of man over man, is the
>   orphan's mother,
> Nanshe, who cares for the widow,
> Who seeks out (?) justice (?) for the poorest (?).
> The queen brings the refugee to her lap,
> Finds shelter for the weak.

In another passage of this hymn, she is pictured as judging mankind on New Year's Day; by her side are Nidaba, the goddess of writing and accounts, and her husband, Haia, as well as numerous witnesses. The evil human types who suffer her displeasure are

> (People) who walking in transgression reached out
>   with high hand, ... ,
> Who transgress the established norms, violate
>   contracts,
> Who looked with favor on the places of evil, ... ,
> Who substituted a small weight for a large weight,
> Who substituted a small measure for a large measure,
> Who having eaten (something not belonging to him)
>   did not say "I have eaten it,"
> Who having drunk, did not say "I have drunk it," . . . . ,
> Who said "I would eat that which is forbidden,"
> Who said "I would drink that which is forbidden."

Nanshe's social conscience is further revealed in lines which read:

> To comfort the orphan, to make disappear the widow,
> To set up a place of destruction for the mighty,
> To turn over the mighty to the weak. . . . ,
> Nanshe searches the heart of the people.

Unfortunately, although the leading deities were assumed to be ethical and moral in their conduct, the fact remained that, in accordance with the world view of the Sumerians, they were also the ones who in the process of establishing civilization had planned evil and falsehood, violence and oppression—in short, all the immoral and unethical modes of human conduct. Thus, for example, among the list of *me*'s, the rules and regulations devised by the gods to make the cosmos run smoothly and effectively, there are not only those which regulate "truth," "peace," "goodness," and "justice," but also those which govern "falsehood," "strife," "lamentation," and "fear." Why, then, one might ask, did the gods find it necessary to plan and create sin and evil, suffering and misfortune, which were so pervasive that one Sumerian pessimist could say, "Never has a sinless child been born to his mother"? To judge from our available material, the Sumerian sages, if they asked the question at all, were prepared to admit their ignorance in this respect; the will of the gods and their motives were at times inscrutable. The proper course for a Sumerian Job to pursue was not to argue and complain in face of seemingly unjustifiable misfortune, but to plead and wail, lament and confess, his inevitable sins and failings.

But will the gods give heed to him, a lone and not very effective mortal, even if he prostrates and humbles himself in heartfelt prayer? Probably not, the Sumerian teachers would have answered. As they saw it, gods were like mortal rulers and no doubt had more important things to attend to; and so, as in the case of kings, man must have an intermediary to intercede in his behalf, one whom the gods would be willing to hear and favor. As a result, the Sumerian thinkers contrived and evolved the notion of a personal god, a kind of good angel to each particular individual and family head, his divine father who had begot him, as it were. It was to him, to his personal deity, that the individual sufferer bared his heart in prayer and supplication, and it was through him that he found his salvation.

From S. N. Kramer, *The Sumerians*, University of Chicago Press, 1963. Reprinted by permission of the publisher.

ANALYSIS AND INTERPRETATION
OF THE READINGS

1. Judging from the letters reproduced here, how would you characterize kingship in ancient Assyria? How do you account for the combination of deference and admonition contained in the letters?

2. S. N. Kramer describes the need that gave rise to the idea of a personal deity. What need might have given rise to belief in the major Sumerian gods?

CHAPTER 3 | Egyptian Civilization

CHRONOLOGY

In the blanks, write the appropriate dates from the list below. All dates are B.C.E.

c. 3100	c. 1750
1151	2770–2200
c. 1560–1087	671
322	c. 2770
525	c. 2050–1786
750	525

_____ Old Kingdom

_____ Assyrian conquest of Egypt

_____ Beginning of Zoser's reign

_____ First unified state in the Nile Valley

_____ Hyksos invasion of Egypt

_____ Middle Kingdom

_____ Persian conquest of Egypt

_____ Death of Ramses II

_____ The New Kingdom (Empire)

_____ Alexander the Great's conquest of Egypt

_____ Kushite king Kashta captures Thebes

IDENTIFICATIONS

You should be able to identify the following:

hieroglyphics	Nefertiti
Hyksos	Tutankhaton (Tutankhamen)
Ahmose	papyrus
polytheism	*Plea of the Eloquent Peasant*
monotheism	"pi" ratio
Amon-Re	Kushites
Osiris	Piankhy
nature myth	Memphis
Amenhotep IV (Akhenaton)	Ethiopia

STUDY QUESTIONS

1. What natural advantages did the Nile Valley have over Mesopotamia as a center for the development of civilization?
2. Why could Herodotus describe Egypt as "the gift of the Nile"?
3. Why can the unification of the northern and southern parts of Egypt be described as the "greatest event in ancient Egyptian political history"?
4. Discuss briefly the nature of the responsibilities of a pharaoh of the Old Kingdom.
5. What is the evidence that the Old Kingdom, unlike so many ancient states, was a peaceful, nonaggressive community?
6. Why has the Twelfth Dynasty been referred to as a "golden age"?
7. "The Hyksos conquest contributed strongly to the rise of Egyptian imperialism and to a decline in the character of Egyptian religion." Discuss this statement.

8. Describe the evolution of the Egyptian system of writing. In what respects did it advance beyond the Mesopotamian system?
9. Why was the Egyptian calendar the best in antiquity?
10. How did the basis of the pharaoh's rule change with the advent of the New Kingdom (Empire)? What were the consequences of this change?
11. Explain the general popularity of the cult of Osiris during the Middle Kingdom.
12. How did belief in an afterlife affect Egyptian religious ideas and funeral practices?
13. How did Amenhotep IV (Akhenaton) try to offset the debasement of religion under the Empire?
14. Explain the statement that the religion of Amenhotep IV (Akhenaton) was a "qualified monotheism."
15. To what extent and in what directions were the Egyptians scientific? How do you explain the limitations in their intellectual achievements?
16. What was the ancient Egyptian view of the origin of diseases? How did this affect medical practices?
17. Why does limestone occupy a prominent place in the history of the twenty-seventh century B.C.E.?
18. What special features of the Great Pyramid of Cheops qualified it to rank as one of the "seven wonders of the world"?
19. The construction of the Egyptian pyramids was extraordinarily difficult, and required tremendous effort. How do you account for their accomplishment if slave labor was not the primary means of organization?
20. During what period were the great Egyptian temples built? Describe their characteristics.
21. How did the sculpture of the Egyptians symbolize their national aspirations?
22. What was the structure of Egyptian society throughout the greater part of its ancient history? What features did Egyptian society have in common with our own and what features were different?
23. How did the position of women in ancient Egypt differ from that in most other ancient societies?
24. To what extent was Egyptian art bound by convention? To what extent was it original and individualistic?
25. How do you account for the remarkable longevity of Egyptian civilization?
26. In what ways was ancient Egyptian civilization indebted to Nubia?
27. Describe the rise of Kushitic civilization. Why did this civilization fall?
28. What were the origins of the Ethiopian civilization? In what respects was the Ethiopian state superior to the Kushite kingdom?
29. Outline Egypt's legacy to world civilization. Which aspects of this legacy would you say are most visible today?

PROBLEMS

1. Compare and contrast the judicial system under the Old Kingdom with that of the United States.
2. Amenhotep IV (Akhenaton) is generally considered one of the splendid failures in history. Why do you think he failed? To what extent might he be called a success?
3. In your judgment, in what ways was Egyptian civilization superior and in what ways inferior to Mesopotamian civilization?
4. Compare the following aspects of the religions of Egypt and Mesopotamia:
   a. Ethical concepts
   b. Notions of the afterlife
   c. Views of human nature
5. Despite their great accomplishments in mathematics, medicine, and astronomy, the Egyptians were limited by their very way of thinking from carrying any science very far. Discuss the reasons for this.
6. In the life and world around you, what are the evidences, direct and indirect, of Egyptian achievements?
7. Geography is sometimes said to be the determining factor in a nation's history. To what extent was this true of ancient Egypt?

AIDS TO AN UNDERSTANDING OF EGYPTIAN CIVILIZATION

ETHICAL DOCTRINES OF THE *Book of the Dead*

. . . I have not done iniquity.
. . . I have not robbed with violence.
. . . I have not done violence to any man.
. . . I have not committed theft.
. . . I have not slain man or woman.
. . . I have not made light the bushel.

. . . I have not acted deceitfully.
. . . I have not purloined the things which belong unto God.
. . . I have not uttered falsehood.
. . . I have not carried away food.
. . . I have not uttered evil words.
. . . I have attacked no man.
. . . I have not killed the beasts, which are the property of God.
. . . I have not acted deceitfully.

. . . I have not laid waste the lands which have been plowed.

. . . I have never pried into matters to make mischief.

. . . I have not set my mouth in motion against any man.

. . . I have not given way to wrath concerning myself without a cause.

. . . I have not defiled the wife of a man.

. . . I have not committed any sin against purity.

. . . I have not struck fear into any man.

. . . I have not encroached upon sacred times and seasons.

. . . I have not been a man of anger.

. . . I have not made myself deaf to the words of right and truth.

. . . I have not stirred up strife.

. . . I have made no man to weep.

. . . I have not committed acts of impurity . . . .

. . . I have not eaten my heart.

. . . I have abused no man.

. . . I have not acted with violence.

. . . I have not judged hastily.

. . . I have not taken vengeance upon the god.

. . . I have not multiplied my speech overmuch.

. . . I have not acted with deceit, and I have not worked wickedness.

. . . I have not uttered curses on the King.

. . . I have not fouled water.

. . . I have not made haughty my voice.

. . . I have not cursed the god.

. . . I have not sought for distinctions.

. . . I have not increased my wealth, except with such things as are justly mine own possessions.

. . . I have not thought scorn of the god who is in my city.

———————

From E. A. Wallis Budge, *The Book of the Dead. The Chapters of Coming Forth by Day.*

ANCIENT EGYPTIAN PYRAMID INSCRIPTIONS

Re-Atum, this Unas comes to you,
A spirit indestructible
Who lays claim to the place of the four pillars!
Your son comes to you, this Unas comes to you,
May you cross the sky united in the dark,
May you rise in lightland, the place in which you shine!
Seth, Nephthys, go proclaim to Upper Egypt's gods
And their spirits:
"This Unas comes, a spirit indestructible,
If he wishes you to die, you will die,
If he wishes you to live, you will live!"

Re-Atum, this Unas comes to you,
A spirit indestructible
Who lays claim to the place of the four pillars!
Your son comes to you, this Unas comes to you,
May you cross the sky united in the dark,
May you rise in lightland, the place in which you shine!
Osiris, Isis, go proclaim to Lower Egypt's gods

And their spirits:
"This Unas comes, a spirit indestructible,
Like the morning star above Hapy,
Whom the water-spirits worship;
Whom he wishes to live will live,
Whom he wishes to die will die!"

Re-Atum, this Unas comes to you,
A spirit indestructible
Who lays claim to the place of the four pillars!
Your son comes to you, this Unas comes to you,
May you cross the sky united in the dark,
May you rise in lightland, the place in which you shine!
Thoth, go proclaim to the gods of the west
And their spirits:
"This Unas comes, a spirit indestructible,
Decked above the neck as Anubis,
Lord of the western height,
He will count hearts, he will claim hearts,
Whom he wishes to live will live,
Whom he wishes to die will die!"

Re-Atum, this Unas comes to you,
A spirit indestructible
Who lays claim to the place of the four pillars!
Your son comes to you, this Unas comes to you,
May you cross the sky united in the dark,
May you rise in lightland, the place in which you shine!
Horus, go proclaim to the powers of the east
And their spirits:
"This Unas comes, a spirit indestructible,
Whom he wishes to live will live,
Whom he wishes to die will die!"

Re-Atum, your son comes to you,
Unas comes to you,
Raise him to you, hold him in your arms,
He is your son, of your body, forever! . . .

THE KING JOINS THE STARS

This Unas comes to you, O Nut,
This Unas comes to you, O Nut,
He has consigned his father to the earth,
He has left Horus behind him.
Grown are his falcon wings,
Plumes of the holy hawk;
His power has brought him,
His magic has equipped him!

THE SKY-GODDESS REPLIES

Make your seat in heaven,
Among the stars of heaven,
For you are the Lone Star, the comrade of Hu!
You shall look down on Osiris,
As he commands the spirits,
While you stand far from him;
You are not among them,
You shall not be among them! . . .

THE KING BECOMES A STAR

Truly, this Great One has fallen on his side,
He who is in Nedyt was cast down.
Your hand is grasped by Re,
Your head is raised by the Two Enneads.
Lo, he has come as Orion,
Lo, Osiris has come as Orion,
Lord of wine at the *wag*-feast.
"Good one," said his mother,
"Heir," said his father,
Conceived of sky, born of dusk.
Sky conceived you and Orion,
Dusk gave birth to you and Orion.
Who lives lives by the gods' command,
You shall live!
You shall rise with Orion in the eastern sky,
You shall set with Orion in the western sky,
Your third is Sothis, pure of thrones,
She is your guide on sky's good paths,
In the Field of Rushes.

From Miriam Lichtheim, *Ancient Egyptian Literature: A Book of Readings*, vol. 1.
pp. 30–31, 32–33, 45–46. University of California Press, 1973.

THE RIDDLE OF THE PYRAMIDS
Kurt Mendelssohn

If man 5000 years ago looked for a great, unifying common task, why did he choose a pyramid instead of something useful, such as an irrigation scheme? Here the answer is simple. Irrigation projects had been in existence in Egypt long before the pyramids but they were always local efforts, giving benefit to a few villages. Even a more ambitious scheme, such as the Bar Yusuf connecting the Nile with Lake Moeris in the Fayum, would hardly have brought the people together in one locality, and its execution demanded a level of hydrological engineering which, at the beginning of the Fourth Dynasty, was well beyond their ability. The same argument also applies to the more basic and straightforward project of damming up the Nile at the apex of the Delta. It is worth remembering that when the French eventually undertook it at Kaliub in about 1860, the dam proved a dismal failure because they had underestimated the seepage of water under its foundations.

No, the construction of an impressive man-made mountain was not a matter of choice. It was the only means of doing something spectacular with the large labour force that they wanted to gather, and a mountain of 50° elevation was, as we have seen, the best they could manage. In Chapter 6 we have traced its development through the escalation of Zoser's monument, which resulted in the Step Pyramid. The building of a distinctive mark in the landscape by making a large heap is still with us in the desire of children making a sand castle. Moreover, this primitive urge is testified to in the Bible (*Genesis*, XI, 4): 'Let us build us a city and a tower whose top may reach unto heaven; and let us make a name'. The Egyptians of the Fourth Dynasty certainly made their name by building the pyramids.

The second question is equally obvious. Why was the building of immense pyramids discontinued? The answer has, to some extent, already been given earlier in this book. Once, through the process of building pyramids the formation of a centralized state had been achieved, there was little point in continuing this activity. Building pyramids in Egypt to bury kings, and in Mexico to sacrifice humans, continued, but these later pyramids were on a scale so much reduced that the primary object of concentrating a large labour force clearly did not apply. In both orbits, pyramid-building had achieved its aim and there was no point in prolonging it. Once the object of creating the centralized state had been attained, independently in the two independent hemispheres, it had found its place in the development of society, and it had not be invented again. It is interesting to note that the only project of commensurable size, the Great Wall of China, followed the pyramids by 2000 years and that its purpose was not in building it but in the use of the final product—to save the state from barbarian incursions.

From Kurt Mendelssohn, *The Riddle of the Pyramids*, pp. 197–98. Praeger Publishers, 1974.

ANALYSIS AND INTERPRETATION OF THE READINGS

1. What is the major theme in the inscriptions from the Egyptian pyramids?
2. How does Kurt Mendelssohn account for both the building of the pyramids and its discontinuance?

| The Hebrew and Early Greek Civilizations

CHRONOLOGY

Number the events listed below in their proper chronological order, from earliest to latest. For the items marked with an asterisk, write in the approximate date. (All events with asterisks —though not necessarily all events in the list—are B.C.E.)

_____ Conquest of the Kingdom of Judah by the Babylonians*

_____ Conquest of Palestine by Alexander the Great

_____ Trojan War (Mycenaean conquest of Troy)*

_____ Beginning of the Roman protectorate over Palestine

_____ Accession of King David*

_____ Philistine conquests in Canaan

_____ Dark Age in Greek history*

_____ Invasion of Greek peninsula by Indo-Europeans

_____ Flourishing of Mycenaean civilization

_____ End of the united Hebrew kingdom

_____ Earliest traces of Minoan civilization*

IDENTIFICATIONS

You should be familiar with the meaning or role of each of the following persons or terms as they relate to Hebrew or early Greek civilization:

Abraham
Moses
Yahweh
Joshua
Philistines
Samuel
Saul
Ark of the Covenant
"Babylonian Captivity"

Judas Maccabeus
diaspora
national monolatry
eschatology
Heinrich Schliemann
Deuteronomic Code
Minos
Michael Ventris
Dorians

STUDY QUESTIONS

1. Explain the origin of the term *Israelite.*
2. How did the region called Palestine get its name?
3. How did the Philistine invasions affect the Hebrews' political history?
4. Describe the changes in Hebrew society and economy under the kings David and Solomon.
5. Why did Solomon consider it essential to build a great temple?
6. Identify the four stages in the evolution of the Hebrew religion. What were the primary characteristics of each stage?
7. Three basic doctrines made up the substance of the teachings of the great prophets Isaiah, Hosea, Amos, and Micah. What were they?
8. What is the real significance of the "prophetic revolution" in the development of the ancient Hebrew religion?
9. Compare the philosophical points of view found in the books of Job and Ecclesiastes.
10. What concept of a messiah is set forth in the Book of Daniel?
11. What is described as "the real Jewish miracle," and what brought about this miracle?

12. Giving specific examples, explain how the Deuteronomic Code represents an ethical advance over the Code of Hammurabi.
13. "The literature of the Hebrews was the finest produced by any ancient civilization of western Asia." Justify this statement.
14. In what ways has the heritage from Judaism affected secular aspects of Western civilization?
15. What was the most important "storybook triumph" in the annals of archaeology?
16. In what ways did Minoan society resemble modern Western societies?
17. Minoan art differed considerably from Egyptian and Mesopotamian art. Show how its art suggests the nature of the Minoans' culture.
18. What were the chief characteristics of the Minoan religion?
19. What aspect of the Minoan social order was the most unusual in comparison with other ancient societies?
20. How did Mycenaean civilization differ from Minoan civilization?
21. What light did the decipherment of Linear B throw on Mycenaean civilization?
22. Both the Minoan and the Mycenaean states have been described as "bureaucratic monarchies." Describe this type of political organization.
23. What is the lasting importance of the Minoan and Mycenaean civilizations?

PROBLEMS

1. Where can the Semitic language family be found today?
2. Compare the portraits of Solomon in I Kings 2–12, I Chronicles 28–29, and II Chronicles 1–10.
3. Read the books of Amos and Micah in the Old Testament and answer the following:
   a. Where are these prophets from and what is their background?
   b. What land is the target of their criticism?
   c. What social and religious conditions are they deploring?
   d. What are their religious and ethical standards?
4. The Book of Job deals with the problem of theodicy, that is, of the origin and explanation of evil. Read it and analyze with citations to the text the problem as presented there. Other than his physical rewards, what is the nature of Job's triumph?
5. Read the Book of Deuteronomy in the Old Testament and sketch the nature of the society that Moses demands.
6. Read either Proverbs or Ecclesiastes and analyze with citations to the text the philosophy set forth there.
7. Read Homer's *Iliad* (Richmond Lattimore's translation is preferred). What character traits are dominant in the heroes of the Greeks and the Trojans? How would you characterize the immortals (the gods)?
8. Explore further any of the following:
   a. The archaeological discoveries of Heinrich Schliemann or Arthur Evans
   b. Recent developments in Aegean archaeology
   c. Sports in the Minoan culture
   d. Cretan writing and attempts to decipher it
   e. Crete's debt to Egypt

AIDS TO AN UNDERSTANDING OF THE HEBREW AND EARLY GREEK CIVILIZATIONS

HEBREW PIETY
Psalm 1

Blessed is the man that walketh not in the counsel of the ungodly, nor standeth in the way of sinners, nor sitteth in the seat of the scornful.

But his delight is in the law of the Lord; and in his law doth he meditate day and night.

And he shall be like a tree planted by the rivers of water, that bringeth forth his fruit in his season; his leaf also shall not wither; and whatsoever he doeth shall prosper.

The ungodly are not so: but are like the chaff which the wind driveth away.

Therefore the ungodly shall not stand in the judgment, nor sinners in the congregation of the righteous.

For the Lord knoweth the way of the righteous: but the way of the ungodly shall perish.

HEBREW PHILOSOPHY
Proverbs 10:5–14

He that gathereth in summer is a wise son: but he that sleepeth in harvest is a son that causeth shame.

Blessings are upon the head of the just, but violence covereth the mouth of the wicked.

The memory of the just is blessed: but the name of the wicked shall rot.

The wise in heart will receive commandments: but a prating fool shall fall.

He that walketh uprightly walketh surely: but he that perverteth his ways shall be known.

He that winketh with the eye causeth sorrow: but a prating fool shall fall.

The mouth of a righteous man is a well of life: but violence covereth the mouth of the wicked.

Hatred stirreth up strifes: but love covereth all sins.

In the lips of him that hath understanding wisdom is found: but a rod is for the back of him that is void of understanding.

Wise men lay up knowledge: but the mouth of the foolish is near destruction.

THE BOOK OF JOB
9:1–17

Then Job answered:

"Truly I know that it is so; But how can a man be just before God?

If one wished to contend with him, one could not answer him once in a thousand times.

He is wise in heart, and mighty in strength—who has hardened himself against him, and succeeded?—

He who removes mountains, and they know it not, when he overturns them in his anger;

who shakes the earth out of its place, and its pillars tremble;

who commands the sun, and it does not rise; who seals up the stars;

who alone stretched out the heavens, and trampled the waves of the sea;

who made the Bear and Orion, the Pleiades and the chambers of the south;

who does great things beyond understanding, and marvelous things without number.

Lo, he passes by me, and I see him not; he moves on, but I do not perceive him.

Behold, he snatches away; who can hinder him? Who will say to him, 'What doest thou'?

"God will not turn back his anger; beneath him bowed the helpers of Rahab.

How then can I answer him, choosing my words with him?

Though I am innocent, I cannot answer him; I must appeal for mercy to my accuser.

If I summoned him and he answered me, I would not believe that he was listening to my voice.

For he crushes me with a tempest, and multiplies my wounds without cause.

10:18–22

"Why didst thou bring me forth from the womb? Would that I had died before any eye had seen me, and were as though I had not been, carried from the womb to the grave.

Are not the days of my life few? Let me alone, that I may find a little comfort before I go whence I shall not return, to the land of gloom and deep darkness, the land of gloom and chaos, where light is as darkness."

19:20–27

My bones cleave to my skin and to my flesh, and I have escaped by the skin of my teeth.

Have pity on me, have pity on me, O you my friends, for the hand of God has touched me!

Why do you, like God, pursue me? Why are you not satisfied with my flesh?

Oh that my words were written! Oh that they were inscribed in a book! Oh that with an iron pen and lead they were graven in the rock for ever!

For I know that my Redeemer lives, and at last he will stand upon the earth;

and after my skin has been thus destroyed, then without my flesh I shall see God, whom I shall see on my side, and my eyes shall behold, and not another. My heart faints within me!

38:1–20

Then the Lord answered Job out of the whirlwind: "Who is this that darkens counsel by words without knowledge? Gird up your loins like a man, I will question you, and you shall declare to me.

"Where were you when I laid the foundation of the earth? Tell me, if you have understanding. Who determined its measurements—surely you know! Or who stretched the line upon it? On what were its bases sunk, or who laid its cornerstone, when the morning stars sang together, and all the sons of God shouted for joy?

"Or who shut in the sea with doors, when it burst forth from the womb; when I made clouds its garment and thick darkness its swaddling band, and prescribed bounds for it, and set bars and doors, and said, 'Thus far shall you come and no farther, and here shall your proud waves be stayed'?

"Have you commanded the morning since your days began, and caused the dawn to know its place, that it might take hold of the skirts of the earth, and the wicked be shaken out of it?

It is changed like clay under the seal, and it is dyed like a garment. From the wicked their light is withheld, and their uplifted arm is broken.

"Have you entered into the springs of the sea, or walked in the recesses of the deep? Have the gates of death been revealed to you, or have you seen the gates of deep darkness? Have you comprehended the expanse of the earth? Declare, if you know all this.

"Where is the way to the dwelling of light, and where is the place of darkness, that you may take it to its territory and that you may discern the paths to its home?

42:1–6

Then Job answered the Lord: "I know that thou canst do all things, and that no purpose of thine can be thwarted.

'Who is this that hides counsel without knowledge?' Therefore I have uttered what I did not understand, things too wonderful for me, which I did not know.

'Hear, and I will speak; I will question you, and you declare to me.' I had heard of thee by the hearing of the ear, but now my eye sees thee; therefore I despise myself, and repent in dust and ashes.''

THE MYCENAEANS AS A GREEK DYNASTY
John Chadwick

One fact stands out at once as of major consequence: the Mycenaeans were Greeks. Schliemann, when he excavated the first grave circle at Mycenae, had no doubt that he had unearthed a Greek dynasty, and in his famous telegram to the king of Greece claimed to have looked upon the face of one of the king's ancestors. But more academic judges were not so certain, and at one time theories of foreign domination were invoked to account for the precocious brilliance of the Mycenaeans at such a remove from the historical Greeks. The proof that the language of their accounts was Greek might be thought to have settled all controversy on this score; but much ingenuity has been expended on attempts to circumvent the implications of this evidence. The language of accounts is not always that of their writers: an Indian business house may find it convenient to keep its accounts in English; a medieval king of England may have had his secretaries write in Latin. But in all such cases which I know of, the language in question is a dominant literary language, and the language replaced by it a local one with restricted currency and often no adequate orthography. If Greek were adopted by foreigners as a written language, as it was in Hellenistic Egypt, then this implies that Greek was already a dominant literary language: a conclusion which on the available evidence is absurd.

Even this does not answer two theories which have been put forward, either that the preserved tablets were written by Greek scribes in Greek at the behest of foreign rulers; or that they were written by foreign scribes in Greek for Greek rulers. The best refutation of these theories is the existence in the tablets of large numbers of transparently Greek personal names, and these are not stratified but belong equally to all classes of society. For instance, a person of the highest standing at Pylos is named *E-ke-ra₂-wo*, which appears to be a well-known type of Greek name *Ekhelawon*; at the other end of the social scale a smith has the delightful name *Mnasiwergos* "Mindful-of-his-work" and a goat-herd has the common name *Philaios*.

Many names of course are much harder to interpret as Greek, and some are certainly foreign; but the presence of an element foreign in origin, if not still in speech, does not contradict the positive evidence that Greeks were widely spread throughout society, and we can feel sure that the Mycenaeans were at least predominantly Greek. The 700 years or so between the coming of the Greeks and the Pylos tablets are time enough to allow the pre-Hellenic inhabitants to have been absorbed.

The presence of Greeks at Knossos is still something of an embarrassment. Professor Wace and a few other archaeologists had demonstrated the close links between Knossos and the mainland in the period preceding the fall of the Palace there, and even proposed to explain them as due to mainland influence on Crete, and not vice versa. The truth is that the limitations of archaeological research preclude deductions about the languages spoken by the people studied. The physical remains may allow an anthropological classification, but people of a given physical type do not all speak the same language. The study of "cultures," peoples using artifacts of similar type, is the archaeologists' main weapon. (It is this, for instance, which enables us to feel sure that about 1900 B.C., a wave of invaders entered and settled in Greece. But the inference that these were the ancestors of the Greeks is based upon the knowledge that Greek was subsequently spoken in that area, and could not be made without recourse to non-archaeological premises.)

Thus a clear statement from the archaeologists of the date when mainland influence first appears at Knossos is a vain hope. When a half-civilized people conquer a civilized one, they try to absorb and adapt as much as they can of the superior civilization, so, especially if the actual conquest is not accompanied by great destruction, the event may easily escape the archaeologist's spade. There is, however, one piece of evidence, not strictly archaeological, which proves that the Greek domination of Crete was a comparatively recent event: the use of Linear A, apparently down to the early fifteenth century, is an indication that Greek had not then replaced Minoan as the language of accounts; unless Linear A too is Greek, a possibility which none but the most determined enthusiasts will admit.

From John Chadwick, *The Decipherment of Linear B*, Cambridge University Press, 1958. Reprinted by permission of the publisher and the author.

ANALYSIS AND INTERPRETATION OF THE READINGS

1. What do the passages from the Book of Job tell us about the Hebrew concept of a deity?
2. What do the "Linear B" tablets tell us about the relationship of the Mycenaeans to Greek civilization?

CHAPTER 5 | Ancient Indian Civilization

CHRONOLOGY

With the exception of Alexander the Great's invasion of the Indus valley, exact chronology is lacking for most of the ancient history of India. Data concerning the pre-Aryan Indus valley civilization will probably become more complete as archaeological exploration continues. The Indo-Aryan invaders, who developed ancient Indian civilization, produced few written records until comparatively late and displayed little interest in precise chronology. Most dates below, therefore, are approximations. It will be helpful, however, to remember the sequence and the approximate duration of the principal cultural periods. From the list of dates below, select the appropriate one for each period or event and write it in the proper space. All dates are B.C.E.

c. 3000–1600	c. 2000–500
c. 322–184	327–326
c. 2000–1500	sixth century
c. 273–232	

_____ Vedic age

_____ Reign of King Ashoka

_____ Indo-Aryan invasions

_____ Indus valley civilization

_____ Maurya Dynasty

_____ Invasion of Alexander the Great into Indus valley

_____ Period of the rise of Jainism and Buddhism

IDENTIFICATIONS

You should be able to identify the following. It will help to write a brief definition of each.

Indo-Aryan	*kshatriya*
Arya	Vedas
raja	Sanskrit
deva	*karma*
Varuna	*nirvana*
Indra	*ahimsa*
varna	*Arthashastra*
brahman	

STUDY QUESTIONS

1. Why might the Ganges River be referred to as "Mother Ganges"?
2. Although distinct in many ways, Indo-Aryan culture absorbed some elements of the Indus valley civilization. Cite examples of this.
3. Discuss the consequences of large-scale migration from central and western Asia beginning in the early second millennium B.C.E.
4. What is the origin of the term "Aryan"?
5. Describe the changing character of religion during the Vedic age.
6. What does it mean to describe a religion as "contractual"?
7. In what respects are the Vedas comparable to the sacred texts of Judaism and Christianity? In what ways are they different from those texts?
8. Explain how the popular belief in transmigration of souls was reinterpreted by philosophers of the *Upanishads*.

9. The idealism of the *Upanishads*, though seemingly negative and pessimistic, is actually optimistic regarding human worth and destiny. Explain how.
10. How does the *Ramayana* differ in style and content from the *Mahabharata*?
11. Why did the epics replace the Vedas as the "bible for the common people"?
12. How do you account for the rise of the caste system in India?
13. What changes in the position of women accompanied the development of the caste system?
14. What were the negative aspects of the caste system? What were its positive aspects?
15. Explain the theoretical bases of Gautama Buddha's ethical teachings.
16. What are the primary differences between Jainism and the teachings of Gautama? What are the primary differences between the teachings of the *Upanishads* and the teachings of Gautama?
17. According to Gautama, what is the root of suffering, and how can one escape suffering?
18. Why has Buddhism been called "the Protestant form of Hinduism"?
19. Explain the origin of the two main divisions of Buddhism, *Hinayana* and *Mahayana*. Where is each found today?
20. What significant contributions to science are derived from ancient Hindu civilization?
21. What were the consequences stemming from Alexander the Great's short-lived invasion of the Indus valley?
22. Describe the characteristics and the accomplishments of the reign of Chandragupta Maurya.
23. Why is Ashoka regarded as one of the most remarkable rulers in the annals of civilization?

PROBLEMS

1. What effects have geography and climate had on society and culture in India?
2. Investigate the origin of the theory that the so-called Indo-European languages bear a family relationship to one another. What scholars first advanced this theory, and where did they find evidence to support it? What is the status of this theory today?
3. Read Aldous Huxley's *Ends and Means*, or one of his later novels, to find examples of the influence of the philosophy of the *Upanishads* on his thinking.
4. Investigate the special characteristics of Buddhism in Tibet, Burma, or Sri Lanka.
5. Compare the development of mathematics and astronomy in ancient India with that in ancient Greece.
6. Investigate the similarities between the pre-Aryan Indus valley civilization and other contemporary civilizations, such as the Babylonian or Egyptian.
7. Investigate further what archaeological explorations have revealed about ancient Indian civilization. What can our current arhaeological knowledge tell us about daily life in the Indus valley civilization?
8. According to legend, Indra was supposed to have conquered drought and refreshed the earth with plentiful water. Compare this legend with other water-related legends from other ancient civilizations (Hebrew, Egyptian, Chinese, and so on). Analyze the place of water in ancient lore and ancient life.
9. Explore the connection between religion and statecraft in India. Compare this with the relationship found in other early civilizations.

AIDS TO AN UNDERSTANDING OF ANCIENT INDIAN CIVILIZATION

HYMNS AND PRAYERS FROM THE VEDAS

TO NIGHT

With all her eyes the goddess Night looks forth approaching many a spot:
She hath put all her glories on.

Immortal, she hath filled the waste, the goddess hath filled height and depth:
She conquers darkness with her light.

The goddess as she comes hath set the Dawn her sister in her place:
And then the darkness vanishes.

So favour us this night, O thou whose pathways we have visited
As birds their nest upon the tree.

The villagers have sought their homes, and all that walks and all that flies,
Even the falcons fain for prey.

Keep off the she-wolf and the wolf; O Ūrmyā, keep the thief away:
Easy be thou for us to pass.

Clearly hath she come nigh to me who decks the dark with richest hues:
O morning, cancel it like debts.

These have I brought to thee like kine. O Night, thou child of
heaven, accept
This laud as for a conqueror.

To Varuna

Sing forth a hymn sublime and solemn, grateful to glorious
Varuna, imperial ruler,
Who hath struck out, like one who slays the victim, earth as a
skin to spread in front of Sūrya.

In the tree-tops the air he hath extended, put milk in kine and
vigorous speed in horses,
Set intellect in hearts, fire in the waters, Sūrya in heaven and
Soma on the mountain.

Varuna lets the big cask, opening downward, flow through the
heaven and earth and air's mid-region.
Therewith the universe's sovran waters earth as the shower of
rain bedews the barley.

When Varuna is fain for milk, he moistens the sky, the land, and
earth to her foundation.
Then straight the mountains clothe them in the rain-cloud: the
heroes, putting forth their vigour, loose them.

I will declare this mighty deed of magic, of glorious Varuna, the
lord immortal,
Who, standing in the firmament, hath meted the earth out with
the sun as with a measure.

None, verily, hath ever let or hindered this the most wise god's
mighty deed of magic,
Whereby with all their flood, the lucid rivers fill not one sea
wherein they pour their waters.

If we have sinned against the man who loves us, have ever
wronged a brother, friend, or comrade,
The neighbour ever with us, or a stranger, O Varuna, remove
from us the trespass.

If we, as gamesters cheat at play, have cheated, done wrong un-
wittingly or sinned of purpose,
Cast all these sins away like loosened fetters, and, Varuna, let
us be thine own beloved.

Prayer for Success in Gambling

The successful, victorious, skilfully gaming Apsarâ, that Apsarâ
who makes the winnings in the game of dice, do I call hither.

The skilfully gaming Apsarâ who sweeps and heaps up (the
stakes), that Apsarâ who takes the winnings in the game of dice,
do I call hither.

May she, who dances about with the dice, when she takes the
stakes from the game of dice, when she desires to win for us,
obtain the advantage by (her) magic! May she come to us full of
abundance! Let them not win this wealth of ours!

The (Apsarâs) who rejoice in dice, who carry grief and
wrath—that joyful and exulting Apsarâ, do I call hither.

From *Hindu Scriptures*, ed. Dr. Nicol MacNicol, Everyman's Library, 1938.
Reprinted by permission of E. P. Dutton & Co.

Philosophy of the Upanishads: The Self as Eternal Essence

Twelfth Khanda

"**F**etch me from thence a fruit of the
Nyagrodha tree."
  "Here is one, Sir."
  "Break it."
  "It is broken, Sir."
  "What do you see there?"
  "These seeds, almost infinitesimal."
  "Break one of them."
  "It is broken, Sir."
  "What do you see there?"
  "Not anything, Sir."
The father said: "My son, that subtle essence which you do
not perceive there, of that very essence this great Nyagrodha
tree exists.
  "Believe it, my son. That which is the subtle essence, in it
all that exists has its self. It is the True. It is the Self, and thou,
O Svetaketu, art it."
  "Please, Sir, inform me still more," said the son.
  "Be it so, my child," the father replied.

Thirteenth Khanda

"Place this salt in water, and then wait on me in the morning."
The son did as he was commanded.
  The father said to him: "Bring me the salt, which you placed
in the water last night."
  The son having looked for it, found it not, for, of course, it
was melted.
  The father said: "Taste it from the surface of the water. How
is it?"
  The son replied: "It is salt."
  "Taste it from the middle. How is it?"
  The son replied: "It is salt."
  "Taste it from the bottom. How is it?"
  The son replied: "It is salt."
  The father said: "Throw it away and then wait on me."
  He did so; but salt exists for ever.
  Then the father said: "Here also, in this body, forsooth, you
do not perceive the True (Sat), my son; but there indeed it is.
  "That which is the subtle essence, in it all that exists has its
self. It is the True. It is the Self, and thou, O Svetaketu, art it."
  "Please, Sir, inform me still more," said the son.
  "Be it so, my child," the father replied.

From *Khandogya Upanishad*, in F. Max Mueller, trans., *The Upanishads* (The Sacred Books of the East), Vol. I, Krishna Press, 1963.

The Four Noble Truths of Buddhism:

From the "Deer Park Sermon"

"**T**he cause of all sorrow lies at the very beginning; it is hidden in the ignorance from which life grows.
Remove ignorance and you will destroy the wrong appetences

that rise from ignorance; destroy these appetences and you will wipe out the wrong perception that rises from them. Destroy wrong perception and there is an end of errors in individualised beings. Destroy errors in individualised beings and the illusions of the six fields will disappear. Destroy illusions and the contact with things will cease to beget misconception. Destroy misconception and you do away with thirst. Destroy thirst and you will be free of all morbid cleaving. Remove the cleaving and you destroy the selfishness of selfhood. If the selfishness of selfhood is destroyed you will be above birth, old age, disease, and death, and you escape all suffering."

The Enlightened One saw the four noble truths which point out the path that leads to Nirvana or the extinction of self:

"The first noble truth is the existence of sorrow. Birth is sorrowful, growth is sorrowful, illness is sorrowful, and death is sorrowful. Sad it is to be joined with that which we do not like. Sadder still is the separation from that which we love, and painful is the craving for that which cannot be obtained.

"The second noble truth is the cause of suffering. The cause of suffering is lust. The surrounding world affects sensation and begets a craving thirst, which clamors for immediate satisfaction. The illusion of self originates and manifests itself in a cleaving to things. The desire to live for the enjoyment of self entangles us in the net of sorrow. Pleasures are the bait and the result is pain.

"The third noble truth is the cessation of sorrow. He who conquers self will be free from lust. He no longer craves, and the flame of desire finds no material to feed upon. Thus it will be extinguished.

"The fourth noble truth is the eightfold path that leads to the cessation of sorrow. There is salvation for him whose self disappears before Truth, whose will is bent upon what he ought to do, whose sole desire is the performance of his duty. He who is wise will enter this path and make an end of sorrow.

"The eightfold path is (1) right comprehension; (2) right resolutions; (3) right speech; (4) right acts; (5) right way of earning a livelihood; (6) right efforts; (7) right thoughts; and (8) the right state of a peaceful mind."

This is the dharma. This is the truth. . . .

From *Classics of Eastern Thought*, Lynn H. Nelson and Patrick Peebles, eds. "The Four Noble Truths of Buddhism." pp. 33–34. Harcourt Brace Jovanovich, 1991.

ANALYSIS AND INTERPRETATION OF THE READINGS

1. In the "Deer Park Sermon," how does Buddha explain the cause of human suffering? What does he prescribe as the solution to the problem?
2. Compare the view of the self found in the selection from the *Upanishads* with that found in the Buddha's "Deer Park Sermon."

CHAPTER 6

Ancient Chinese Civilization

CHRONOLOGY

From the list below, select the correct dates for each epoch or person and write the dates in the appropriate blanks. All dates are B.C.E., and all are approximate.

8000	2200–1750
551–477	1100–771
5000–3000	1750–1100
771–250	373–288

_____ Shang dynasty

_____ Western Zhou dynasty

_____ Mencius

_____ Transition to Neolithic culture

_____ Eastern Zhou dynasty

_____ Confucius

_____ Yangshao painted pottery culture

_____ Xia dynasty

IDENTIFICATIONS

You should be able to explain the meaning and importance of each of the following terms.

monsoon	"Warring States"
Neolithic	*Analects*
"oracle bones"	"Middle Kingdom"
"mandate of heaven"	

In the blanks provided, write the name of the person identified with each of the following statements.

1. His major contributions to Confucian thought were the ideas that all humans were basically good and therefore improvable through education, and that a tyrannical ruler had no right to remain in power.

_____

2. This person, whose historical existence is open to question, set forth a philosophy that advocated as little human interference with nature as possible, and promoted minimal government.

_____

3. The brother of the leader who defeated the Shang dynasty, he seemed to eschew personal power, instead selflessly serving the state and becoming a model for later Confucians.

_____

4. A great teacher concerned with the problem of creating a well-ordered society, he urged that ethics and moral principles be enshrined as the guiding principles in government.

_____

5. This philosopher argued that a life of private cultivation of inner strength was more desirable than a life of government service.

_____

6. Unlike many Confucian thinkers, this man held a pessimistic view of human nature and believed that laws were necessary to control human impulses.

_____

STUDY QUESTIONS

1. What were some of the major effects of geography on the development of Chinese civilization?
2. What were the major consequences of the development of permanent settlements in China?
3. Discuss the importance of kinship in ancient Chinese state and society.
4. In what respects was the Shang dynasty a formative period for Chinese civilization?
5. How does the Chinese concept of "Heaven" differ from Judeo-Christian views of God?
6. How did the five-class hierarchy in ancient Chinese society promote order and harmony? What was the basis for this system?
7. The development of much of classical Chinese thought coincides with the turbulent period known as "Warring States." How do you account for this convergence of warfare and intense philosophical development?
8. What functions did religion serve in ancient China? How would you compare them with the role of religion in other civilizations?
9. How did the *disunity* of the late Zhou period pave the way for the unity brought about by the state of Qin?

Circle the letter in parentheses that precedes the correct completion in each of the following multiple-choice questions.

1. The Confucian concept of the ideal state was based on the assumption that (a) all men are equal; (b) church and state should be separate; (c) the purpose of government is to promote the welfare of the people; (d) that government is best which governs least.
2. Confucius believed that the state should be governed by an aristocracy determined by (a) wealth; (b) talent; (c) birth; (d) hard work.
3. In spite of the differences in emphasis, members of the Confucian school of thought agreed that (a) people can become better if properly guided; (b) human nature is hopelessly corrupt; (c) politics and ethics are entirely separate.
4. Laozi is noted for affirming (a) the virtue of unrestrained individualism; (b) the superiority of nature over human institutions; (c) that all governments are inherently evil; (d) the importance of the ruler's keeping a close watch on his subjects.
5. The Legalist school of thought (a) provided a basis for the rule of law in later Chinese history; (b) emphasized the virtue of the common people; (c) argued for a smaller, but more efficient, government than the Daoists; (d) believed the best way to motivate people was through reward and punishment.
6. The concept of *yin* and *yang* would tend to promote a view of the universe characterized by (a) constancy and solidity; (b) change and fluidity.

PROBLEMS

1. Study the archaeology of China's stone and bronze ages. What elements suggest indigenous origins for Chinese civilization? Are there elements that argue for outside influence?
2. What are the limitations in using the term "feudal" to describe the Zhou period? What are the advantages? (After studying chapter 13, you may want to compare this period with the feudal period in western Europe.)
3. Discuss the ways in which classical Chinese thought is a product of the realities of its time. Compare classical Chinese thought with classical Greek, Roman, Indian, or Egyptian thought.
4. Explore the role and importance of ritual (*li*) in ancient Chinese society.
5. Investigate the origins of agriculture in China, and explore the impact of the development of agriculture on Chinese civilization.
6. What is meant by the term "stimulus diffusion"? How does understanding this process help us understand ancient Chinese history?
7. From any of the available English translations, analyze the moral and ethical teachings of the *Daodejing*. Compare these teaching with those found in the *Analects* of Confucius.
8. Explore the origins of writing in China. When and why did writing develop? To what purposes was writing put? What was the long-term impact of the development of a Chinese writing system? Compare this with the development of writing in other cultures.
9. Did ancient Chinese thinkers agree on the basic problems of Chinese society? If so, how and why did their answers differ? What did the "Confucian" thinkers—Confucius, Mencius, Xunzi—have in common?
10. Compare the ideas of China's Legalists with those of Machiavelli. Do the same for China's Confucians.

AIDS TO AN UNDERSTANDING OF ANCIENT CHINESE CIVILIZATION

CONFUCIUS: From the *Analects*

Confucius said, "The gentleman concerns himself with the Way; he does not worry about his salary. Hunger may be found in plowing; wealth may be found in studying. The gentleman worries about the Way, not about poverty."

Confucius said, "When he eats, the gentleman does not seek to stuff himself. In his home he does not seek luxury. He is diligent in his work and cautious in his speech. He associates with those who possess the Way, and thereby rectifies himself. He may be considered a lover of learning."

Tzu Kung inquired about being a gentleman. Confucius said, "First he behaves properly and then he speaks, so that his words follow his actions."

Ssu-ma Niu asked about the nature of the gentleman. Confucius replied, "The gentleman does not worry and is not fearful." Ssu asked, "Then, can not fearing and not worrying be considered the essence of being a gentleman?" Confucius responded, "If you can look into yourself and find no cause for dissatisfaction, how can you worry and how can you fear?"

Confucius said, "The gentleman reveres three things. He reveres the mandate of Heaven; he reveres great people; and he reveres the words of the sages. Petty people do not know the mandate of Heaven and so do not revere it. They are disrespectful to great people and they ridicule the words of the sages."

Confucius said, "The gentleman must exert caution in three areas. When he is a youth and his blood and spirit have not yet settled down, he must be on his guard lest he fall into lusting. When he reaches the full vigor of his manhood in his thirties and his blood and spirit are strong, he must guard against getting into quarrels. When he reaches old age and his blood and spirit have begun to weaken, he must guard against envy."

Confucius said, "The gentleman understands integrity; the petty person knows about profit."

Confucius said, "For the gentleman integrity is the essence; the rules of decorum are the way he puts it into effect; humility is the way he brings it forth; sincerity is the way he develops it. Such indeed is what it means to be a gentleman."

Confucius said that Tzu Ch'an possessed the way of the gentleman in four areas. In his personal conduct he was respectful; in serving his superiors he was reverent; in nourishing the people he was kind; in governing the people he was righteous.

Confucius said, "The gentleman has nine concerns. In seeing he is concerned with clarity. In hearing he is concerned with acuity. In his expression he wishes to be warm. In his bearing he wishes to be respectful. In his words he is concerned with sincerity. In his service he is concerned with reverence. When he is in doubt, he wants to ask questions. When he is angry, he is wary of the pitfalls. When he sees the chance for profit, he keeps in mind the need for integrity."

Confucius said, "The gentleman is easy to serve but difficult to please. When you try to please him, if your manner of pleasing is not in accord with the Way, then he will not be pleased. On the other hand, he does not expect more from people than their capacities warrant. The petty individual is hard to serve and easy to please. When you try to please him, even if your method of pleasing him is not in accord with the Way, he will be pleased. But in employing people he expects them to be perfectly accomplished in everything."

Confucius said, "The gentleman is in harmony with those around him but not on their level. The small man is on the level of those around him but not in harmony with them."

Confucius said, "The gentleman aspires to things lofty; the petty person aspires to things base."

Confucius said, "The gentleman looks to himself; the petty person looks to other people."

Confucius said, "The gentleman feels bad when his capabilities fall short of some task. He does not feel bad if people fail to recognize him."

Confucius said, "The gentleman fears that after his death his name will not be honored."

Confucius said, "The gentleman does not promote people merely on the basis of their words, nor does he reject words merely because of the person who uttered them."

Confucius said, "The gentleman is exalted and yet not proud. The petty person is proud and yet not exalted."

Tzu Hsia said, "The gentleman has three transformations. Seen from afar he appears majestic. Upon approaching him you see he is amiable. Upon hearing his words you find they are serious."

Confucius said, "If the gentleman is not dignified, he will not command respect and his teachings will not be considered solid. He emphasizes sincerity and honesty. He has no friends who are not his equals. If he finds a fault in himself, he does not shirk from reforming himself."

Tzu Kung said, "When the gentleman falls into error, it is like the eclipse of the sun and moon: everyone sees it. When he corrects it, everyone will look up to him again."

Tzu Kung said, "Does not the gentleman also have his hatreds?" Confucius replied. "Yes, he has his hatreds. He hates those who harp on the weak points of others. He hates those who are base and yet slander those who are exalted. He hates those who are bold but do not observe the proprieties. He hates those who are brash and daring and yet have limited outlook." Confucius then asked, "You too have your hatreds, do you not?" Tzu Kung replied. "I hate those who pry into things and consider it wisdom. I hate those who are imprudent and consider it courage. I hate those who leak out secrets and consider it honesty."

Tseng-tzu said, "The gentleman knows enough not to exceed his position."

Confucius said, "The gentleman is not a tool."

From Confucius, *The Analects*, reprinted in *Chinese Civilization and Society*, Patricia Buckley Ebrey, ed. pp. 13–14. The Free Press, 1981.

THE DAOIST VIEWS IN LIFE: From the *Daodejing*

1 The way that can be spoken of
Is not the constant way;
The name that can be named
Is not the constant name.

2 The nameless was the beginning of heaven and earth;
The named was the mother of the myriad creatures.

3 Hence always rid yourself of desires in order to observe
its secrets;
But always allow yourself to have desires in order to
observe its manifestations.

3a These two are the same
But diverge in name as they issue forth.
Being the same they are called mysteries,
Mystery upon mystery—
The gateway of the manifold secrets. . . .

11 The way is empty, yet use will not drain it.
Deep, it is like the ancestor of the myriad creatures.

12 Blunt the sharpness;
Untangle the knots;
Soften the glare;
Let your wheels move only along old ruts.

13 Darkly visible, it only seems as if it were there.
I know not whose son it is.
It images the forefather of God. . . .

43 Exterminate the sage, discard the wise,
And the people will benefit a hundredfold;
Exterminate benevolence, discard rectitude,
And the people will again be filial;
Exterminate ingenuity, discard profit,
And there will be no more thieves and bandits.

43a These three, being false adornments, are not enough
And the people must have something to which they can
attach themselves:
Exhibit the unadorned and embrace the uncarved block,
Have little thought of self and as few desires as possible. . . .

147 Do that which consists in taking no action; pursue that
which is not meddlesome; savour that which has no flavor.

148 Make the small big and the few many; do good to him
who has done you an injury.

149 Lay plans for the accomplishment of the difficult before it
becomes difficult; make something big by starting with it
when small.

149a Difficult things in the world must needs have their beginnings in the easy; big things must needs have their beginnings in the small.

150 Therefore it is because the sage never attempts to be great
that he succeeds in becoming great.

151 One who makes promises rashly rarely keeps good faith;
one who is in the habit of considering things easy meets
with frequent difficulties.

151a Therefore even the sage treats some things as difficult.
That is why in the end no difficulties can get the better of
him. . . .

184 Is not the way of heaven like the stretching of a bow?
The high it presses down,
The low it lifts up;
The excessive it takes from,
The deficient it gives to.

184a It is the way of heaven to take from what has in excess in
order to make good what is deficient. The way of man is
otherwise. It takes from those who are in want in order to
offer this to those who already have more than enough.
Who is there that can take what he him self has in excess
and offer this to the empire? Only he who has the way.

185 Therefore the sage benefits them yet exacts no gratitude,
Accomplishes his task yet lays claim to no merit.

185a Is this not because he does not wish to be considered a
better man than others? . . .

From *Tao te Ching*, D. C. Lau., trans. Penguin Books. verses 1–3a, 11–13, 43, 43a, 147–151a, and 184–185a. © D. C. Lau, 1963.

THE LEGALIST RULER: From Han Feizi

The enlightened ruler controls his ministers by means of two handles alone. The two handles are punishment and favor. What do I mean by punishment and favor? To inflict mutilation and death on men is called punishment; to bestow honor and reward is called favor. Those who act as ministers fear the penalties and hope to profit by the rewards. Hence, if the ruler wields his punishments and favors, the ministers will fear his sternness and flock to receive his benefits. But the evil ministers of the age are different. They cajole the ruler into let-ting them inflict punishment themselves on men they hate and bestow rewards on men they like. Now if the ruler of men does not insist upon reserving to himself the right to dispense profit in the form of rewards and show his sternness in punishments, but instead hands them out on the advice of his ministers, then the people of the state will all fear the ministers and hold the ruler in contempt, will flock to the ministers and desert the ruler. This is the danger that arises when the rule loses control of punishments and favors.

The tiger is able to overpower the dog because of his claws and teeth, but if he discards his claws and teeth and lets the dog use them, then on the contrary he will be overpowered by the dog. In the same way the ruler of men uses punishments and fa-vors to control his ministers, but if he discards his punishments and favors and lets his ministers employ them, then on the con-trary he will find himself in the control of his ministers. . . .

From Han Fei Tzu, "The Two Handles." From *Basic Writings of Mo Tzu, Hsün Tzu, and Han Fei Tsu.* Burton Watson, trans. p. 30. Columbia University Press, 1967.

ANALYSIS AND INTERPRETATION OF THE READINGS

1. How does Confucius define the "gentleman"? What is the relevance of such characteristics to the gentleman's task of governing?
2. Was Confucius an idealist? Explain.
3. To what extent are the ideas of Confucius and Laozi (as represented in the *Daodejing*) antithetical? To what extent are they compatible or complementary?
4. How did the Legalists' view of government differ from that of the Confucians?

Near Eastern Empires

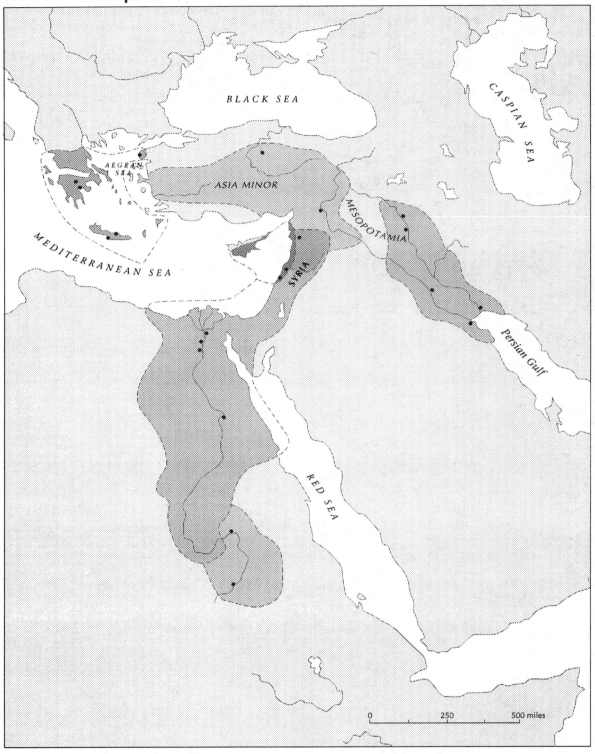

BLACK SEA

CASPIAN SEA

AEGEAN SEA

ASIA MINOR

MESOPOTAMIA

MEDITERRANEAN SEA

SYRIA

Persian Gulf

RED SEA

0   250   500 miles

Near Eastern Empires and Ancient India Maps
(Chapters 1–6)

NEAR EASTERN EMPIRES

1. On the "Near Eastern Empires" map (opposite), place the appropriate name in the shaded area that most closely approximates the geographic extent of the empire or civilization at the time indicated.

    a. Old Babylonian Empire (c. 1750 B.C.E.)
    b. Kushitic Kingdom (c. 800 B.C.E.)
    c. Minoan-Mycenaean civilization (c. 2200–1000 B.C.E.)
    d. Hittite Empire (c. 1600–1200 B.C.E.)
    e. Egyptian Empire (c. 1450 B.C.E.)

2. Locate the following on the map.

Tigris River	Mycenae
Euphrates River	Troy
Nile River	Thebes
Nineveh	Memphis
Babylon	Knossos
Ur	

ANCIENT INDIA

1. Label the following locations on the map of ancient India (see page 30, over).

Himalaya Mountains	Indus River
the Deccan	Ganges River
Hindustan	Pataliputra (Patna)
Hindu Kush Mountains	Mohenjo Daro

Ancient India, 500 B.C.E.

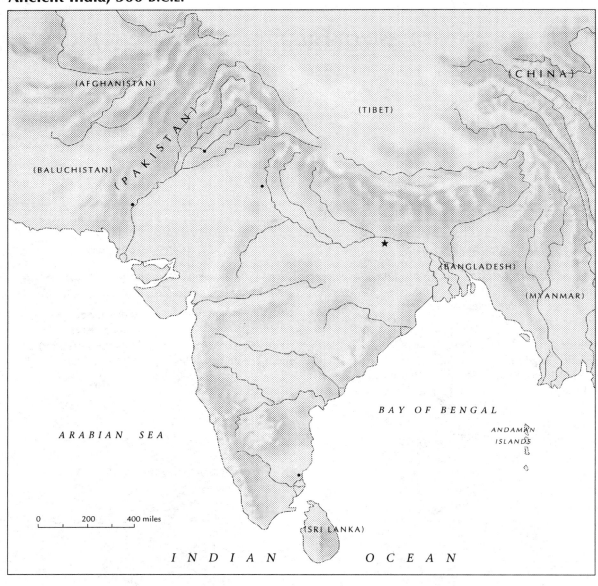

CHAPTER 7 | Greek Civilization

CHRONOLOGY

Following is a list of events in Greek history with which you should be familiar. Arrange them in the spaces below according to their proper chronological order (earliest to latest). After each event write its date (or approximate date).

rule of Cleisthenes
rise of Greek city-states
Peloponnesian War
appointment of Solon as magistrate
life of Aristotle
Persian Wars
Dark Ages
Age of Pericles

1. _____

2. _____

3. _____

4. _____

5. _____

6. _____

7. _____

8. _____

IDENTIFICATIONS

You should be able to identify the following. Be sure you understand the importance of each to an understanding of Greek civilization.

basileus	syllogism
polis	*polity*
phalanx	*Iliad*
helot	*Odyssey*
Solon	Parthenon
Pisistratus	Doric order
Xerxes	Ionic order
Pre-Socratics	*paideia*
the *Republic*	

Each of the following descriptions applies to one of the three men named in the brackets after it. In each blank, write the number of the man described:

_____ The earliest of the Pre-Socratics, he believed that the basic substance in nature was water. [1. Anaximenes, 2. Thales, 3. Pythagoras]

_____ The "father of Athenian democracy," he greatly enlarged both the size of the citizen population and its political powers late in the sixth century B.C.E. [1. Solon, 2. Lycurgus, 3. Cleisthenes]

_____ A native of Abdera who taught in Athens, his dictum, "Man is the measure of all things," contained the essence of the Sophist philosophy. [1. Protagoras, 2. Thrasymachus, 3. Scopas]

_____ The "father of medicine," he emphasized that every disease has a natural cause. [1. Hippocrates, 2. Empedocles, 3. Anaximander]

_____ He was a benevolent tyrant, but his son's rule was so oppressive that it was forcefully overthrown. [1. Solon, 2. Pisistratus, 3. Hippias]

_____ One of the three great Greek tragic playwrights, he displays a greater interest in the particular, unique features of his characters, and focuses less on universal qualities. [1. Aeschylus, 2. Sophocles, 3. Euripides]

_____ Though he left no writings himself, his determination to question every assumption and his emphasis on proper conduct fostered through pursuit of truth had a profound and lasting effect on later thinkers. [1. Parmenides, 2. Socrates, 3. Aristotle]

_____ An advocate of scientific history, he wrote a famous, dispassionate account of the Peloponnesian War. [1. Herodotus, 2. Plato, 3. Thucydides]

_____ One of the most famous of Greek sculptors, he created the giant statue of Athena in the Parthenon, along with other notable works. [1. Praxiteles, 2. Phidias, 3. Myron]

STUDY QUESTIONS

1. Describe the character of government in Greece during the "Dark Ages."
2. What was the Greek conception of religious piety? How did this relate to the Greek view of the gods, their powers, and their expectations of humans?
3. Discuss how the Greek view of Hades and of the fate of humans after death compares with the idea of the transmigration of souls found in ancient India. How would these two views affect ideas about the purpose of life?
4. What supplied the foundations of Greek ethics and morality?
5. Discuss the consequences of relatively widespread literacy in Greece.
6. Evaluate the effects of intense militarism on the political and social life of Sparta.
7. How did the origins of Sparta differ from those of Athens? How did those differences affect their respective destinies?
8. Trace the evolution of Athenian democracy from Solon to Pericles. At the peak of its development, what were the limitations of that democracy?
9. Discuss the advantages and disadvantages of the Athenian system of "direct" democracy.
10. Describe the similarities and differences between Athenian democracy and twentieth-century American democracy.
11. What were the consequences for Greece (both positive and negative) of the Persian War?
12. What were the causes of the Peloponnesian War? What were its results?
13. Describe the roles of women in ancient Greece, and the reasons for their subordination.
14. Identify the most important social changes in Greek society in the fifth to fourth centuries B.C.E.
15. "Although the various conclusions of the Pre-Socratics would not stand up to later questioning and testing, their insistence on looking for natural laws and rational explanations was pathfinding." Explain the meaning of this statement.

16. Cicero said of the Sophists that they "brought philosophy down from heaven to the dwellings of men." What did he mean?
17. What did Plato mean when he referred to an "Idea"?
18. Aristotle's philosophy "was a compromise between Platonism, which tended to ignore matter, and the purest materialism, which saw no patterns in the universe other than the accidents of matter impinging on matter." Show how this statement is justified by Aristotle's philosophy.
19. Explain the differences between epic poetry and lyric poetry. Keep in mind themes as well as performance styles.
20. What was the Greek conception of tragedy?
21. How did the art of the Greeks illustrate their social, political, and aesthetic ideals?
22. In what ways did Athenian social life differ from that of other peoples of the ancient world, including other Greeks?
23. The Hellenic Greeks are often described as humanists. What is meant by this description? To what extent is this description appropriate, and what were the limitations of Greek humanism?

PROBLEMS

1. Why did Athenians turn to imperialism at the peak of their democratic development? Is there any parallel in the history of other countries in modern times?
2. Read a play by Sophocles and another by Euripides. Compare their themes and attitudes. Which playwright do you prefer? Why?
3. Investigate further any of the following:
   a. Homeric religion
   b. The nature of Spartan militarism
   c. Greek tactics in the Persian War
   d. Athenian government under Pericles
   e. Thucydides' account of the Peloponnesian War
   f. Socrates and his thought
   g. Plato's *Republic*
   h. Aristotle's ideas on biology
   I. Greek sculpture
   j. Athenian life in the Golden Age
4. Compare Athenian ideals as described in the Funeral Oration of Pericles (found in Thucydides, *The Peloponnesian War*) with those of Sparta as described by Plutarch in his life of Lycurgus (found in Plutarch, *Lives of Illustrious Men*).
5. Discuss the effects of wars on Hellenic civilization.
6. It is said that "the Greeks invented philosophy." What does it mean to "invent" philosophy? Explore the thought of the Pre-Socratics, the Sophists, Socrates, Plato, and Aristotle. Analyze the main features of the ideas of these philosophers. Pay particular attention to the questions they sought to answer, and the approaches they adopted in searching for answers.

7. Study the philosophy of Plato as contained in *The Republic*. What aspects of his ideal state would you like to see in put into practice today? In your opinion, what are the weaknesses or dangers inherent in his prescription for the ideal state?

8. Trace as many elements of Greek civilization as possible to their origins in the civilization of western Asia.

9. Read the discussion of Euripides in Edith Hamilton's *The Greek Way*. Why does she disagree with the dictum that he was the most tragic of the dramatists? Why does she consider him the exponent of "the modern mind"?

10. Explore this statement: "To a startling degree the very concept of 'humanity' itself . . . comes to us from the Greeks."

AIDS TO AN UNDERSTANDING OF GREEK CIVILIZATION

THE SPARTAN SYSTEM
Plutarch

And this was the reason why he (Lycurgus) forbade them to travel abroad, and go about acquainting themselves with foreign rules of morality, the habits of ill-educated people, and different views of government. Withal he banished from Lacedæmon all strangers who would not give a very good reason for their coming thither; not because he was afraid lest they should inform themselves of and imitate his manner of government (as Thucydides says), or learn any thing to their good; but rather lest they should introduce something contrary to good manners. With strange people, strange words must be admitted; these novelties produce novelties in thought; and on these follow views and feelings whose discordant character destroys the harmony of the state. He was as careful to save his city from the infection of foreign bad habits, as men usually are to prevent the introduction of a pestilence.

Hitherto I, for my part, see no sign of injustice or want of equity in the laws of Lycurgus, though some who admit them to be well contrived to make good soldiers, pronounce them defective in point of justice. The Cryptia, perhaps (if it were one of Lycurgus's ordinances, as Aristotle says it was), gave both him and Plato, too, this opinion alike of the lawgiver and his government. By this ordinance, the magistrates despatched privately some of the ablest of the young men into the country, from time to time, armed only with their daggers, and taking a little necessary provision with them; in the daytime, they hid themselves in out-of-the-way places, and there lay close, but, in the night issued out into the highways, and killed all the Helots they could light upon; sometimes they set upon them by day, as they were at work in the fields, and murdered them. As, also, Thucydides, in his history of the Peloponnesian war, tells us, that a good number of them, after being singled out for their bravery by the Spartans, garlanded, as enfranchised persons, and led about to all the temples in token of honors, shortly after disappeared all of a sudden, being about the number of two thousand; and no man either then or since could give an account how they came by their deaths. And Aristotle, in particular, adds that the ephori, so soon as they were entered into their office, used to declare war against them, that they might be massacred without a breach of religion. It is confessed, on all hands, that the Spartans dealt with them very hardly; for it was a common thing to force them to drink to excess, and to lead them in that condition into their public halls, that the children might see what a sight a drunken man is; they made them to dance low dances, and sing ridiculous songs, forbidding them expressly to meddle with any of a better kind. And accordingly, when the Thebans made their invasion into Laconia, and took a great number of the Helots, they could by no means persuade them to sing the verses of Terpander, Aleman, or Spendon, "For," said they, "the masters do not like it." So that it was truly observed by one, that in Sparta he who was free was most so, and he that was a slave there, the greatest slave in the world. . . .

From Plutarch, *Lives of Illustrious Men* (Lycurgus), A. H. Clough trans.

ATHENIAN IDEALS: As Described by Pericles in his Famous Funeral Oration
Thucydides

Our form of government does not enter into rivalry with the institutions of others. We do not copy our neighbours, but are an example to them. It is true that we are called a democracy, for the administration is in the hands of the many and not of the few. But while the law secures equal justice to all alike in their private disputes, the claim of excellence is also recognised; and when a citizen is in any way distinguished, he is preferred to the public service, not as a matter of privilege, but as the reward of merit. Neither is poverty a bar, but a man may benefit his country whatever be the obscurity of his condition. There is no exclusiveness in our public life, and in our private intercourse we are not suspicious of one another, nor angry with our neighbour if he does what he likes; we do not put on sour looks at him which, though harmless, are not pleasant. While we are thus unconstrained in our private intercourse, a spirit of reverence pervades our public acts; we are prevented from doing wrong by respect for authority and for the laws, having an especial regard to those which are ordained for the protection of the injured as well as to those unwritten laws which bring upon the transgressor of them the reprobation of the general sentiment.

And we have not forgotten to provide for our weary spirits many relaxations from toil; we have regular games and sacrifices throughout the year; at home the style of our life is refined; and the delight which we daily feel in all these things helps to banish melancholy. Because of the greatness of our city the fruits of the whole earth flow in upon us; so that we enjoy the goods of other countries as freely as of our own.

Then, again, our military training is in many respects superior to that of our adversaries. Our city is thrown open to the world, and we never expel a foreigner or prevent him from seeing or learning anything of which the secret if revealed to an enemy might profit him. We rely not upon management or trickery, but upon our own hearts and hands. And in the matter of education, whereas they from early youth are always undergoing laborious exercises which are to make them brave, we live at ease, and yet are equally ready to face the perils which they face. . . .

For we are lovers of the beautiful, yet with economy, and we cultivate the mind without loss of manliness. Wealth we employ, not for talk and ostentation, but when there is a real use for it. To avow poverty with us is no disgrace; the true disgrace is in doing nothing to avoid it. An Athenian citizen does not neglect the state because he takes care of his own household; and even those of us who are engaged in business have a very fair idea of politics. We alone regard a man who takes no interest in public affairs, not as a harmless, but as a useless character; and if few of us are originators, we are all sound judges of a policy. The great impediment to action is, in our opinion, not discussion, but the want of that knowledge which is gained by discussion preparatory to action. For we have a peculiar power of thinking before we act and of acting too, whereas other men are courageous from ignorance but hesitate upon reflection. And they are surely to be esteemed the bravest spirits who, having the clearest sense both of the pains and pleasures of life, do not on that account shrink from danger. In doing good, again, we are unlike others; we make our friends by conferring, not by receiving favours. Now he who confers a favour is the firmer friend, because he would fain by kindness keep alive the memory of an obligation; but the recipient is colder in his feelings, because he knows that in requiting another's generosity he will not be winning gratitude but only paying a debt. We alone do good to our neighbours not upon a calculation of interest, but in the confidence of freedom and in a frank and fearless spirit.

To sum up: I say that Athens is the school of Hellas, and that the individual Athenian in his own person seems to have the power of adapting himself to the most varied forms of action with the utmost versatility and grace. This is no passing and idle word, but truth and fact; and the assertion is verified by the position to which these qualities have raised the state. For in the hour of trial Athens alone among her contemporaries is superior to the report of her. No enemy who comes against her is indignant at the reverses which he sustains at the hands of such a city; no subject complains that his masters are unworthy of him. And we shall assuredly not be without witnesses; there are mighty monuments of our power which will make us the wonder of this and of succeeding ages; we shall not need the praises of Homer or of any other panegyrist whose poetry may please for the moment, although his representation of the facts will not bear the light of day. For we have compelled every land and every sea to open a path for our valour, and have everywhere planted eternal memorials of our friendship and of our enmity. Such is the city for whose sake these men nobly fought and died; they could not bear the thought that she might be taken from them; and every one of us who survives should gladly toil on her behalf.

I have dwelt upon the greatness of Athens because I want to show you that we are contending for a higher prize than those who enjoy none of these privileges, and to establish by manifest proof the merit of these men whom I am now commemorating. Their loftiest praise has been already spoken. For in magnifying the city I have magnified them, and men like them whose virtues made her glorious. And of how few Hellenes can it be said as of them, that their deeds when weighed in the balance have been found equal to their fame! It seems to me that a death such as theirs has been given the true measure of a man's worth; it may be the first revelation of his virtues, but is at any rate their final seal.

From Thucydides, *The Peloponnesian War*, Benjamin Jowett trans.

PLATO'S IDEAL STATE: The Life of the Guardians
Plato

Then now let us consider what will be their way of life, if they are to realize our idea of them. In the first place, none of them should have any property of his own beyond what is absolutely necessary; neither should they have a private house or store closed against any one who has a mind to enter; their provisions should be only such as are required by trained warriors, who are men of temperance and courage; they should agree to receive from the citizens a fixed rate of pay, enough to meet the expenses of the year and no more; and they will go to mess and live together like soldiers in a camp. Gold and silver we will tell them that they have from God; the diviner metal is within them, and they have therefore no need of the dross which is current among them, and ought not to pollute the divine by any such earthly admixture; for that commoner metal has been the source of many unholy deeds, but their own is undefiled. And they alone of all the citizens may not touch or handle silver or gold, or be under the same roof with them, or wear them, or drink from them. And this will be their salvation, and they will be the saviors of the State. But should they ever acquire homes or lands or moneys of their own, they will become housekeepers and husbandmen instead of guardians, enemies and tyrants instead of allies of the other citizens; hating and being hated, plotting and being plotted against, they will pass their whole life in much greater terror of internal than of external enemies, and the hour of ruin, both to themselves and to the rest of the State, will be at hand. For all which reasons may we not say that thus shall our State be ordered, and that these shall be the regulations appointed by us for our guardians concerning their houses and all other matters?

Yes, said Glaucon. . . .

I said: *Until philosophers are kings, or the kings and princes of this world have the spirit and power of philosophy, and political greatness and wisdom meet in one, and those commoner natures who pursue either to the exclusion of the other are compelled to stand aside, cities will never have rest from their evils,—no, nor the human race, as I believe,—and then only will this our State have a possibility of life and behold the light of day.*

From Benjamin Jowett trans., *The Dialogues of Plato* (Republic).

WOMEN IN CLASSICAL ATHENS
Sarah Pomeroy

The separation of the sexes was spatially emphasized. While men spent most of their day in public areas such as the marketplace and the gymnasium, respectable women remained at home. In contrast to the admired public buildings, mostly frequented by men, the residential quarters of Classical Athens were dark, squalid, and unsanitary.

Women stayed home not only because their work did not allow them much chance to get out but because of the influence of public opinion. Many families were likely to own at least one female slave, but even a woman with slaves was tied down by the demands of her household, husband, and infants. Wealthier women were most likely to stay home and send their slaves on errands. But poor women, lacking slaves, could not be kept in seclusion, and in fact women found pleasure in the company of other women, for they gossiped while fetching water, washing clothes, and borrowing utensils.

Women of all economic classes went out for festivals and funerals. The close association of women and mourning noted for earlier periods continued in Classical Athens. In an effort to promote democratization, Solonian legislation had curtailed the participation of women in funerals, for mourning by large numbers of women had been a means for ostentatious families to parade their wealth. The *prothesis* (lying-in-state) formerly held in the courtyard was to take place indoors. Only women

over sixty years of age or within the degree of children of cousins were permitted to enter the room of the deceased and to accompany the dead when the corpse was carried to the tomb, following the men in the funeral procession. Xanthippe's visit to Socrates on the day he was to die was not warmly received, but Socrates' behavior was unusual. When some men were condemned to death by the notorious Thirty, they summoned their sisters, mothers, wives, or other female relatives to see them in prison.

Whether women attended dramatic performances has been much disputed. It seems likely that they did, but the contrary can be maintained with plausibility. Dramatic festivals evolved from the worship of Dionysus, and all the roles were acted by male actors; but, as Euripides' *Bacchae* demonstrates, women were highly enthusiastic participants in the cult of this god. On the other hand, women who did not have slaves to tend their babies were probably not able to attend a full day's performance, or even to see one play. What is interesting about this controversy is that, numerous though they probably were over the years, the women, absent or present, were not noticed by our ancient authorities.

The separation of the sexes was expressed in private architecture by the provision of separate quarters for men and women. Women usually inhabited the more remote rooms, away from the street and from the public areas of the house. If the house had two stories, the wife along with female slaves lived upstairs. The sexes were separated to restrain the household slaves from breeding without the master's permission.

From Sarah B. Pomeroy, *Goddesses, Whores, Wives, and Slaves: Women in Classical Antiquity.* pp. 79–80. Schocken Books, 1975.

ANALYSIS AND INTERPRETATION OF THE READINGS

1. Was it really true that in Sparta, "he who was free was most so, and he that was a slave there, the greatest slave in the world"?
2. What proofs does Pericles offer, in his Funeral Oration, of the greatness of Athens? Do you think these proofs are valid?
3. Do you think that Plato actually believed his ideal state could become a reality?
4. What purposes did separation of the sexes serve in classical Athens? How did this vary from one social class to another?

CHAPTER 8 | The Hellenistic Civilization

CHRONOLOGY

c. 600   323
559   301
490   338

From the list above, select the correct date for each of the items below and write it in the blank (all dates are B.C.E.):

Death of Alexander _____

Battle of Ipsus _____

Zoroaster _____

Battle of Chaeronea _____

Battle of Marathon _____

Accession of Cyrus to Persian throne _____

IDENTIFICATIONS

The people of the Hellenistic Age most memorable to us now were its intellectuals—its writers, philosophers, and scientists. In the blanks below, write the name of the appropriate individuals selected from the following list:

Carneades   Polybius
Archimedes   Menander
Epicurus   Eratosthenes
Theocritus   Hipparchus
Erasistratus   Euclid
Ptolemy   Zeno
Diogenes   Aristarchus
Herophilus

1. "Hellenistic Copernicus"

_____

2. Like Thucydides, a practitioner of "scientific" history

_____

3. Leading Skeptic

_____

4. Exponent of Cynic philosophy

_____

5. Greatest geographer of his age

_____

6. Athenian comic playwright

_____

7. Author of *Elements of Geometry*

_____

8. "Greatest anatomist of antiquity"

_____

9. Founder of the Stoic philosophy

_____

10. Laid the foundations of trigonometry

_____

11. Author of the *Almagest*

_____

12. Discoverer of specific gravity

_____

13. Founder of a philosophy which, though based on materialism, stressed the possibility of human freedom

_____

14. Founder of physiology

_____

15. Pastoral poet of the third century B.C.E.

_____

You should be able to define or explain each of the following:

satrap	Orphic cult
eclecticism	religious dualism
Achaean League	the *Laocoön* group
Aetolian League	Hellenistic cosmopolitanism

STUDY QUESTIONS

1. "The supreme tragedy of the Greeks was their failure to solve the problem of political conflict." Discuss this statement and explain how it contributes to an understanding of the Hellenistic Age.
2. Explain the basic teachings of Zoroastrianism. How was it both a universal and a personal religion?
3. Point out the parallels between Zoroastrianism, Judaism, and Christianity.
4. What is meant by the claim that "Zoroaster was probably the first real theologian in history"?
5. What would you describe as the enlightened aspects of Persian imperial rule?
6. Explain the eclectic character of Persian culture. Illustrate this with reference to Persian architecture.
7. Explain why Philip, ruler of relatively uncivilized Macedon, was able to conquer the more civilized cities of Greece.
8. In what ways did Alexander lay the foundations of Hellenistic civilization? In what respects did he break with Greek tradition and ideals?
9. To what extent should the Hellenistic civilization be considered as distinct from the Hellenic rather than a further development of it? What elements of continuity were there between the two civilizations?
10. How did the dominant political pattern of the Hellenistic Age differ from Hellenic political institutions or traditions?
11. Evaluate the economic conditions in the Hellenistic Age. Explain the reasons behind the growth of trade.
12. How do you explain the rapid growth of cities in spite of the fact that agriculture remained the chief source of wealth?
13. Describe the ways in which Hellenistic science diverged from the philosophy of Aristotle.
14. In what ways were Epicureanism and Stoicism alike, and in what ways were they different?
15. Do you agree that "the Stoic philosophy was one of the noblest products of the Hellenistic Age"? Why or why not?
16. How did the Epicurean philosophy differ from that of the Cynics and that of the Skeptics?
17. Compare the popular religion of the Hellenistic Age with the "civil religion" of the Greeks.
18. Which genres of Hellenistic literature most clearly exhibit a penchant for escapism?
19. What were the primary characteristics of Hellenistic sculpture?
20. How do you account for the flowering of science during the Hellenistic Age?
21. Compare the Hellenistic Age with our own. What are the apparent similarities between that age and this? What significant differences can be noted?

PROBLEMS

1. In your view, during Hellenistic times did sculpture retrogress or progress from Greek standards?
2. Read Plutarch's life of Alexander and assess the validity of the notion that "history is the lengthened shadow of a great man."
3. Explain the importance of the Hellenistic Age as a period in world history. What were this age's major contributions to world history?
4. Compare the science, literature, and art of the Hellenistic Age with those of the Hellenic Greeks. How do you account for the differences?
5. Compare the philosophy and religion of the Hellenistic Age with those of the Hellenic Greeks. How do you account for the differences?
6. Compare the estimate of Alexander in Wicken, *Alexander the Great* with that in Burn, *Alexander the Great and the Hellenistic World*.
7. Investigate further any of the following aspects of Hellenistic civilization:
   a. cities and city life
   b. medical science and practice
   c. the spread of Mithraism and other mystery cults
8. Analyze the Hellenistic Age as an "intermediary" between Greece and Rome.

AIDS TO AN UNDERSTANDING OF THE HELLENISTIC CIVILIZATION

THE LAST DAYS OF ALEXANDER
Plutarch

When once Alexander had given way to fears of supernatural influence, his mind grew so disturbed and so easily alarmed, that if the least unusual or extraordinary thing happened, he thought it a prodigy or a presage, and his court was thronged with diviners and priests whose business was to sacrifice and purify and foretell the future. So miserable a thing is incredulity and contempt of divine power on the one hand, and so miserable, also, superstition on the other, which like water, where the level has been lowered, flowing in and never stopping, fills the mind with slavish fears and follies, as now in Alexander's case. But upon some answers which were brought him from the oracle concerning Hephæstion, he laid aside his sorrow, and fell again to sacrificing and drinking; and having given Nearchus a splendid entertainment, after he had bathed as was his custom, just as he was going to bed, at Medius's request he went to supper with him. Here he drank all the next day, and was attacked with a fever, which seized him, not as some write, after he had drunk of the bowl of Hercules; nor was he taken with any sudden pain in his back, as if he had been struck with a lance, for these are the inventions of some authors who thought it their duty to make the last scene of so great an action as tragical and moving as they could. Aristobulus tells us, that in the rage of his fever and a violent thirst, he took a draught of wine, upon which he fell into delirium, and died on the thirtieth of the month Dæsius.

But the journals give the following record. On the eighteenth of the month, he slept in the bathing-room on account of his fever. The next day he bathed and removed into his chamber, and spent his time in playing at dice with Medius. In the evening he bathed and sacrificed, and ate freely, and had the fever on him through the night. On the twentieth, after the usual sacrifices and bathing, he lay in the bathing-room and heard Nearchus's narrative of his voyage, and the observations he had made in the great sea. The twenty-first he passed in the same manner, his fever still increasing, and suffered much during the night. The next day the fever was very violent, and he had himself removed and his bed set by the great bath, and discoursed with his principal officers about finding fit men to fill up the vacant places in the army. On the twenty-fourth he was much worse, and was carried out of his bed to assist at the sacrifices, and gave order that the general officers should wait within the court, whilst the inferior officers kept watch without doors. On the twenty-fifth he was removed to his palace on the other side the river, where he slept a little, but his fever did not abate, and when the generals came into his chamber, he was speechless, and continued so the following day. The Macedonians, therefore, supposing he was dead, came with great clamors to the gates, and menaced his friends so that they were forced to admit them, and let them all pass through unarmed along by his bedside. The same day Python and Seleucus were despatched to the temple of Serapis to inquire if they should bring Alexander thither, and were answered by the god, that they should not remove him. On the twenty-eighth, in the evening, he died. This account is most of it word for word as it is written in the diary.

From Plutarch, *Lives of Illustrious Men* (Alexander), A. H. Clough

A CHARACTER SKETCH OF ALEXANDER THE GREAT
Robin Lane Fox

Most historians have had their own Alexander, and a view of him which is one-sided is bound to have missed the truth. There are features which cannot be disputed; the extraordinary toughness of a man who sustained nine wounds, breaking an ankle bone and receiving an arrow through his chest and the bolt of a catapult through his shoulder. He was twice struck on the head and neck by stones and once lost his sight from such a blow. The bravery which bordered on folly never failed him in the front line of battle, a position which few generals since have considered proper; he set out to show himself a hero, and from the Granicus to Multan he left a trail of heroics which has never been surpassed and is perhaps too easily assumed among all his achievements. There are two ways to lead men, either to delegate all authority and limit the leader's burden or to share every hardship and decision and be seen to take the toughest labour, prolonging it until every other man has finished. Alexander's method was the second, and only those who have suffered the first can appreciate why his men adored him; they will also remember how lightly men talk of a leader's example, but how much it costs both the will and the body to sustain it.

Alexander was not merely a man of toughness, resolution and no fear. A murderous fighter, he had wide interests outside war, his hunting, reading, his patronage of music and drama and his lifelong friendship with Greek artists, actors and architects; he minded about his food and took a daily interest in his meals, appreciating quails from Egypt or apples from western orchards; from the naphtha wells of Kirkuk to the Indian 'people of Dionysus' he showed the curiosity of a born explorer. He had an intelligent concern for agriculture and irrigation which he had learnt from his father; from Philip, too, came his constant favour for new cities and their law and formal design. He was famously generous and he loved to reward the same show of spirit which he asked of himself; he enjoyed the friendship of Iranian nobles and he had a courteous way, if he chose, with women. Just as the eastern experience of later crusaders first brought the idea of courtly love to the women's quarters of Europe, so Alexander's view of the East may have brought this courtesy home to him. It is extraordinary how Persian courtiers learnt to admire him, but the double sympathy with the lives of Greece and Persia was perhaps Alexander's most unusual characteristic. Equally he was impatient and often conceited; the same officers who worshipped him must often have found him

impossible, and the murder of Cleitus was an atrocious reminder of how petulance could become blind rage. Though he
drank as he lived, sparing nothing, his mind was not slurred by
excessive indulgence; he was not a man to be crossed or to be
told what he could not do, and he always had firm views on exactly what he wanted.

With a brusque manner went discipline, speed and shrewd
political sense. He seldom gave a second chance, for they usually let him down; he had a bold grasp of affairs, whether in his
insistence that his expedition was the Greeks' reverse of Persian sacrilege, though most Greeks opposed it, or in his brilliant
realization that the ruling class of the Empire should draw on
Iranians and Macedonians together, while the court and army
should stand open to any subject who could serve it. He was
generous, and he timed his generosity to suit his purpose; he
knew better than to wait and be certain that conspirators were
guilty. As a grand strategist, he took risks because he had to, but
he always attempted to cover himself, whether by 'defeating'
the Persian fleet on dry land or terrorizing the Swat highlands
above his main road to the Indus: his delay till Darius could do
pitched battle at Gaugamela was splendidly aggressive and his
plan to open the sea route from India to the Red Sea was proof
of that wider insight into economic realities to which his
Alexandria in Egypt still bears witness. The same boldness encouraged the fatal march through Makran; he had tactical sense,
whether on the Hydaspes or in the politics of Babylon and
Egypt, but self-confidence could override it and luck would not
always see self-confidence through. Here, it is very relevant
that rational profit was no more the cause of his constant search
for conquest than of most other wars in history. Through Zeus
Ammon, Alexander believed he was specially favoured by
heaven; through Homer, he had chosen the ideal of a hero, and
for Homer's heroes there could be no turning back from the demands of honour. Each ideal, the divine and the heroic, pitched
his life too high to last; each was the ideal of a romantic. . . .

From Robin Lane Fox, *Alexander the Great*, pp. 495–97. © 1973 by Robin Lane Fox.

THE STOIC PHILOSOPHY: As Described by Diogenes Laertius

The first instinct which the animal has is the
impulse to self-preservation with which nature endows it at the
outset. The first possession which every animal acquires is its
own organic unity and the perception thereof. If this were not
so, nature must either have estranged from itself the creature
which she has made or left it utterly indifferent to itself, neither
of which assumptions is tenable. The only alternative is that she
should have designed the creature to love itself. For in this way
it repels what harms it and welcomes what benefits it. It is not
true, as some say, that the first instinct of animals is toward
pleasure. For pleasure, if it is an end at all, is a concomitant of
later growth which follows when the nature of the animal in
and by itself has sought and found what is appropriate to it.
Under like circumstances animals sport and gambol and plants

grow luxuriant. Nature has made no absolute severance between plants and animals: in her contrivance of plants she
leaves out impulse and sensation, while certain processes go on
in us as they do in plants. But when animals have been further
endowed with instinct, by whose aid they go in search of the
things which benefit them, then to be governed by nature means
for them to be governed by instinct. When rational animals are
endowed with reason, in token of more complete superiority, in
them life in accordance with nature is rightly understood to
mean life in accordance with reason. For reason is like a crafts-
man shaping impulse and desire. Hence Zeno's definition of the
end is to live in conformity with nature, which means to live a
life of virtue, since it is to virtue that nature leads. On the other
hand, a virtuous life is a life which conforms to our experience
of the course of nature, our human natures being but parts of
universal nature. Thus the end is a life which follows nature,
whereby is meant not only our own nature, but the nature of the
universe, a life wherein we do nothing that is forbidden by the
universal law, *i.e.*, by right reason, which pervades all things
and is identical with Zeus, the guide and governor of the universe. The virtue of the happy man, his even flow of life, is re-
alised only when in all the actions he does his individual genius
is in harmony with the will of the ruler of the universe. Virtue is
a disposition conformable to reason, desirable in and for itself
and not because of any hope or fear or any external motive. And
well-being depends on virtue, on virtue alone, since the virtuous soul is adapted to secure harmony in the whole of life.
When reason in the animal is perverted, this is due to one of
two causes, either to the persuasive force of external things or
to the bad instruction of those surrounding it. The instincts
which nature implants are unperverted.

From R. D. Hicks, *Stoic and Epicurean*, Charles Scribner's Sons, 1910.

THE HELLENIZATION OF THE NEAR EAST
Moses Hadas

When imperialist historians speak of their na-
tion's armies "liberating" the regions they conquer and bringing them the blessings of civilization we are entitled to remain
skeptical. . . . But of the peoples newly subjected to helleniza-
tion it may be said that they welcomed the innovations, despite,
or it may be because of, the fact that they were themselves heirs
to venerable civilizations. Because they were they had much to
give the Greeks in return, but by far the stronger current ran
from west to east. The western influences affected the upper
classes directly, whereas the slighter influence from the east
touched mainly the lower classes, whence it forced its way up
into respectable Greek society only gradually. And so far from
resisting hellenism the upper classes, in the Near if not the Middle East, welcomed it with open arms.

The language of the Greek city, and the official language in
all the dominions of the Successors, was Greek. In the beginning natives may have learned it out of necessity, for the uses of
commerce or government, or by the compulsion of snobbery,

but they continued to use it out of choice, and it soon became at least a second vernacular among a considerable proportion of the population. Upper-class natives must of course have known their native vernaculars, but they spoke to each other in Greek and were literate only in Greek. The use of a new language is not only a sign manifest that a new culture is being accepted but a key to the culture as a whole. We shall see that even books written by natives as propaganda for native values and intended mainly for a native audience were written in Greek, and that even books written in native languages were affected, in form and content, by Greek models.

Some native languages did of course survive, to become the basis for vernaculars in the Near East today, and it is interesting to see to what degree religion was a factor in the survival. The clearest case is hieroglyphic, which Egyptian priests continued to use though they understood it very imperfectly. On the other hand, Egypt was traditionally literate as well as conservative, and there continued to be lower-class Egyptians who could write demotic. In a remote place like Palmyra Aramaic continued to be an official language. But Syriac was able to produce a religious literature in the early centuries of Christianity because it had served as a subliterary vehicle for religion in the preceding period. Neither would Hebrew have survived but for religious motivations. Aramaic, not Hebrew, was the vernacular, and even before the coming of the Greeks Hebrew had something of the position of Latin in the Middle Ages as the language of Scripture and religion. That position it could retain even if Greek became the vernacular; it was only after the fall of Jerusalem in A.D. 70 and the rise of Christianity that the study of Greek was frowned upon on religious grounds.

In the pre-Christian period literary and other remains of the Jews afford abundant, and for our purposes highly relevant, evidence for the spread of Greek. The Bible was translated into Greek not, as Aristeas alleges in the beginning of his book, as a literary curiosity to be deposited in Ptolemy Philadelphus' library, but, as the end of the book indicates, for the use of a Jewish community who could receive their Scriptures in no other way. It is very doubtful that so devout a man as Philo knew any Hebrew or even Aramaic at all; certainly he makes the phrasing of the Septuagint the basis for his exegesis. Passages of prayer or psalmody which occur in such Greek books as III and IV Maccabees and the Wisdom of Solomon show similarities with Septuagint phraseology even when they are not quotations, and it has been thought that such passages are therefore translations of Hebrew originals. A more probable explanation is that "Septuagint Greek" had become normal for devotional compositions and that they were written in that language—just as a twentieth-century minister will use the style of the King James Bible for a prayer of his own composition. St. Paul did not receive Greek as part of his enlightenment on the road to Damascus; he must have learned the Greek poets he quotes (and expected his Jewish auditors to know) when he was a faithful Jew.

For the diaspora, then, which came to be more numerous than the population of Palestine, it is plain that Greek was the vernacular and that public worship was conducted in that language. But we know that Greek was a familiar language in Palestine itself. At a relatively early period we find evidence that classical Greek literature was known in Palestine, and the rabbinic writings of the later period contain a high proportion of Greek loan words. When the anti-humanist trend was at its strongest a new and more literal Greek version of the Bible was made, that called Aquila's, in order to reduce the possibilities of latitudinarian interpretation. When Paul addressed a Jerusalem crowd in Hebrew (Acts 22.2) they were pleased; apparently they expected him to speak in Greek and would have understood him if he had done so; in the diaspora Paul did address Jewish congregations in Greek. It would be very strange if the Jewish literature written in Greek in Alexandria and Antioch were not read and even emulated in Palestine.

The most forcible evidence that Greek had become the vernacular comes from epigraphy. Inscriptions in languages other than Greek are extremely rare in hellenized areas, and this is true not only of official inscriptions but even of grave inscriptions, and even in the case of quite humble burials. And it is fully as true of Jewish as of other burials, not only in Alexandria and Rome but in Palestine itself, and during the entire span of Greek and Roman sway. A city like Tiberias, which was a great center for rabbinic study, has yielded very numerous Greek inscriptions and very few Hebrew. Greek inscriptions, along with Greek decoration, appear in the ruins of synagogues, and the directional signs in the temple were in Greek.

Adoption of Greek architectural forms certainly caused a revision in ritual practices to approach Greek modes of worship, and even among the Jews. Mosaic and other Greek decoration, sometimes with distinctly pagan themes, has been discovered in synagogues, significantly in such as came to some catastrophic end, like those in Galilee or in Dura-Europus. On the basis of rabbinic literature it had been firmly believed that such decoration was impossible; but the literature was crystallized after the anti-humanist tendency had become a condition of survival. It is easy to imagine that before the crises which called forth official prohibitions the Jews, like other native peoples, would be attracted by the pomp and elegance of the Greek temples and forms of worship and so far as possible emulate them. It is not unlikely that Greek music was also influential. Certainly the Church adapted Greek musical forms; the best key for studying ancient Greek music today are the chants of the Russian Orthodox Church.

From Moses Hadas, *Hellenistic Culture-Fusion and Diffusion*, Columbia University Press, 1959. Reprinted by permission of the publisher.

ANALYSIS AND INTERPRETATION OF THE READINGS

1. Why should a man so powerful and successful as Alexander have fallen a victim of superstition?
2. What do you suppose Robin Lane Fox means in saying that "each ideal, the divine and the heroic, pitched [Alexander's] life too high to last"?
3. To what extent is Stoicism fatalistic?
4. What is the relationship of reason and instinct, according to the Stoics?

| # Roman Civilization

CHRONOLOGY

Fill in the blanks in the simplified chronological narrative below:

Sometime around the year _____ a group of Italic people founded Rome on the Tiber River. After a period of subjection to Etruscan rule during the _____ century, the Romans conquered neighboring peoples until by the year _____ they had subdued the entire Italian peninsula. Expansion led to further expansion, the most famous example of which came about through the Punic Wars. The first of these struggles was launched in _____ , but the long intermittent contest was not over until the destruction of Carthage in _____ . As early as _____ , Rome had become a republic, the early history of which was marked by a contest for control of the state between the patricians and plebeians. Notable triumphs of the latter class occurred in _____ when the office of tribune was created, and in _____ when the Law of the Twelve Tables was set down. With the passage of a law granting full legislative powers to the assembly in _____ , the plebeians achieved, at least nominally, their final victory. Conquest of the Mediterranean rim brought more troubles to the Republic. Attempted agrarian reforms by the Gracchi in the _____ and _____ decades of the second century B.C.E. failed; the nation drifted into one-man rule. Among those who exercised it were Marius, who, first elected consul in _____ , served six more terms until his death in _____ , and Sulla, dictator on behalf of the patrician Senate from _____ to _____ . But it was Julius Caesar who, between the time he crossed the Rubicon in _____ and his assassination in _____ , effectively ended the Republic. His grandnephew and heir, Augustus, established the Principate or Early Empire in _____ , which brought both Roman culture and territo-

rial expansion to their highest points and maintained relative peace for _____ . The death of the "good emperor" Marcus Aurelius, in _____ , ushered in a period of crisis and civil war with fatal results for Roman civilization, although strong rule was reimposed in _____ .

IDENTIFICATIONS

Fill in each blank below with the appropriate term.

1. The first written Roman law, it was set down on tablets of wood.

_____

2. Among the branches or divisions of Roman law, this classification was held to be the law common to all men of whatever nation.

_____

3. A judicial official, he defined the law and instructed the judge in a particular suit.

_____

4. Originally named for their capacity to provide their own cavalry equipment, these men were the *parvenus* of the late Republic.

_____

5. The work of a great poet of the Augustan age, this epic poem celebrated the founding of Rome, its imperial triumphs, and glorious destiny.

_____

Fill in each blank below with the name of the individual described.

1. Killed in a conflict with the conservative aristocracy, this tribune had sought to limit the amount of land any citizen might hold.

_____

2. This general terrorized the Italian peninsula for sixteen years and outfought the Roman armies, but in the end lost the war.

_____

3. An orator and philosopher, he affirmed the natural law as a legal principle.

_____

4. One of the most philosophical of golden-age writers, he was influenced by both Epicureanism and Stoicism.

_____

5. This escaped slave led a revolt of other slaves in southern Italy until his death in battle.

_____

6. A gullible encyclopedist, this "scientist" put together a famous and misleading *Natural History* in the first century C.E.

_____

7. A brilliant and ironic historian of the first century C.E., he sought not merely to record the past but to indict the present.

_____

8. The founder of a mystical philosophy, he taught that the universe is a series of emanations from the divine.

_____

9. The leading Roman exponent of Epicurean philosophy, he was also a majestic poet.

_____

10. An emperor in the late second century C.E., he was also a famous Stoic.

_____

STUDY QUESTIONS

*Circle the correct number **or numbers** in each of the following multiple-choice questions. Where none of the choices is correct, write the proper answer in the space provided at the end of the question.*

1. The founders of Rome were (1) Etrucsans from Asia Minor; (2) Greek colonists who had earlier settled in southern Italy; (3) obscure Italic people who were descended from Indo-European invaders; (4)_____

_____

_____

2. The early Roman Senate was (1) an elected body; (2) appointed by the king; (3) composed of the heads of clans; (4)_____

_____

_____

3. The old Roman king (1) was an absolute monarch unrestrained by law; (2) exercised patriarchal authority with powers limited by custom; (3) could best be described as a strong constitutional monarch; (4)_____

_____

_____

4. The Romans were brought into direct contact with Greek culture through (1) the Punic Wars; (2) their conquest of the Etruscans; (3) their conquest of southern Italy; (4)_____

_____

_____

5. The overthrow of the Roman monarchy brought several political changes. Among them were (1) a quick settlement of the ancient differences between patricians and plebeians; (2) the substitution of two elected consuls for the king; (3) the establishment of the office of dictator in times of crisis; (4)_____

_____

_____

6. The plebeians of the early Republic were (1) conquered peoples of Italy; (2) small farmers and craftsmen; (3) an urban proletariat; (4)_____

_____

_____

7. In religion (1) the Romans early developed a highly ethical set of beliefs; (2) Rome took over the Greek religion intact; (3) the Romans clearly showed the worldly, practical nature of their character; (4)_____

_____

_____

8. The final conquest of Carthage by Rome (1) led directly to further Roman expeditions to Greece and the Middle East in the third century B.C.E.; (2) contributed to the decline of the small farmer; (3) brought an era of peace and prosperity for the next hundred years; (4)_____

_____

_____

9. The revision of the Roman calendar on the Egyptian model was enacted by (1) Augustus Caesar; (2) Marcus Aurelius; (3) Pompey; (4)_____

_____

_____

10. Cicero (1) borrowed heavily from Stoicism; (2) leaned strongly, as did many other Romans, toward Epicureanism; (3) strongly influenced European medieval and Renaissance writers through his eloquent Latin prose; (4)_____

_____

_____

You should be able to answer the following:

1. Describe how the geography of Italy affected Roman civilization. Compare this with the effects of geography on Greek civilization.
2. What did Roman civilization obtain from the Greeks?
3. Why was it so difficult to bring about major changes in the law in the old Roman monarchy?
4. Tradition says that the overthrow of the Roman monarchy in the sixth century B.C.E. was a revolt against a foreign oppressor. What other and more important factors contributed to that overthrow? What were its results?
5. What effects did the wars of the Early Republic have on Roman civilization?
6. The plebeians had a number of grievances, and won a number of apparent victories. How significant were the changes that came from their struggles?
7. Compare the religion of the Romans with that of the Greeks.
8. How did Rome's victory in the Punic Wars contribute to fatal problems for Roman civilization?

9. How did Cicero's political philosophy differ from that of the earlier Stoics?
10. Why did Stoicism have a stronger appeal to Romans than Epicureanism?
11. Show how the political troubles of the Principate were an outgrowth of the civil strife of the late Republic and of the nature of the Roman constitution.
12. Discuss the flaws in the economy of the Principate.
13. What were the major accomplishments of Julius Caesar?
14. Describe the position of women of the upper class under the Principate.
15. In what way was the "natural law" a concept superior to the "civil law"?
16. "For all their achievements in engineering, the Romans accomplished little in science." Justify this assertion.
17. How did the Roman attitude toward manual labor contribute to the decline of Roman culture?
18. Explain the statement: "Roman history is the real beginning of Western history as we know it."

PROBLEMS

1. Do you agree with the authors that the similarities between Roman civilization and our own are overstated? Why or why not?
2. The art and architecture of a people usually reveal a great deal about their aspirations, ideals, and character. With this in mind, compare Roman art and architecture with any of the following: (a) Egyptian; (b) Aegean; (c) Assyrian; (d) Hellenic.
3. "Even without political problems the Roman Empire would probably have been fated to extinction for economic reasons." Discuss the validity of this statement.
4. Read the *Meditations* of Marcus Aurelius and compare them with Hellenistic Stoicism.
5. Compare in as many ways as you can ancient Rome and the United States. (You may wish to consult, among other works, Guglielmo Ferrero's *Ancient Rome and Modern America*.)
6. Attempt to determine the extent of Etruscan influence on Roman society and culture.
7. Machiavelli (*Discourses on Livy*, I, 37) asserted that the Gracchan agrarian reforms and the dissension they led to were a prime cause of the decline of the Roman Republic. Do you agree? Why or why not?
8. In assessing the causes of Rome's decline, compare Arnold Toynbee's discussion in *A Study of History* (Vol. I, Part IV: "The Breakdown of Civilizations") with that of Michael Rostovtzev in *A History of the Ancient World* (Vol. II, Chap. XXV: "Causes of the Decline of Ancient Civilization").

9. How was Roman civilization modified by contact with other peoples? Were these contacts beneficial or detrimental to Rome?
10. Why were Roman achievements in the field of law so outstanding?
11. How do you account for the fact that the Romans made little advancement in science despite the fact that the vast contribution of Hellenistic science was at their disposal?
12. What do you think were the chief drawbacks of the civilization of ancient Rome?
13. Examine in detail the various theories regarding the decline and fall of the Roman empire.
14. In Chapter 14 of his *The Revolt of the Masses*, José Ortega y Gasset identified Julius Caesar as one of the two "really clear heads" of the ancient world. Evaluate Ortega's judgment in the light of Roman history and of later European history.
15. If it is appropriate to your locale, examine the influence of Roman architecture on contemporary Western buildings.

AIDS TO AN UNDERSTANDING OF ROMAN CIVILIZATION

A ROMAN OF THE OLD SCHOOL: As Described by Plutarch

Ten years after his consulship, Cato stood for the office of censor, which was indeed the summit of all honor, and in a manner the highest step in civil affairs; for besides all other power, it had also that of an inquisition into every one's life and manners. For the Romans thought that no marriage or rearing of children, nay, no feast or drinking-bout ought to be permitted according to every one's appetite or fancy without being examined and inquired into; being indeed of opinion, that a man's character was much sooner perceived in things of this sort than in what is done publicly and in open day. They chose, therefore, two persons, one out of the patricians, the other out of the commons, who were to watch, correct, and punish, if any one ran too much into voluptuousness, or transgressed the usual manner of life of his country; and these they called Censors. They had power to take away a horse, or expel out of the senate any one who lived intemperately and out of order. It was also their business to take an estimate of what every one was worth, and to put down in registers everybody's birth and quality; besides many other prerogatives. And therefore the chief nobility opposed his pretensions to it. Jealousy prompted the patricians, who thought that it would be a stain to everybody's nobility, if men of no original honor should rise to the highest dignity and power; while others conscious of their own evil practices, and of the violation of the laws and customs of their country, were afraid of the austerity of the man; which, in an office of such great power, was likely to prove most uncompromising and severe. And so, consulting among themselves, they brought forward seven candidates in opposition to him, who sedulously set themselves to court the people's favor by fair promises, as though what they wished for was indulgent and easy government. Cato, on the contrary, promising no such mildness, but plainly threatening evil livers, from the very hustings openly declared himself, and exclaiming, that the city needed a great and thorough purgation, called upon the people, if they were wise, not to choose the gentlest, but the roughest of physicians; such a one, he said, he was, and Valerius Flaccus, one of the patricians, another; together with him, he doubted not but he should do something worth the while, and that, by cutting to pieces and burning like a hydra, all luxury and voluptuousness. He added, too, that he saw all the rest endeavoring after the office with ill intent, because they were afraid of those who would exercise it justly, as they ought. And so truly great and so worthy of great men to be its leaders was, it would seem, the Roman people, that they did not fear the severity and grim countenance of Cato, but rejecting those smooth promisers who were ready to do all things to ingratiate themselves, they took him, together with Flaccus; obeying his recommendations not as though he were a candidate, but as if he had had the actual power of commanding and governing already.

From Plutarch, *Lives of Illustrious Men* (Marcus Cato), A. H. Clough trans.

THE LAW OF THE TWELVE TABLES

TABLE IV: *Concerning the Rights of a Father and of Marriage*

LAW I

A father shall have the right of life and death over his son born in lawful marriage, and shall also have the power to render him independent, after he has been sold three times.

LAW II

If a father sells his son three times, the latter shall be free from paternal authority.

LAW III

A father shall immediately put to death a son recently born, who is a monster, or who has a form different from that of members of the human race.

LAW IV

When a woman brings forth a son within the next ten months after the death of her husband, he shall be born in lawful marriage, and shall be the legal heir of his estate. . . .

TABLE VII: *Concerning Crimes*

LAW IV

If anyone who has arrived at puberty, secretly, and by night, destroys or cuts and appropriates to his own use, the crop of another, which the owner of the land has laboriously obtained by plowing and the cultivation of the soil, he shall be sacrificed to Ceres, and hung.

If he is under the age of puberty, and not yet old enough to be accountable, he shall be scourged, in the discretion of the Praetor, and shall make good the loss by paying double its amount.

LAW V

Anyone who turns cattle on the land of another, for the purpose of pasture, shall surrender the cattle, by way of reparation.

LAW VI

Anyone who, knowingly and maliciously, burns a building, or a heap of grain left near a building, after having been placed in chains and scourged, shall be put to death by fire. If, however, he caused the damage by accident, and without malice, he shall make it good; or, if he has not the means to do so, he shall receive a lighter punishment.

LAW VII

When a person, in any way, causes an injury to another which is not serious, he shall be punished with a fine of twenty asses.

LAW VIII

When anyone publicly abuses another in a loud voice, or writes a poem for the purpose of insulting him, or rendering him infamous, he shall be beaten with a rod until he dies.

LAW IX

When anyone breaks a member of another, and is unwilling to come to make a settlement with him, he shall be punished by the law of retaliation.

From S. P. Scott. *The Civil Law*, The Central Trust Company, Cincinnati, 1932, Vol. I. Reprinted by permission of the Samuel P. Scott Trust and the Jefferson Medical College of Philadelphia.

LATE ROMAN STOICISM: As Exemplified by The Philosophy of Marcus Aurelius

What then is that which is able to conduct a man? One thing and only one, philosophy. But this consists in keeping the daemon within a man free from violence and unharmed, superior to pains and pleasures, doing nothing without a purpose, nor yet falsely and with hypocrisy, not feeling the need of another man's doing or not doing anything; and besides, accepting all that happens, and all that is allotted, as coming from thence, wherever it is, from whence he himself came;

and, finally, waiting for death with a cheerful mind, as being nothing else than a dissolution of the elements of which every living being is compounded. But if there is no harm to the elements themselves in each continually changing into another, why should a man have any apprehension about the change and dissolution of all the elements? For it is according to nature, and nothing is evil which is according to nature.

•   •   •

Does another do me wrong? Let him look to it. He has his own disposition, his own activity. I now have what the universal nature wills me to have; and I do what my nature now wills me to do.

Let the part of thy soul which leads and governs be undisturbed by the movements in the flesh, whether of pleasure or of pain; and let it not unite with them, but let it circumscribe itself and limit those affects to their parts. But when these affects rise up to the mind by virtue of that other sympathy that naturally exists in a body which is all one, then thou must not strive to resist the sensation, for it is natural: but let not the ruling part of itself add to the sensation the opinion that it is either good or bad.

Live with the gods. And he does live with the gods who constantly shows to them that his own soul is satisfied with that which is assigned to him, and that it does all that the daemon wishes, which Zeus hath given to every man for his guardian and guide, a portion of himself. And this is every man's understanding and reason.

•   •   •

As thou intendest to live when thou art gone out . . . so it is in thy power to live here. But if men do not permit thee, then get away out of life, yet so as if thou wert suffering no harm. The house is smoky, and I quit it. Why dost thou think that this is any trouble? But so long as nothing of the kind drives me out, I remain, am free, and no man shall hinder me from doing what I choose; and I choose to do what is according to the nature of the rational and social animal.

•   •   •

Soon, very soon, thou wilt be ashes, or a skeleton, and either a name or not even a name; but name is sound and echo. And the things which are much valued in life are empty and rotten and trifling, and [like] little dogs biting one another, and little children quarrelling, laughing, and then straightway weeping. But fidelity and modesty and justice and truth are fled.

Up to Olympus from the wide-spread earth.

HESIOD, *Works, etc.*, v. 197.

What then is there which still detains thee here? if the objects of sense are easily changed and never stand still, and the organs of perception are dull and easily receive false impressions; and the poor soul itself is an exhalation from blood. But to have good repute amidst such a world as this is an empty thing. Why then dost thou not wait in tranquility for thy end, whether it is extinction or removal to another state? And until that time comes, what is sufficient? Why, what else than to venerate the gods and bless them, and to do good to men, and to practise tolerance and self-restraint. . . .

From George Long trans., *The Thoughts of the Emperor Marcus Aurelius.*

ANALYSIS AND INTERPRETATION
OF THE READINGS

1. Why was Cato, despite his severity, chosen Censor by the pleasure-loving Romans?
2. Do you consider that the law of the Romans showed an advance over the law of the Mesopotamian peoples and of the ancient Hebrews? Explain.
3. Compare the philosophy of Marcus Aurelius with the teachings of Jesus in the Sermon on the Mount (Matthew 5 and 6; see chapter 10).

CHAPTER 10 | Christianity and the Transformation of the Roman World

CHRONOLOGY

Write the correct date or dates in the blank preceding each event listed below:

_____ Death of St. Augustine

_____ Founding of Constantinople

_____ Reign of Diocletian

_____ Execution of Boethius

_____ Council of Nicaea

_____ Edict of Toleration by Galerius

_____ Assumption of the title "King of Rome" by a German chieftain

_____ Sack of Rome by the Visigoths

_____ Life of St. Benedict (approximate)

_____ Battle of Adrianople

IDENTIFICATIONS

In each blank below write the correct term or title:

1. Tradition and theory that justifies papal authority.

_____

2. Christian sect which believed that Christ was inferior to God the Father and not coeternal with Him.

_____

3. A bishop who ruled over any of several of the oldest and largest Christian communities, such as Antioch, Alexandria, and Constantinople.

_____

4. Autobiography of a famous theologian who held church office in Africa.

_____

5. Name given to St. Jerome's Latin translation of the Bible.

_____

6. A famous book joining classical and Christian ideals, whose author was put to death by the ruler he had served.

_____

7. A bishop of a large city whose authority extended over the clergy of an entire province.

_____

8. A lasting achievement of Justinian which includes "the most important lawbook that the world has ever seen."

_____

9. A Germanic people that established a kingdom in northwest Africa and sacked Rome in 455.

_____

10. Major work of a great Church father incorporating a philosophy of history predominant throughout the Middle Ages.

_____

In each blank below write the name of the person described:

1. Roman emperor who named his capital after himself and made the succession hereditary.

_____

2. Fourth-century ascetic who laid down a set of rules for a monastic order widely followed in eastern Christendom.

_____

3. Native of Tarsus who proclaimed Christianity a universal religion and greatly expanded its early character.

_____

4. Roman aristocrat and polished Latinist whose writings forged a link between ancient Greek thinkers and the Middle Ages.

_____

5. Monastic figure who did more than any other to establish the Benedictine monasteries as centers of learning and of transcribing texts.

_____

6. Last ruler of a united Roman Empire, cruel in vengeance but titled "the Great."

_____

7. Archbishop of Milan who humbled this same Roman emperor.

_____

8. Roman emperor who, after trying vainly to exterminate Christianity, issued an edict of toleration.

_____

9. Extreme ascetic who spent nearly forty years on the top of a pillar.

_____

10. Founder of western monasticism whose rule was almost universally used in Latin Christendom.

_____

11. Bishop of Hippo and greatest of the Latin Church fathers, whose writings have been held in esteem by both Roman Catholics and Protestants.

_____

12. Ostrogothic conqueror who gave Italy an intelligent and progressive rule in contrast to many native Roman emperors.

_____

STUDY QUESTIONS

1. Explain the statement that when the Roman Empire turned away from the West and consolidated its strength in the East, "antiquity clearly came to an end."
2. Describe the political structure of the Roman Empire as reorganized by Diocletian. By what means did he strengthen the empire? In what significant ways did he change its character?
3. What does it mean to say that Diocletian "orientalized" the Empire?
4. Explain this comment on Diocletian's regime: "It was almost as if the defeat of Antony and Cleopatra at Actium was now being avenged."
5. Explain the advantages of Constantinople as a center of government.
6. Explain the relationship between the growth of bureaucracy during the third and fourth centuries and the widening gap between rich and poor.
7. What were the fundamentals of Jesus' teachings?
8. Describe the contributions of Paul to Christianity.
9. How did the conditions of the Roman world aid the growth of Christianity?
10. Trace the development of a clear distinction between clergy and laity in Christianity.
11. What factors helped Christianity triumph over other contemporary competing religions?
12. How did doctrinal disputes within the Church contribute to separation between East and West?
13. Describe the development of Christian organization down to the year 400, and explain its importance in the context of a collapsing Roman Empire.
14. Explain this statement: "In many respects the Christianity of the late fourth century was a very different religion from the one persecuted by Diocletian and Galerius."
15. What were the chief causes of the rise of Christian asceticism in the third and fourth centuries?
16. What were the differences between the dominant rules of Eastern and Western monasticism?
17. What were the major contributions of Benedictine monasticism to Western civilization?
18. Discuss the effects of the Germanic invasions in the West. Why was the East much less affected?
19. What is the doctrine of predestination? How did St. Augustine defend this doctrine?
20. What changes were made in Christianity as a result of the work of the Church fathers?

21. Describe the role of women in early Christian teachings and organization.
22. What elements of classical or pagan culture were carried over into the culture of the Middle Ages? By what means?
23. How does the Justinian Code reflect changes in the philosophy of Roman law between the third and sixth centuries C.E.? What did the Code contribute to modern legal or political theory?
24. Why was Justinian's attempt to reconquer the West a failure in spite of military victories?

PROBLEMS

1. Read any two of the synoptic Gospels (Matthew, Mark, or Luke) and compare the accounts of the life of Jesus. (Then, if you like, compare the approach of the synoptics with that of John.)

2. Read some of the major epistles of St. Paul in the New Testament and consider what they reveal about the nature of early Christianity.
3. Investigate in further detail any of the following:
   a. Early monasticism
   b. The Arian controversy
   c. The rise of papal supremacy in the Western Church
4. Compare and contrast the teachings of Jesus with those of the Hebrew prophets.
5. Compare the teachings of the Apostle Paul and St. Augustine. What teachings of St. Augustine have been carried over into modern Christianity?
6. Examine the relationship between early Christianity and competing salvationist cults such as Mithraism and Gnosticism.

AIDS TO AN UNDERSTANDING OF CHRISTIANITY AND THE TRANSFORMATION OF THE ROMAN WORLD

EARLY CHRISTIANITY: The Sermon on the Mount

And seeing the multitudes, he went up into a mountain: and when he was set, his disciples came unto him:

And he opened his mouth, and taught them, saying,

Blessed are the poor in spirit: for theirs is the kingdom of heaven.

Blessed are they that mourn: for they shall be comforted.

Blessed are the meek: for they shall inherit the earth.

Blessed are they which do hunger and thirst after righteousness: for they shall be filled.

Blessed are the merciful: for they shall obtain mercy.

Blessed are the pure in heart: for they shall see God.

Blessed are the peacemakers: for they shall be called the children of God.

Blessed are they which are persecuted for righteousness' sake: for theirs is the kingdom of heaven.

Blessed are ye, when men shall revile you, and persecute you, and shall say all manner of evil against you falsely, for my sake.

Rejoice, and be exceeding glad: for great is your reward in heaven: for so persecuted they the prophets which were before you.

Ye are the salt of the earth: but if the salt have lost its savour, wherewith shall it be salted? it is thenceforth good for nothing, but to be cast out, and to be trodden under foot of men.

Ye are the light of the world. A city that is set on a hill cannot be hid.

Neither do men light a candle, and put it under a bushel, but on a candlestick; and it giveth light unto all that are in the house.

Let your light so shine before men, that they may see your good works, and glorify your Father which is in heaven.

Think not that I am come to destroy the law, or the prophets: I am not come to destroy, but to fulfil.

For verily I say unto you, Till heaven and earth pass, one jot or one tittle shall in no wise pass from the law, till all be fulfilled.

Whosoever therefore shall break one of these least commandments, and shall teach men so, he shall be called the least in the kingdom of heaven: but whosoever shall do and teach them, the same shall be called great in the kingdom of heaven.

For I say unto you. That except your righteousness shall exceed the righteousness of the scribes and Pharisees, ye shall in no case enter into the kingdom of heaven.

Ye have heard that it was said by them of old time. Thou shalt not kill; and whosoever shall kill shall be in danger of the judgment:

But I say unto you, That whosoever is angry with his brother without a cause shall be in danger of the judgment: and whosoever shall say to his brother, Raca, shall be in danger of the council: but whosoever shall say, Thou fool, shall be in danger of hell fire.

Therefore if thou bring thy gift to the altar, and there rememberest that thy brother hath aught against thee; leave there thy gift before the altar, and go thy way; first be reconciled to thy brother, and then come and offer thy gift.

Agree with thine adversary quickly, while thou art in the way with him; lest at any time the adversary deliver thee to the judge, and the judge deliver thee to the officer, and thou be cast into prison.

Verily I say unto thee, Thou shalt by no means come out thence, till thou hast paid the uttermost farthing.

Ye have heard that it was said by them of old time, Thou shalt not commit adultery:

But I say unto you, That whosoever looketh on a woman to lust after her hath committed adultery with her already in his heart.

And if thy right eye offend thee, pluck it out, and cast it from thee: for it is profitable for thee that one of thy members should perish, and not that thy whole body should be cast into hell,

And if thy right hand offend thee, cut it off, and cast if from thee: for it is profitable for thee that one of thy members should perish, and not that thy whole body should be cast into hell.

It hath been said, Whosoever shall put away his wife, let him give her a writing of divorcement:

But I say unto you, That whosoever shall put away his wife, saving for the cause of fornication, causeth her to commit adultery: and whosoever shall marry her that is divorced committeth adultery.

Again, ye have heard that it hath been said by them of old time, Thou shalt not forswear thyself, but shalt perform unto the Lord thine oaths:

But I say unto you, Swear not at all; neither by heaven; for it is God's throne:

Nor by the earth; for it is his footstool: neither by Jerusalem; for it is the city of the great King.

Neither shalt thou swear by the head, because thou canst not make one hair white or black.

But let your communication be, Yea, yea; Nay, nay: for whatsoever is more than these cometh of evil.

Ye have heard that it hath been said, An eye for an eye, and a tooth for a tooth:

But I say unto you, That ye resist not evil: but whosoever shall smite thee on thy right cheek, turn to him the other also.

And if any man will sue thee at the law, and take away thy coat, let him have thy cloak also.

And whosoever shall compel thee to go a mile, go with him twain.

Give to him that asketh thee, and from him that would borrow of thee turn not thou away.

Ye have heard that it hath been said, Thou shalt love thy neighbour and hate thine enemy.

But I say unto you, Love your enemies, bless them that curse you, do good to them that hate you, and pray for them which despitefully use you, and persecute you;

That ye may be the children of your Father which is in heaven: for he maketh his sun to rise on the evil and on the good, and sendeth rain on the just and on the unjust.

For if ye love them which love you, what reward have ye? do not even the publicans the same?

And if ye salute your brethren only, what do ye more than others? do not even the publicans so?

Be ye therefore perfect, even as your Father which is in heaven is perfect.

• • •

No man can serve two masters: for either he will hate the one, and love the other; or else he will hold to the one, and despise the other. Ye cannot serve God and mammon.

Therefore I say unto you, Take no thought for your life, what ye shall eat, or what ye shall drink; not yet for your body, what ye shall put on. Is not the life more than meat, and the body than raiment?

Behold the fowls of the air: for they sow not, neither do they reap, nor gather into barns; yet your heavenly Father feedeth them. Are ye not much better than they?

Which of you by taking thought can add one cubit unto his stature?

And why take ye thought for raiment? Consider the lilies of the field, how they grow; they toil not; neither do they spin:

And yet I say unto you, That even Solomon in all his glory was not arrayed like one of these.

Wherefore, if God so clothe the grass of the field, which to day is, and to morrow is cast into the oven, shall he not much more clothe you, O ye of little faith?

Therefore take no thought, saying, What shall we eat? or, What shall we drink? or, Wherewithal shall we be clothed?

(For after all these things do the Gentiles seek:) for your heavenly Father knoweth that ye have need of all these things.

But seek ye first the kingdom of God, and his righteousness, and all these things shall be added unto you.

Take therefore no thought for the morrow: for the morrow shall take thought for the things of itself. Sufficient unto the day is the evil thereof.

———

Matthew 5:6:24–34

EARLY CHRISTIANITY: The Theology of the Apostle Paul

And we know that all things work together for good to them that love God, to them who are the called according to his purpose.

For whom he did foreknow, he also did predestinate to be conformed to the image of his Son, that he might be the firstborn among many brethren.

Moreover, whom he did predestinate, them he also called: and whom he called, them he also justified: and whom he justified, them he also glorified.

What shall we then say to these things? If God be for us, who can be against us?

He that spared not his own Son, but delivered him up for us all how shall he not with him also freely give us all things?

Who shall lay any thing to the charge of God's elect? It is God that justifieth.

Who is he that condemneth? It is Christ that died, yea rather, that is risen again, who is even at the right hand of God, who also maketh intercession for us.

Who shall separate us from the love of Christ? shall tribulation, or distress, or persecution, or famine, or nakedness, or peril, or sword?

As it is written, For thy sake we are killed all the day long; we are accounted as sheep for the slaughter.

Nay, in all these things we are more than conquerors through him that loved us.

For I am persuaded, that neither death, nor life, nor angels, nor principalities, nor powers, nor things present, nor things to come,

Nor height, nor depth, nor any other creature, shall be able to separate us from the love of God, which is in Christ Jesus our Lord.

• • •

What shall we say then? Is there unrighteousness with God? God forbid.

For he saith to Moses, I will have mercy on whom I will have mercy, and I will have compassion on whom I will have compassion.

So then it is not of him that willeth, nor of him that runneth, but of God that sheweth mercy.

For the Scripture saith unto Pharaoh, Even for this same purpose have I raised thee up, that I might shew my power in thee, and that my name might be declared throughout all the earth.

Therefore hath he mercy on whom he will have mercy, and whom he will he hardeneth.

Thou wilt say then unto me, Why doth he yet find fault? For who hath resisted his will?

Nay but, O man, who art thou that repliest against God? Shall the thing formed say to him that formed it, Why hast thou made me thus?

Hath not the potter power over the clay, of the same lump to make one vessel unto honour, and another unto dishonour?

Romans 8:28–39; 9:14–21

EARLY CHRISTIANITY: Excerpt from St. Augustine's Confessions

It is certain, O Lord, that theft is punished by your law, the law that is written in men's hearts and cannot be erased however sinful they are. For no thief can bear that another thief should steal from him, even if he is rich and the other is driven to it by want. Yet I was willing to steal, and steal I did, although I was not compelled by any lack, unless it were the lack of a sense of justice or a distaste for what was right and a greedy love of doing wrong. For of what I stole I already had plenty, and much better at that, and I had no wish to enjoy the things I coveted by stealing, but only to enjoy the theft itself and the sin. There was a pear-tree near our vineyard, loaded with fruit that was attractive neither to look at nor to taste. Late one night a band of ruffians, myself included, went off to shake down the fruit and carry it away, for we had continued our games out of doors until well after dark, as was our pernicious habit. We took away an enormous quantity of pears, not to eat them ourselves, but simply to throw them to the pigs. Perhaps we ate some of them, but our real pleasure consisted in doing something that was forbidden.

Look into my heart, O God, the same heart on which you took pity when it was in the depths of the abyss. Let my heart now tell you what prompted me to do wrong for no purpose, and why it was only my own love of mischief that made me do it. The evil in me was foul, but I loved it. I loved my own perdition and my own faults, not the things for which I committed wrong, but the wrong itself. My soul was vicious and broke away from your safe keeping to seek its own destruction, looking for no profit in disgrace but only for disgrace itself. . . .

From Augustine, *Confessions.* R. S. Pine-Coffin, trans. p. 47. © 1961 by R. S. Pine-Coffin. Penguin Books.

EARLY CHRISTIANITY: Excerpts from the Rule of St. Benedict

Concerning obedience. The first grade of humility is obedience without delay. This becomes those who, on account of the holy service which they have professed, or on account of the fear of hell or the glory of eternal life consider nothing dearer to them than Christ: so that, so soon as anything is commanded by their superior, they may not know how to suffer delay in doing it, even as if it were a divine command. Concerning whom the Lord said: "As soon as he heard of me he obeyed me." And again he said to the learned men: "He who heareth you heareth me."

Therefore let all such, straightway leaving their own affairs and giving up their own will, with unoccupied hands and leaving incomplete what they were doing—the foot of obedience being foremost,—follow with their deeds the voice of him who orders. And, as it were, in the same moment, let the aforesaid command of the master and the perfected work of the disciple—both together in the swiftness of the fear of God,—be called into being by those who are possessed with a desire of advancing to eternal life. And therefore let them seize the narrow way of which the Lord says: "Narrow is the way which leadeth unto life." Thus, not living according to their own judgment nor obeying their own desires and pleasures, but walking under another's judgment and command, passing their time in monasteries, let them desire an abbot to rule over them. Without doubt all such live up to that precept of the Lord in which he says: "I am not come to do my own will but the will of him that sent me.". . .

Concerning silence. Let us do as the prophet says: "I said, I will take heed to my ways that I sin not with my tongue, I have kept my mouth with a bridle: I was dumb with silence, I held my peace even from good; and my sorrow was stirred." Here the prophet shows that if one ought at times, for the sake of silence, to refrain from good sayings; how much more, as a punishment for sin, ought one to cease from evil words. . . . And therefore, if anything is to be asked of the prior, let it be asked with all humility and subjection of reverence; lest one seem to speak more than is fitting. Scurrilities, however, or idle words and those exciting laughter, we condemn in all places with a lasting prohibition: nor do we permit a disciple to open his mouth for such sayings.

Concerning humility. . . . The sixth grade of humility is, that monk be contented with all lowliness or extremity, and consider himself, with regard to everything which is enjoined on him, as a poor and unworthy workman; saying to himself with the prophet: "I was reduced to nothing and was ignorant; I was made as the cattle before thee, and I am always with thee." The seventh grade of humility is, not only that he, with his tongue, pronounce himself viler and more worthless than all; but that he also believe it in the innermost workings of his heart; humbling himself and saying with the prophet, etc. . . . The eighth degree of humility is that a monk do nothing except what the common ruleof the monastery, or the example of his elders, urges him to do. The ninth degree of humility is that a monk restrain his tongue from speaking; and, keeping silence, do not speak until he is spoken to. The tenth grade of humility is that he be not ready, and easily inclined, to laugh. . . . The eleventh grade of humility is that a monk, when he speaks, speak slowly and without laughter, humbly with gravity, using few and reasonable words; and that he be not loud of voice. . . . The twelfth grade of humility is that a monk, shall not only with his heart but also with his body, always show humility to all who see him: that is, when at work, in the oratory, in the monastery, in the garden, on the road, in the fields. And everywhere, sitting or walking or standing, let him always be with head inclined, his looks fixed upon the ground; remembering every hour that he is guilty of his sins. . . .

* * *

Whether the monks should have any thing of their own. More than any thing else is this special vice to be cut off root and branch from the monastery, that one should presume to give or receive anything without the order of the abbot, or should have anything of his own. He should have absolutely not anything: neither a book, nor tablets, nor a pen—nothing at all.—For indeed it is not allowed to the monks to have their own bodies or wills in their own power. But all things necessary they must expect from the Father of the monastery; nor is it allowable to have anything which the abbot did not give or permit. All things shall be common to all, as it is written: "Let not any man presume or call anything his own." But if any one shall have been discovered delighting in this most evil vice: being warned once and again, if he do not amend, let him be subjected to punishment.

———

From E. F. Henderson, *Select Historical Documents of the Middle Ages*, G. Bell and Sons, Ltd., 1925. Reprinted by permission of the publisher.

ANALYSIS AND INTERPRETATION OF THE READINGS

1. What doctrines of the Apostle Paul do you not find explicit in the teachings of Jesus?
2. How does the incident involving the young Augustine help explain the problem of evil?
3. Is the Rule of St. Benedict an example of primitive communism? Explain your answer.
4. Does the Rule incorporate an extreme and uncompromising asceticism?
5. Can you see any reasons why the Benedictine Rule became the standard for the monks of Latin Christendom?

CHAPTER 11

Asia and Africa in Transition (c. 200 B.C.E.–900 C.E.)

CHRONOLOGY

Plot in the proper position on the chart below the events or epochs listed for India, China, Japan, and Africa. The Tang Dynasty (China) is plotted as an example.

	300	100	C.E.	100	300	500	700	900
INDIA:								
King Vikramaditya								
King Harsha								
Invasion of the White Huns								
Ajanta cave paintings								
Building of the great *stupa* at Sanchi								
CHINA:								
Han Dynasty								
Tang Dynasty								▓▓▓▓
Invention of paper								
Period of disunity								
Introduction of Buddhism								
JAPAN:								
Introduction of Buddhism								
Introduction of writing								
Taika Reform Edict								
AFRICA:								
Wide diffusion of iron technology								
Kingdom of Ghana								
Zaghawa Berber Dynasty								

IDENTIFICATIONS

You should be able to identify each of the following, and describe their importance for an understanding of this period:

Fa Xian	Magic Canal
White Huns	*Admonitions for Women*
Krishna	Sima Qian
bhakti movement	"Pure Land" Buddhism
dharma	Sun Goddess
Kalidasa	*Shinto*
stupa	Taika Reform Edict
Khmers	*Tale of Genji*
Angkor Wat	Nubians
"Greater India"	Berber
"First Emperor" (China)	Awkar

STUDY QUESTIONS

1. How was the influence of Buddhism manifested in Indian civilization of the Gupta period? What factors tended to undermine the strength of Buddhism in India?
2. Why did the Chinese pilgrim Fa Xian go to India in the early fifth century? What do we learn about India from his account?
3. How did the government of Harsha differ from that of the earlier Gupta Dynasty?
4. What similarities and differences were there between Gupta-era sculpture and classical Hellenic sculpture?
5. Compare and contrast the cults of Vishnu and Shiva.
6. Explain the meaning of this statement: "What the Periclean Age and the Augustan Age were for the classical civilizations of the West the reigns of Vikramaditya and Harsha were for India."
7. Explain the significance of the *Bhagavad Gita* in the Indian religious tradition.
8. Contrast Sanskrit drama with Western drama.
9. What kinds of influence did India of this period exert on the West?
10. Explain the assertion that the dominance of the state has been both China's greatest strength and its greatest weakness.
11. The Qin Dynasty was very brief. Why was it so important for Chinese history?
12. What were the major achievements of Shihuangdi, China's "first emperor"?
13. In what ways was the Han Dynasty of lasting significance for Chinese history?
14. Explain Emperor Han Wudi's major contributions to the strength of the Chinese state, examining both internal and external policies.
15. What is referred to as the "Han compromise"? What were the effects of this compromise on later Chinese history?
16. In what ways was China's period of disunity similar to the period in Western Europe following the downfall of the Roman Empire? In what ways was it different?
17. What were the major factors that contributed to the reunification of China after the period of disunity?
18. What did the short-lived Sui Dynasty accomplish that proved to be beneficial to the Tang Dynasty?
19. Explain the purpose and effects of the Chinese civil service examination system.
20. Describe changes in the position and role of the following groups in Chinese society: the aristocracy, farmers, women.
21. What role did eunuchs play in Chinese history?
22. What effects did the abolition of the practice of primogeniture have on later Chinese history?
23. Outline the major economic changes in China from the Han to the Tang, with particular attention to the role of the state.
24. List some specific technological advances in China from the Han through the Tang dynasties.
25. In what sense is it incorrect to refer to Confucianism as a religion?
26. What was Dong Zhongshu's contribution to Confucian thought?
27. What are the advantages and disadvantages of Japan's geographic location and climate?
28. How do you account for the fact that the position of women in Japanese society seems to have been higher in ancient times than later?
29. What factors aided the spread of Buddhism in Japan? What effect did it have on the native *Shinto* religion?
30. Japan imported many cultural items from China. Which were the easiest for the Japanese to assimilate, and which were the hardest?
31. Why did Chinese characters prove to be inadequate in the development of a system for writing Japanese?
32. What important differences were there between the Japanese imperial government and the imperial government of China on which it was modeled?
33. Why is it claimed that the Taika Reforms represent "the founding of the Japanese imperial system"? Why did these reforms not completely succeed?
34. What climatic and other factors hampered the growth of human societies in Africa?
35. How do you account for the emphasis on collectivism rather than individualism in African societies?
36. What impact did the introduction of iron tools have on African societies?
37. Explain the origins of the terms "Sahara" and "Sudan."
38. What effect did the introduction of the camel have on African economic development?
39. Summarize the role of Bantu-speaking peoples in the evolution of civilization in Africa.

PROBLEMS

1. Read the Sanskrit drama *Shakuntala* and compare it with a drama of Aeschylus or Sophocles.
2. Compare the role of Buddhist monks in education in India during this period with the role of Christian monks in education in the West during the Middle Ages.
3. Read translations of poems by Li Bo and Du Fu to determine why the Tang period is considered a high point of Chinese poetry.
4. Investigate the evolution of sculpture in northwestern India.
5. Investigate the problem of the Ainu in the population of Japan. Explore their ethnic characteristics, probable origins, and present status.
6. Compare the descriptions of India by the Chinese Buddhist pilgrims Fa Xian (fifth century) and Xuanzang (seventh century). (Translations can be found in Samuel Beal, *Buddhist Records of the Western World*.)
7. Compare the sculpture and painting of the classical age in India with those of the classical (Hellenic) age in Greece.
8. To what extent was the government of China's "First Emperor" totalitarian? From what sources did he derive his ideas about government?
9. Examine the impact of Buddhism on philosophical thought in Tang-period China.
10. Compare ancient Japanese and Chinese societies and social structures.
11. Compare the impact of Bantu expansion in Africa with the impact of nomadic invasions in China.
12. Compare Confucian and Buddhist views of women. Then compare the impact of Confucianism on women's daily lives with that of Buddhism.
13. Explore further the idea that with regard to science, "the Western model favored analysis; the Chinese model favored synthesis."
14. Examine the impact of Buddhism on artistic and literary developments throughout Asia.

AIDS TO AN UNDERSTANDING OF ASIA AND AFRICA IN TRANSITION

HINDU EPIC: A Man of Steady Wisdom
Bhagavad Gita

Arjuna said:

54. O Keshava, what are the signs of the man of steady wisdom, one who has attained God-consciousness? How does the man of steady wisdom speak? How does he sit? How does he walk?

The Blessed Lord said:

55. O Partha, when a man is satisfied in the Self by Self alone and has completely cast out all desires from the mind, then he is said to be of steady wisdom.

56. He whose mind is not agitated in calamities and who has no longing for pleasure, free from attachment, fear and anger, he indeed is said to be a saint of steady wisdom.

57. He who is free from all attachment and neither rejoices on receiving good nor is vexed on receiving evil, his wisdom is well-established.

58. When he completely withdraws his senses from sense-objects as the tortoise withdraws its limbs, then his wisdom becomes well-established.

59. The embodied, through the practice of abstinence (i.e. not giving food to the senses) can deaden the feelings of the senses, but longing still lingers in the heart; all longings drop off when he has seen the Supreme.

60. O son of Kunti, dangerous are the senses, they even carry away forcibly the mind of a discriminative man who is striving for perfection.

61. The man of steady wisdom, having subdued them all (senses), becomes fixed in Me, the Supreme. His wisdom is well-established whose senses are under control.

62. Thinking of sense-objects, man becomes attached thereto. From attachments arises longing and from longing anger is born.

63. From anger arises delusion; from delusion, loss of memory is caused. From loss of memory, the discriminative faculty is ruined and from the ruin of discrimination, be perishes.

64. But the self-subjugated attains peace and moves among objects with the senses under control, free from any longing or aversion.

65. In peace there is an end to all misery and the peaceful mind soon becomes well-established in wisdom.

66. There is no wisdom for the unsteady and there is no meditation for the unsteady and for the unmeditative there is no peace. How can there be any happiness for the peaceless?

67. For the mind that yields to the uncontrolled and wandering senses, carries away his wisdom just as a boat on water is carried away by wind.

68. Therefore, O mighty-armed, his wisdom is established whose senses are well-restrained from all objects of sense.

69. That which is night to all beings, therein the self-subjugated remains awake; and in that where all beings are awake, that is night for the knower of Self.

70. As the ocean remains calm and unaltered though the waters flow into it, similarly a self-controlled saint remains unmoved when desires enter into him; such a saint alone attains peace, but not he who craves the objects of desire.

71. That man attains peace who, abandoning all desires, moves about without attachment and longing, without the sense of "I" and "mine."

72. O son of Pritha, this is the state of dwelling in Brahman (absolute Truth), having attained this, no one is ever deluded. Being established in this knowledge even at the end of life, one attains oneness with Brahman (the Supreme).

From The Blessed Lord's Song, Swami Paramananda, trans. Reprinted by permission of The Vedanta Center, Cohasset, Mass.

CHINESE PHILOSOPHY AND SCIENCE: Yin and Yang in an Early Medical Text

The Yellow Emperor said: "The principle of Yin and Yang is the foundation of the entire universe. It underlies everything in creation. It brings about the development of parenthood; it is the root and source of life and death; it is found within the temples of the gods. In order to treat and cure diseases one must search for their origins.

"Heaven was created by the concentration of Yang, the force of light; Earth was created by the concentration of Yin, the force of darkness. Yang stands for peace and serenity; Yin stands for confusion and turmoil. Yang stands for destruction; Yin stands for conservation. Yang brings about disintegration; Yin gives shape to things. . . .

"The pure and lucid element of light is manifested in the upper orifices, and the turbid element of darkness is manifested in the lower orifices. Yang, the element of light, originates in the pores. Yin, the element of darkness, moves within the five viscera. Yang, the lucid force of light, truly is represented by the four extremities; and Yin, the turbid force of darkness, stores the power of the six treasures of nature. Water is an embodiment of Yin, as fire is an embodiment of Yang. Yang creates the air, while Yin creates the senses, which belong to the physical body. When the physical body dies, the spirit is restored to the air, its natural environment. The spirit receives its nourishment through the air, and the body receives its nourishment through the senses. . . .

"If Yang is overly powerful, then Yin may be too weak. If Yin is particularly strong, then Yang is apt to be defective. If the male force is overwhelming, then there will be excessive heat. If the female force is overwhelming, then there will be excessive cold. Exposure to repeated and severe cold will lead to fever. Exposure to repeated and severe heat will induce chills.

Cold injures the body while heat injures the spirit. When the spirit is hurt, severe pain will ensue. When the body is hurt, there will be swelling. Thus, when severe pain occurs first and swelling comes on later, one may infer that a disharmony in the spirit has done harm to the body. Likewise, when swelling appears first and severe pain is felt later on, one can say that a dysfunction in the body has injured the spirit. . . .

"Nature has four seasons and five elements. To grant long life, these seasons and elements must store up the power of creation in cold, heat, dryness, moisture, and wind. Man has five viscera in which these five climates are transformed into joy, anger, sympathy, grief, and fear. The emotions of joy and anger are injurious to the spirit just as cold and heat are injurious to the body. Violent anger depletes Yin; violent joy depletes Yang. When rebellious emotions rise to Heaven, the pulse expires and leaves the body. When joy and anger are without moderation, then cold and heat exceed all measure, and life is no longer secure. Yin and Yang should be respected to an equal extent." . . .

The Yellow Emperor asked, "Is there any alternative to the law of Yin and Yang?"

Ch'i Po answered: "When Yang is the stronger, the body is hot, the pores are closed, and people begin to pant; they become boisterous and coarse and do not perspire. They become feverish, their mouths are dry and sore, their stomachs feel tight, and they die of constipation. When Yang is the stronger, people can endure winter but not summer. When Yin is the stronger, the body is cold and covered with perspiration. People realize they are ill; they tremble and feel chilly. When they feel chilled, their spirits become rebellious. Their stomachs can no longer digest food and they die. When Yin is the stronger, people can endure summer but not winter. Thus Yin and Yang alternate. Their ebbs and surges vary, and so does the character of their diseases." . . .

From *Chinese Civilization and Society*, Patricia Buckley Ebrey, ed. pp. 36–37. The Free Press, 1981.

COURTLY LOVE IN JAPAN: The Tale of Genji

At this they all laughed and To no Chujo continued: "But now it is Shikibu's turn and he is sure to give us something entertaining. Come Shikibu, keep the ball rolling!" "Nothing of interest ever happens to humble folk like myself" said Shikibu; but To no Chujo scolded him for keeping them waiting and after reflecting for a while which anecdote would best suit the company, he began: "While I was still a student at the University, I came across a woman who was truly a prodigy of intelligence. One of Uma no Kami's demands she certainly fulfilled, for it was possible to discuss with her to advantage both public matters and the proper handling of one's private affairs. But not only was her mind capable of grappling with any problems of this kind; she was also so learned that ordinary scholars found themselves, to their humiliation, quite unable to hold their own against her.

"I was taking lessons from her father, who was a Professor. I had heard that he had several daughters, and some accidental circumstance made it necessary for me to exchange a word or two with one of them who turned out to be the learned prodigy of whom I have spoken. The father, hearing that we had been seen together, came up to me with a wine-cup in his hand and made an allusion to the poem of The Two Wives.* Unfortunately I did not feel the least inclination towards the lady. However I was very civil to her; upon which she began to take an affectionate interest in me and lost no opportunity of displaying her talents by giving me the most elaborate advice how best I might advance my position in the world. She sent me marvelous letters written in a very far-fetched epistolary style and entirely in Chinese characters; in return for which I felt bound to visit her, and by making her my teacher I managed to learn how to write Chinese poems. They were wretched, knock-kneed affairs, but I am still grateful to her for it. She was not however at all the sort of woman whom I should have cared to have as a wife, for though there may be certain disadvantages in marrying a complete dolt, it is even worse to marry a blue-stocking. Still less do princes like you and Genji require so huge a stock of intellect and erudition for your support! Let her but be one to whom the *karma* of our past lives draws us in natural sympathy, what matter if now and again her ignorance distresses us? Come to that, even men seem to me to get along very well without much learning."

Here he stopped, but Genji and the rest, wishing to hear the end of the story, cried out that for their part they found her a most interesting woman. Shikibu protested that he did not wish to go on with the story, but at last after much coaxing, pulling a comical wry face he continued: "I had not seen her for a long time. When at last some accident took me to the house, she did not receive me with her usual informality but spoke to me from behind a tiresome screen. Ha, Ha, thought I foolishly, she is sulking; now is the time to have a scene and break with her I might have known that she was not so little of a philosopher as to sulk about trifles; she prided herself on knowing the ways of the world and my inconstancy did not in the least disturb her.

"She told me (speaking without the slightest tremor) that having had a bad cold for some weeks she had taken a strong garlic-cordial, which had made her breath smell rather unpleasant and that for this reason she could not come very close to me. But if I had any matter of special importance to discuss with her she was quite prepared to give me her attention. All this she had expressed with solemn literary perfection. I could think of no suitable reply, and with an 'at your service' I rose to go. Then, feeling that the interview had not been quite a success, she added, raising her voice, 'Please come again when my breath has lost its smell.' I could not pretend I had not heard. I had however no intention of prolonging my visit, particularly as the odour was now becoming definitely unpleasant, and looking cross I recited the acrostic 'On this night marked by the strange behaviour of the spider, how foolish to bid me come back to-morrow' and calling over my shoulder 'There is no excuse for you!' I ran out of the room. But she, following me, 'If night by night and every night we met, in daytime too I should grow

bold to meet you face to face.' Here in the second sentence she had cleverly concealed the meaning, 'If I had had any reason to expect you, I should not have eaten garlic.'"

————

From *Tale of Genji*, Arthur Waley, trans., Houghton Mifflin Company, 1935. Reprinted by permission of the publisher.

THE RISE OF SUDANIC STATES
Roland Oliver and J. D. Fage

The historian cannot be content to postulate vague notions about "waves of conquest." He must approach the problem through the known history of the states concerned, and must seek chronological evidence wherever it is available. Judged by this test, many of the "Sudanic" states can be written off as comparatively recent extensions from others already existing in their neighborhood. But in at least three geographically widely spread cases there would seem to be evidence that states of this kind were in existence by as early as the end of the first millennium a.d. The kingdom of Ghana, with its centre some five hundred miles to the north-west of its modern namesake's nearest boundary, was first mentioned in writing by an Arab author of the eighth century, Al Fazari. Three centuries later, when Ghana was well known to the Muslin world by its export of gold to North Africa, the Moorish geographer Al Bakri of Cordoba described what was still a sturdily pagan kingship ritual:

"The audience is announced by the beating of a drum which they call *daba*, made from a long hollow log. When the people . . . approach [the king], they fall on their knees and sprinkle their heads with dust, for this is their way of showing respect. . . . The religion of the people of Ghana is paganism and the worship of idols. When their king dies, they build over the place where his tomb will be an enormous dome of *saj* wood. Then they bring him on a bed covered with a few carpets and put him inside the dome. At his side they place his ornaments, his weapons, and the vessels from which he used to eat and drink, filled with various kinds of food and beverages. They also place there the men who had served his meals. They close the door of the dome and cover it with mats and materials, and then they assemble the people, who heap earth upon it until it becomes like a large mound. Then they dig a ditch around the mound so that can be reached only at one place. They sacrifice victims for their dead and make offerings of intoxicating drinks."

The kingdom of Kanem, lying to the north-east of Lake Chad, was mentioned, together with its Zaghawa rulers, by Al Yaqubi, writing in the ninth century, while the tenth-century writer. Al Muhallabi, made it quite clear that this was a divine kingdom of the "Sudanic" type:

"The kingdom of the Zaghawa is said to be a great kingdom among the kings of the Sudan. On their eastern boundary is the kingdom of the Nuba who are above upper Egypt. Between them there is a distance of ten days' journey. They are many tribes. The length of their land is a fifteen days' journey through habitations and cultivations all the way. Their houses are all of gypsum and so is the castle of their king. Him they respect and worship to the neglect of Allah the most High; and they falsely imagine that he does not eat food. His food is taken into his house secretly, and if any one of his subjects happens to meet the camels carrying it, he is immediately killed on the spot. He has absolute power over his subjects and takes what he will of their belongings. Their cattle are goats and cows and camels and horses. Millet chiefly is cultivated in their land, and beans, also wheat. Most of the ordinary people are naked, covering themselves with skins. They spend their time cultivating and looking after their cattle; and their religion is the worship of their kings, for they believe that it is they who bring life and death and sickness and health."

And finally the great traveller and geographical writer Al Masudi of Baghdad, who himself journeyed by sea from the Persian Gulf down the east coast of Africa to Sofala in modern Moçambique in or about 922 A.D., clearly recorded the existence of a substantial trade in gold and ivory, which was shipped from Sofala to Oman and thence to China and India, and which originated in a large African state in the Southern Rhodesian hinterland. The king of this state bore sublime titles such as "son of the great master, the god of the earth and the sky," and was the foremost of all the African rulers known to the Arabs who frequented the east coast. It is highly probable that Masudi was referring to the state whose rulers were responsible for the earliest stages of stone building at Great Zimbabwe, currently attributed by archaeologists, on the basis of carbon-dating, to approximately the eleventh century. It is very clear, from Portuguese descriptions of the societies they found in this region five centuries later, that although political fragmentation had set in, political structure was uniform and showed most of the typical features of "Sudanic" divine kingship.

The geographical spread of those African states for which we happen to have evidence stretching back into the first millennium A.D. is such as to make it highly improbable that they were the only states of their kind in existence, even at this early period. Rather we must assume that they were the only ones which happened to attract the attention of literate people in the outside world; and we must assume that with the further development of Iron Age archaeology in Africa, with its new methods of absolute dating, a steady stream of fresh evidence will come to light, pointing to other early centres of the "Sudanic" civilization, and perhaps carrying its origins back to a period considerably earlier than our existing documentary references. Belgian archaeologists, for example, have recently found on the banks of the upper Lualaba extensive cemeteries, provisionally carbon-dated to the eighth and ninth centuries A.D., with rich burials, showing that at this period the copper of the Katanga was already being mined and forged into jewellery and into small H-shaped ingots which must have been used for currency. No distinctive royal tomb or capital site has yet been found to prove that these technologically very advanced Africans, whose skeletons do not differ significantly from those of the present Luba population, were organized into a state of the "Sudanic" type; but judging by the historical traditions of this area, it

would seem highly likely that they were so. Further north, in Uganda, Ruanda-Urundi, and the adjoining parts of the Kivu province of the Congo, where the formation and re-formation of "Sudanic" states can be traced in some detail through five hundred years or so of traditional history, the recent discovery of earthwork sites typologically ancestral to those of the traditional period may well lead to new chronological evidence carrying the history of this region back to a period nearer to that of the Rhodesian and Katangan cultures. North-eastwards from Uganda, the pagan states of south-west Ethiopia, notably Kaffa and Enarea, may well provide comparable evidence.

If the antiquity of "Sudanic" political organization in north-eastern and Bantu Africa is still (with the exception of Rhodesia) highly speculative, that of sub-Saharan Africa west of Kanem is much less so, though here again the relative precision of archaeological evidence is badly needed. Traditions recorded by literate Muslim Sudanese in the sixteenth and seventeenth centuries A.D. suggest, however, that the origins of at least one other "Sudanic" state, that of Songhai on the eastern arm of the great Niger bend, were approximately as ancient as those of Kanem and ancient Ghana. In Northern Nigeria and the adjacent Niger Republic, the origins of the Hausa states (again from traditional evidence) are almost certainly to be placed about the end of the first millennium. The southward extension of these systems towards the lands of the upper Volta in the centre of the Niger bend, and towards Nupe and Yorubaland in central and western Nigeria, certainly occurred later, though how much later remains to be discovered.

The essential conclusions that emerge from this brief survey would thus seem to be, first, that the formation of states, alike in sub-Saharan and in Bantu Africa, was a process which involved the deployment of a considerable fund of common political ideas; secondly, that the earliest lines of deployment seem to have been interior lines, running out in two long arms westwards and southwards from a common point of origin in the upper Nile valley; thirdly, that this fund of common ideas was pre-Muslim and pre-Christian, in the sense that the basic ideas of the system ran sharply counter to the tenets of both these religions, and therefore that if the Nile valley was the point of departure, they must have started to disperse outwards from that region before either Christianity or Islam became firmly established there. Islam did not seriously begin to penetrate the Nilotic Sudan until the eleventh century. Christianity, however, spread from Egypt to Nubia in the late sixth century, and by the seventh was strongly enough established there to resist the southward spread of Islam for more than four centuries. In our search for the sources of the "Sudanic" civilization, we are therefore driven back to the history of the Sudan during the first six centuries A.D. At the beginning of that period the Meroitic state was still at the height of its power, and there can be little doubt that the ideas of ancient Egypt, percolating through the Meroitic filter, formed the basic element in the "Sudanic" civilization.

From Roland Oliver and J. D. Fage, *A Short History of Africa*, Penguin Books, 1962, 1966, 1970. Reprinted by permission of the publisher.

ANALYSIS AND INTERPRETATION
OF THE READINGS

1. Compare the yin/yang explanation with other fundamental medical explanations from other early civilizations. Is the Chinese conception any more or less rational than others? Why or why not?

2. On the evidence of the passage from *The Tale of Genji*, what qualities in women did Japanese men consider desirable?

3. In their account of "The Rise of Sudanic States," Oliver and Fage make a number of assumptions. What are they? Do these assumptions appear to be well founded? Why or why not?

Tang Dynasty, 618–907

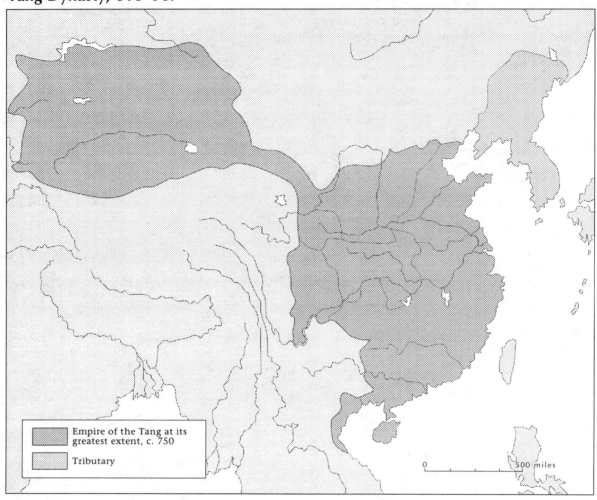

Empire of the Tang at its
greatest extent, c. 750

Tributary

0   500 miles

Tang Dynasty (618–907) Map
(Chapters 7–11)

1. On the map of the Tang Dynasty (opposite page), label the following locations:

   Seas: Yellow, South China, East China
   Rivers: Yellow (Huang Ho), Yangtze, West (Hsi)

2. Locate and mark the ancient city of Changan.

3. Show the extent of the Great Wall, and the route of the Grand Canal.

4. Locate and mark Manchuria, Mongolia, Korea, Annam, India, and Tibet.

CHAPTER 12 | Rome's Three Heirs: The Byzantine, Islamic, and Early-Medieval Western Worlds

CHRONOLOGY

Number the events listed below in their correct chronological sequence from earliest to latest:

_____ Separation of Greek and Roman branches of the Church

_____ The *Hijrah* (Hegira)

_____ Coronation of Charlemagne as emperor

_____ Beginning of the Umyyad caliphate

_____ Beginning of Iconoclastic movement

_____ Death of Muhammad

_____ Beginning of Abbasid caliphate

_____ Destruction of Baghdad by Mongols

_____ Accession to papacy of St. Gregory the Great

_____ Battle of Tours

_____ Fall of Constantinople to the Ottoman Turks

_____ Battle of Manzikert

_____ Crusaders' capture of Constantinople

_____ Accession of Pepin the Short

IDENTIFICATIONS

You should be familiar with the following:

Seljuk Turks	*Arabian Nights*
Iconoclasts	ulama
Bedouins	sufis
Kabah	faylasufs
Quraish (tribe)	alchemy
Koran	mayor of the palace
caliph	*Beowulf*
Shiites	*Book of Kells*

In the blanks below write the name of the person described:

1. A Persian poet who wrote the *Rubaiyat*.

_____

2. An emperor whose successful defense of Constantinople against the Arabs ranks as one of the most significant battles in European history.

_____

3. A princess whose writings testify to a high educational level among Byzantine women.

_____

4. An emperor who paved the way for his state's downfall by appealing to the West for help against the Turks.

_____

5. A Russian ruler who, by accepting baptism by a Byzantine missionary, provided a strong bastion for Eastern Orthodox Christianity.

_____

6. An Abbasid caliph of regal splendor who sent an elephant as a gift to Charlemagne.

_____

7. An Islamic philosopher known as "the Commentator" by Western medieval writers, whom he greatly influenced by his interpretation of Aristotle.

_____

8. The greatest clinical physician of the medieval world, who first discovered the real nature of smallpox.

_____

9. The Prophet's son-in-law, who posthumously became identified with a militant Muslim minority.

_____

10. Discoverer of the contagious nature of tuberculosis and author of the *Canon*, regarded as a medical authority until the seventeenth century.

_____

11. An eighth-century emperor who provoked a famous religious controversy.

_____

12. A brutal Frankish chieftain who founded the Merovingian dynasty.

_____

13. A Church father who wrote a life of St. Benedict and worked to strengthen papal authority.

_____

14. A military figure nicknamed "the Hammer" and reputed to be the second founder of the Frankish state.

_____

15. A leader of the English Benedictines who aided the accession of the Carolingian dynasty.

_____

16. An Anglo-Saxon Benedictine who wrote a remarkable Latin *History of the English Church.*

_____

STUDY QUESTIONS

1. Why is it difficult to date the beginning of the Byzantine Empire? What is the justification for choosing the accession of the emperor Heraclius as a starting point?
2. Why was Byzantine political history marked by intrigues and palace revolts?
3. How did changes in agriculture and the farming classes affect the welfare of the Byzantine state?
4. Explain the issues in the Iconoclastic Controversy. What were its results?
5. What significant differences in religious trends and emphases can you detect between the Byzantine and Roman churches?
6. Considering its constant difficulties, how do you account for the long life of the Byzantine Empire?
7. If it is true that "what the Byzantines themselves cared about most was usually religion," how did this attitude affect Byzantine history?
8. "The structural design of Santa Sophia was something altogether new in the history of architecture." Explain the meaning of this statement.
9. In what ways was Byzantine civilization superior to that of Western Europe?
10. Through what channels did Byzantium, both in its own day and later, influence the West?
11. What are the main doctrines of Islam?
12. Compare the views of Jesus held by Muhammad and the Apostle Paul.
13. What factors other than religion account for the rapidity and extent of the Arab conquests?
14. Judaism, Christianity, and Islam, the three great Semitic religions, are closely related. What are the main points of difference among them?
15. Explain the statement that "the Umayyad caliphate appears to some extent like a Byzantine successor state."
16. In what ways might it be said that early and medieval Islamic society was more progressive than most societies of its day? What limitations were there to its democratic or equalitarian aspects?
17. What were the major elements of Islamic philosophy?
18. What were the leading Islamic accomplishments in science and medicine?
19. What specific contributions did Islamic mathematicians make to mathematical knowledge?
20. "Islamic art often seems more secular and 'modern' than any other art of premodern times." Why is this the case?
21. What, for the West, has been the "legacy" of Islam?
22. What contribution did the Frankish monarchy make to the future of Western civilization?
23. What did Gregory the Great add to the work of the earlier Latin Church fathers?

24. How did papal ambition and the spread of Benedictine monasticism contribute to the growth of Frankish power and the Carolingian accession?
25. Why does Charlemagne rank as one of the most important rulers of the medieval period?
26. What was the nature of the "Carolingian Renaissance"? What were its limitations?
27. In spite of a relatively low level of civilization in western Europe at the end of the tenth century, what had been accomplished that held the promise of a brighter future?

PROBLEMS

1. Investigate further any of the following:
   a. The migration of the Slavs
   b. The architecture of Santa Sophia
   c. The Judaic-Christian roots of Islam
   d. Muslim science
   e. The legacy of Islam to the West
   f. The split between the Eastern and Western churches
   g. The coronation of Charlemagne
   h. The reign of Alfred the Great
2. "If the Byzantines had not prospered and defended Europe, Western Christian civilization might well have been snuffed out." Explore further what reasons there might be for accepting this statement.
3. In what respects are Islam and Christianity contradictory? In what respects are they similar?
4. Read *History of the Franks* by Bishop Gregory of Tours and try to account for that churchman's apparently complacent attitude toward the crimes of King Clovis.

AIDS TO AN UNDERSTANDING OF THE BYZANTINE, ISLAMIC, AND EARLY MEDIEVAL WESTERN WORLDS

LIFE IN THE BYZANTINE EMPIRE
Steven Runciman

Already by the Fifth Century the population of Constantinople, excluding its suburbs, must have numbered about a million persons, and it remained roughly at that level till the Latin conquest, after which it declined rapidly, to be well under a hundred thousand in 1453. The area of the City was even greater than such a population would justify. The base of the triangle on which it stood was some five miles across, where the land-walls built by Theodosius II stretched across in a double line from the Marmora to the Golden Horn, pierced by eleven gates, the military alternating with the civil. From either end the sea-walls ran for some seven miles each before they met at the blunted apex on the Bosphorus. Within the walls were various crowded towns and villages separated by orchards and parks. Like Old Rome, Constantinople could boast of seven hills. These rose steep over the Bosphorus and the Golden Horn, but from the Sea of Marmora the slopes were gentler and the lay-out more spacious.

• • •

The smartest shopping district lay inland. Along the central ridge from the entrance of the Palace and the Hippodrome for two miles there ran westward the street called Mesê, the Central Street, a wide street with arcades on either side, passing through two forums—open spaces decorated with statues—the Forum of Constantine, close to the Palace, and the larger Forum of Theodosius, and finally branching into two main roads, the one going through the Forums of the Bull and of Arcadius to Studium and the Golden Gate and the Gate of Pegæ, the other past the Church of the Holy Apostles to Blachernæ and the Charisian Gate. Along the arcades of the Mesê Street were the more important shops, arranged in groups according to their wares—the goldsmiths and next them the silversmiths, the clothiers, the furniture-makers and so on. The richest of all were near the Palace, at the Baths of Zeuxippus. There were the silk emporia in the great bazaar known as the House of Lights because its windows were illuminated by night.

There was no particular fashionable residential district. Palaces, hovels and tenements all jostled together. The houses of the rich were built in the old Roman manner, two stories high, presenting a blank exterior and facing inward round a courtyard, sometimes covered in, and usually adorned with a fountain and any exotic ornament that fancy might suggest. Poorer houses were constructed with balconies or windows overhanging the street, from which the idler ladies of the household could watch their neighbours' daily life. The residential streets had mostly been built by private contractors, but a law of Zeno's attempted to introduce some order. Streets had to be 12 feet wide, and balconies might not extend to within 10 feet of the opposite wall and must be 15 feet above the ground. Outside staircases were forbidden, and where the streets had already been built less than 22 feet wide windows for prospect were not allowed, only gratings for ventilation. This law remained the basic charter of Byzantine town-planning. There were strict regulations about drainage. All the drains led carefully to the sea, and no one, except an Imperial personage, could be buried within the City. Medical officers in each parish gave further attention to the public health.

• • •

The poor of Constantinople lived in great squalor, their slums jostling against the palaces of the rich, but they were perhaps better off than the poor of most nations. The Circus, their one recreation, was open to them free. The distribution of free bread had been stopped by Heraclius, but free food was still provided for men that undertook work for the State, such as keeping parks and aqueducts in repair or helping in the State bakeries. It was the Qurestor's business to see that the destitute were thus given useful work and that there was no unemployment. To further this, no one was allowed to enter the City except on authorised business. There were, moreover, alms-houses and hospitals for the old and infirm, founded usually by the Emperor or some noble and attached to and managed by a monastery or convent. We possess the title-deeds of several of the foundations of the Comneni. For the children of the poor there were the State orphanages. The Orphanotrophus, the official in charge of the orphanages, had early become an important member of the State hierarchy, with enormous sums under his control. Under the Iconoclasts the Church for a while captured the management of the orphanages, but the Macedonian Emperors restored it to the civil powers and enhanced the position of the Orphanotrophus. The biggest orphanage was in the precincts of the Great Palace. An earthquake destroyed it in Romanus III's reign, but Alexius I refounded it, forgetting the cares of State as he watched over the children.

With all these charitable institutions there was probably very little actual starvation. It is noticeable that when the populace rose up in riot, it was never prompted by anarchical or communistic desires. The rabble might wish to depose an oppressive minister or destroy hated foreigners, but it never sought to alter the structure of society. Indeed, it was to rescue the purple Imperial blood from the overboldness of some usurper that the People most often gave expression to its basic sovereignty.

————————

From Steven Runciman, *Byzantine Civilization*, Edward Arnold and Company, 1933. Reprinted by permission of the publisher.

THE ISLAMIC FAITH: Excerpts from the Koran

SURA XXXV: *The Creator, or the Angels*

In the Name of God, the Compassionate, the Merciful.

Praise be to God, Maker of the Heavens and of the Earth! Who employeth the ANGELS as envoys, having two and three and four pairs of wings: He addeth to his creature what He will! Truly God hath power over all things.

The Mercy which God layeth open for man no one can withhold; and what He withholdeth, none can afterwards send forth. And He is the Mighty, the Wise.

O men! bear in mind the favour of God towards you. Is there a creator other than God who nourisheth you out of heaven and earth? There is no God but He! How then are ye turned aside from Him?

If they treat thee as an impostor, then before thee have apostles been treated as impostors—But to God shall all things return.

O men! verily the promise of God is true: let not then the present life deceive you with vain hopes: and let not the Deceiver deceive you as to God.

Yes, Satan is your foe. For a foe then hold him. He summoneth his followers only to become inmates of the flame.

The unbelievers,—for them a terrible punishment!—

But believers and doers of good works, for them is mercy, and a great reward!

Shall he, the evil of whose deeds are so tricked out to him that he deemeth them good, be treated like him who seeth things aright? Verily God misleadeth whom He will, and guideth whom He will. Spend not thy soul in sighs for them: verily God knoweth their doings.

It is God who sendeth forth the winds which raise the clouds aloft; then drive We them on to some land dead from drought, and give life thereby to the earth after its death. So shall be the Resurrection.

If any one desireth greatness, greatness is wholly with God. The good word riseth up to Him, and the righteous deed doth He exalt. But a severe punishment awaiteth the plotters of evil things; and the plots of such will be in vain.

Moreover God created you of dust—then of the germs of life—then made you two sexes and no female conceiveth or bringeth forth without his knowledge, and the aged ageth not, nor is aught minished from man's age, but in accordance with the Book. An easy thing truly is this to God.

Nor are the two seas alike: the one is fresh, sweet, pleasant for drink, and the other salt, bitter; yet from both ye eat fresh fish, and take forth for yourselves ornaments to wear; and thou seest the ships cleaving the waters that ye may go in quest of his bounties; and haply ye will be thankful.

He causeth the night to enter in upon the day, and the day to enter in upon the night, and He hath given laws to the sun and to the moon, so that each journeyeth to its appointed goal: This is God your Lord: All power is his: But the gods whom ye call on beside Him have no power over the husk of a date-stone!

• • •

SURA LVI: *The Inevitable*

In the Name of God, the Compassionate, the Merciful.

Day that shall abase! Day that shall exalt!
When the earth shall be shaken with a shock,
And the mountains shall be crumbled with a crumbling,
And become scattered dust,
And into three bands shall ye be divided;
Then the people of the right hand—how happy the people of the right hand!
And the people of the left hand—how wretched the people of the left hand!
And they who were foremost on earth—the foremost still.
[Probably the first to embrace Islam.]
These are they who shall be brought nigh to God,
In gardens of delight;
A crowd from the ancients,

And few from later generations;
On inwrought couches
Reclining on them face to face:
Immortal youths go round about to them
With goblets and ewers and a cup from a fountain;
Their brows ache not from it, nor fails the sense;
And with such fruits as they shall make choice of,
And with flesh of such birds as they shall long for:
And theirs shall be the Houris with large dark eyes like close-
kept pearls,
A recompense for their labours past.
No vain discourse shall they hear therein, nor charge of sin,
But only the cry, "Peace! Peace!"
And the people of the right hand—how happy the people of the
right hand!
Amid thornless lote-trees
And bananas clad with flowers,
And extended shade,
And flowing waters,
And abundant fruits,
Unfailing, and unforbidden,
And lofty couches.
Verily of a rare creation have We created the Houris,
And We have made them ever virgins,
Dear to their spouses, of equal age with them,
For the people of the right hand,
A crowd from the ancients,
And a crowd from later generations.
But the people of the left hand—how wretched shall be the peo-
ple of the left hand!
Amid pestilential winds and in scalding water,
And the shadow of a black smoke.
Not cooling, and not pleasant.
They truly, ere this, were blessed with worldly goods,
But persisted in heinous wickedness,
And were wont to say,
"When we have died, and become dust and bones, shall we in-
deed be raised?
And our fathers the men of yore?"
Say: Aye, the former and the latter:
Gathered shall they surely be for the time of a known day.
Then verily ye, O ye the erring, the imputers of falsehood
Shall surely eat of the tree Zakkoum,
And fill your bellies with it,
And thereupon shall ye drink of the boiling water,
And ye shall drink as the thirsty camel drinketh.
This shall be their repast in the day of reckoning!

From J. M. Rodwell trans., *The Koran.*

THE CHARACTER OF ISLAMIC CIVILIZATION
Bernard Lewis

Islam—the offspring of Arabia and the Arabian Prophet—was not only a system of belief and cult. It was also a system of state, society, law, thought, and art—a civiliza-tion with religion as its unifying, eventually dominating, factor. From the Hijra onwards Islam meant submission not only to the new faith, but to the community—in practice, to the suzerainty of Medina and the Prophet, later of the Empire and Caliph. Its code was the *Shari'a*, the holy law developed by jurists from the Qur'an and the traditions of the Prophet. The *Shari'a* was not only a normative code of law but also, in its social and po-litical aspects, a pattern of conduct, an ideal towards which people and society must strive. Islam admitted no legislative power since law could emanate only from God through revela-tion, but customary law and civil legislation, the will of the ruler, survived unofficially with occasional limited recognition from the jurists. The divinely granted *Shari'a* regulated every aspect of life, not only belief and cult, but also public law, con-stitutional and international, and private law, criminal and civil. Its ideal character is clearest in its constitutional aspect. Ac-cording to the *Shari'a*, the head of the community is the Caliph, the chosen vicegerent of God with supreme power in all mili-tary, civil, and religious matters and with the duty of maintain-ing intact the spiritual and material legacy of the Prophet. The Caliph had no spiritual powers himself. He could not change doctrine, nor create new doctrine; he was supported by no priesthood, but only by the semiclerical class of the 'Ulama', the doctors of the divine law. In practice, the Caliph became the puppet of military commanders and political adventurers who, from the ninth century onwards, were the real rulers of Islam. By the eleventh century the Sultan emerged as supreme secular ruler alongside the Caliph, with powers recognized *post facto* and reluctantly by the jurists. In the administration of law we see the same contrast. Alongside the Qadi, administering the Holy Law, there were other courts, the ostensible purpose of which was to deal with matters not falling within the Qadi's jurisdiction and to remedy injustices by the use of discretionary powers.

Both these gifts of the Arabs, their language and their faith, were of course subject from the earliest times to external influ-ences. There are foreign words even in pre-Islamic poetry and in the Qur'an, many more in the period of the conquests. Ad-ministrative terms from Persian and Greek, theological and re-ligious terms from Hebrew and Syriac, scientific and philosophic terms from Greek show the immense influence of the older civilizations of the area on the new one that was being born. Islamic society of the classical period was a complex de-velopment incorporating within itself many elements of diverse origin: Christian, Jewish, and Zoroastrian ideas of prophecy, legal religion, eschatology, and mysticism, Sasanid and Byzan-tine administrative and imperial practices. Perhaps the most im-portant was the impact of Hellenism, especially in science, philosophy, art, and architecture, and even to some slight extent in literature. So great is the Hellenistic influence that Islam has been described as the third heir, alongside Greek and Latin Christendom, of the Hellenistic legacy. But the Hellenism of Islam was the later Near Eastern Hellenism, semi-orientalized by Aramaic and Christian influences, the uninterrupted continu-ation of late antiquity rather than a rediscovery, as in the West, of classical Athens.

From Bernard Lewis, *The Arabs in History.* Hutchinson University Library, 1950.

THE NEED TO UNDERSTAND ISLAM
Harvey Cox

Odious Western images of Muhammad and of Islam have a long and embarrassingly honorable lineage. Dante places the prophet in that circle of hell reserved for those stained by the sin he calls *seminator di scandalo e di scisma*. As a schismatic, Muhammad's fitting punishment is to be eternally chopped in half from his chin to his anus, spilling entrails and excrement at the door of Satan's stronghold. His loyal disciple Ali, whose sins of division were presumably on a lesser scale, is sliced only "from forelock to chin." There is scandal, too. A few lines later, Dante had Muhammad send a warning to a contemporary priest whose sect was said to advocate the community of goods and who was also suspected of having a mistress. The admonition cautions the errant padre that the same fate awaits him if he does not quickly mend his ways. Already in Dante's classic portrait, we find the image of the Moslem linked with revolting violence, distorted doctrine, a dangerous economic idea, and the tantalizing hint of illicit sensuality.

Nothing much has changed in the 600 years since. Even the current wave of interest in Eastern spirituality among many American Christians has not done much to improve the popular estimate of Islam. It is fashionable now in the West to find something of value in Buddhism or Hinduism, to peruse the *Sutras* or the *Bhagavad Gita*, to attend a lecture by Swami Muktananda or the Dalai Lama, even to try a little yoga or meditation. But Americans in general and Christians in particular seem unable to find much to admire in Islam. As G. H. Hansen observes, with only a modicum of hyperbole, in his book *Militant Islam*, the mental picture most Westerners hold of this faith of 750 million people is one of ". . . strange bearded men with burning eyes, hieratic figures in robes and turbans, blood dripping from the amputated hands and from the striped backs of malefactors, and piles of stones barely concealing the battered bodies of adulterous couples." Lecherous, truculent, irrational, cruel, conniving, excitable, dreaming about lascivious heavens while hypocritically enforcing oppressive legal codes: the stereotype of the Moslem is only partially softened by a Kahlil Gibran who puts it into sentimental doggerel or a Rudolph Valentino who does it with zest and good humor. . . .

The first thing we probably need to recognize is that the principal source of the acrimony underlying the Christian–Moslem relationship is a historical equivalent of sibling rivalry. Christians somehow hate to admit that in many ways their faith stands closer to Islam than to any other world religion. Indeed, that may be the reason Muhammad was viewed for centuries in the West as a charlatan and an imposter. The truth is, theologically speaking at least, both faiths are the offspring of an earlier revelation through the Law and the Prophets to the people of Israel. Both honor the Virgin Mary and Jesus of Nazareth. Both received an enormous early impetus from an apostle—Paul for Christianity and Muhammad for Islam—who translated a particularistic vision into a universal faith. The word "Allah" (used in the core formula of Islam: "There is no God but Allah and Muhammad is his prophet") is not an exclusively Moslem term at all. It is merely the Arabic word for God, and is used by Arabic Christians when they refer to the God of Christian faith.

There is nothing terribly surprising about these similarities since Muhammad, whose preaching mission did not begin until he reached forty, was subjected to considerable influence from Christianity during his formative years and may have come close—according to some scholars—to becoming an Abyssinian Christian. As Arend van Leeuwen points out in his thoughtful treatment of Islam in *Christianity in World History*, "The truth is that when Islam was still in the initial stages of its development, there was nothing likely to prevent the new movement from being accepted as a peculiar version of Arabian Christianity." Maybe the traditional Christian uneasiness with Islam is that it seems just a little too similar. We sense the same aversion we might feel toward a twin brother who looks more like us than we want him to and whose habits remind us of some of the things we like least in ourselves.

The metaphor of a brother, or perhaps a cousin, is entirely germane. Muhammad considered himself to be in a direct line with the great biblical prophets and with Jesus. The title he preferred for himself was *al-nabi al-ummi*, the "prophet of the nations" (or of the "gentiles"). He believed he was living proof that the God who had called and used previous prophets such as Abraham and Job, neither of whom was Jewish, could do the same thing again. Later on, Moslem theologians liked to trace the genealogy of Muhammad back to Hagar, the bondwoman spouse of Abraham. The Old Testament story says that Hagar's giving birth to Ishmael stirred up such jealousy between her and Sarah, Abraham's first wife and the mother of Isaac, that Sarah persuaded Abraham to banish the bondwoman and her child into the desert. There Hagar gave up hope and left the child under a shrub to die. But God heard the child's weeping, created a well of water in the desert to save them both, and promised Hagar that from her son also, as from Isaac, He would "create a great nation." According to the symbolism of this old saga, the Jews and the Arabs (and by extension all Moslems) are the common offspring of Abraham (called "Ibrahim" in Arabic). This makes Christians and Moslems cousins, at least by legendary lineage.

The similarity between Christians and Moslems does not stop with religious genealogy. The actual elements of the Koran's message—faith, fasting, alms, prayer, and pilgrimage—all have Christian analogues. Despite its firm refusal to recognize any divine being except God (which is the basis for its rejection of Christ's divinity), Islam appears sometimes to be a pastiche of elements from disparate forms of Christianity molded into a potent unity. Take the Calvinist emphasis on faith in an omnipotent deity, the pietistic cultivation of daily personal prayer, the medieval teaching on charity, the folk-Catholic fascination with pilgrimage, and the monastic practice of fasting, and you have all the essential ingredients of Islam. All, that is, except the confluence of forces which, through the personality of Muhammad and the movement he set off, joined these elements in the white heat of history and fused them into a coherent faith of compelling attractiveness.

Like Paul, who said his apostleship was to both Jews and gentiles, Muhammad believed his mission was twofold. He felt called by God to bring the law and the Gospel to the heretofore neglected peoples of Arabia. But he also felt he had a mission *to* those very peoples—Christians and Jews (whom he called "peoples of the book")—*from* whom the original message of salvation had come. In one important respect, therefore, Muhammad's mission was different from St. Paul's. Since Muhammad carried on his preaching in the early decades of the seventh century, he not only had to deal with a Judaism he considered corrupted (as Paul had too); he also had to face an even more corrupted form of Christianity. Fortunately for St. Paul, since the Christian movement was only a decade or so old when he lived, he had to cope only with a few legalizers and gnostics. The infant Church had not yet tasted the corruption that comes, perhaps inevitably, from power and longevity. From a certain Christian perspective, Muhammad was as much a reformer as an apostle. A prophet of the gentiles, he also saw himself as a purifier of the faith of all the "people of the book," Christians and Jews, calling them away from the ornate and decadent versions of the faith they had fallen into and back to its simple essence, at least as he understood it. There is always something of this urge to simplify, to return *ad fontes*, in any reformer. And Muhammad was no exception.

No one should minimize the fact that in any genuine conversation between Christians and Moslems certain real differences in theology and practice will have to be faced, what scholars often call "rival truth claims." But such conflicting assertions can be properly understood only against the flesh-and-blood history that has somehow made them rivals. Religious teachings do not inhabit a realm apart. They mean what they do to people because of the coloration given to them by long historical experience. Therefore a previous question has to be asked. It is this: If Christianity and Islam share such common roots and, despite real differences, some striking similarities, why have they grown so bitter toward each other over the centuries? Why did the average white American feel less sympathetic to Islam than to any other world religion even *before* our current flap with the ayatollahs?

The explanation for this hostility is not a pretty story. Its major lineaments can be indicated with the names of three figures who symbolize its most critical stages. The first is Alexander the Great, whose career corresponds to what might be called the prehistory of Christianity. The second is Constantine the Great, who exemplifies its early period. The third is Pope Urban II, who expresses its classical phase, one of the most formative in the Christian–Moslem interaction.

Christopher Dawson, the late Roman Catholic cultural historian, once remarked that "Muhammad is the Orient's answer to Alexander the Great." At first this sounds like one of those wonderfully sweeping but highly improbable aphorisms. Muhammad, after all lived and preached a full thousand years after Alexander. The prodigious Macedonian disciple of Aristotle conquered everything between Greece and northern India before he was thirty-three and spread the culture and values of Hellenism wherever his soldiers trod. But a thousand years is not a long time when one is dealing with cultural domination and the backlash it ultimately elicits. This is what Dawson had in mind.

Alexander did more than conquer everything before him. Unlike previous conquerors, who sought mainly booty and tribute, he wanted to convert his colonized peoples into Hellenists.

Alexander's conquest mixed military, political, and religious power. It was obviously going to require a comparable fusion of elements to throw off his conquest. After a thousand years that response finally came. It was Islam.

When the Islamic response to Roman–Hellenistic domination exploded in the early seventh century, the entire world was stunned by its vitality. In retrospect, however, we can understand its religious ideology in large measure as a reverse mirror image of what it was overthrowing. Take its rejection of the divinity of Christ, for example. Alexander had allowed himself to be viewed as a divine being, a god-emperor, and this ideology persisted through centuries of European culture in one form or another. The Koran's strenuous insistence that there was only one God, and its rejection of all semidivine beings, must be seen at least in part as a rejection of the political use of Christology to sacralize various forms of human rule.

The Moslem rejection of the divinity of Christ is not just simpleminded monotheistic stubbornness. It began as "political theology." For the Arabians, living on what were then the outskirts of the Eastern Empire, it marked a rejection not only of the non-Semitic categories in which the doctrine of Christ's divinity were elaborated in the Church councils (the "being of one substance with the Father") but also of the political hierarchy the doctrine helped to sanctify, especially in the Byzantine environment. When the Pantocrator Christ began to sacralize an empire in which the Arabians were the underdogs, their refusal of the doctrine made perfect sense. Alexander the Great had created the cultural imperium for which Christianity eventually supplied the sacred ideology. The Islamic revolt against this system was a revólt not against the Gospel as they understood it but against what Christianity had come to be. Islam's implacable insistence on one God not only freed thousands of people from their fear of the evil jinns and united the feuding tribes of Arabia (and later a vast part of the known world); it also served as a counterideology to the political function that Christian trinitarianism was beginning to serve. No "rival truth claim" debate between Christians and Moslems can begin until this history is recognized.

Islam began as a liberation theology, but, like Christianity, which had a comparable beginning, it could not resist the wiles of worldly power. As in the case of most successful liberation movements, Islam incorporated many of the cultural and political characteristics of its enemies. Though Muhammad was hounded out of Mecca by its local power elites, one hundred years after his death a glittering capital for the new Islamic empire was founded at Baghdad, the "Constantinople of Islam." Moslems became imperialists themselves, although in most instances they allowed Christians and Jews to practice their faiths. Forced conversions were rare. Above all, Moslems became the supreme masters and cultivators of the very Greek wisdom that had been imposed on them by Alexander. They became devout disciples of the same Aristotle whose zealous pupil had set out to spread his master's learning in their lands a millennium before. It was the Arabs, after all, who brought Aristotle back to the West and eventually to the cluttered desk of Thomas Aquinas. At its height, Islamic culture vastly outshone that of the Christian West, which most Moslems more or less accurately regarded as a barren outpost. But at the same time, the original liberating impulse of Islam had begun to run out. Today, paradoxically, this very spoiling by success may provide a needed bridge between Christians and Moslems, since Christians have experienced the same sad, familiar story in their own history.

Muhammad's judgment on the Christianity of his day is one of the great ironies of history. This Christianity, which began in the life of a Palestinian Jew who was executed because he was viewed as a threat to the Roman Empire and to the Hellenistically inclined rulers of his colonized nation, was seen a few centuries later by Muhammad, the prophet of another downtrodden nation, as the religious sanction for his own people's domination. What is remarkable about Muhammad is not that he rejected current theories about the divinity of Christ but that he did not reject Jesus himself. Rather he tried, from his own vantage point, to bypass the caricature of the Gospel which imperial Christianity had elaborated and to reclaim the faith of a people much like his own who had once looked to Allah for justice and mercy.

Jesus, then, is another vital link between the two faiths. To this day, Jesus holds a central place in Islamic teaching and is sometimes even depicted as a kind of supreme exemplar of what is meant by "submission to God" (the meaning of the word "Islam"). In popular Islamic belief, Jesus often occupies an even more important position. Thus many Moslems believe that when the long awaited "Twelfth Iman," whose name is *al-Mahdi*, finally appears to usher in the reign of justice on earth (not in the sky, incidentally), he will either be accompanied by Jesus or will turn out to be the same one whose "coming in Glory" the Christian creeds confess. Obviously there is much to discuss here between these two "Jesus traditions," if the ground can be cleared of spiteful stereotypes and the sibling rivalry can be held at bay.

Both Christianity and Islam began as visions of captive peoples who yearned for deliverance and caught a glimpse of hope in the promise of God. The two can understand each other only when both begin to acknowledge these common roots, step out of the long shadow of Alexander the Great, and try to learn from each other what has gone so terribly wrong over the years of their common history.

From Harvey Cox, "Understanding Islam—No More Holy Wars," *The Atlantic Monthly*, January 1981. Reprinted by permission of the publisher.

ANALYSIS AND INTERPRETATION OF THE READINGS

1. Was the Byzantine conception of popular sovereignty similar to the modern conception?
2. What resemblances do you find between the doctrines of the Koran and the doctrines of the Old and New Testament?
3. Explain Cox's quotation from Christopher Dawson: "Muhammad is the Orient's answer to Alexander the Great."

CHAPTER 13 | The High Middle Ages (1050–1300): Economic, Social, and Political Institutions

CHRONOLOGY

In the blanks below, write the following events in their correct chronological order: Norman conquest of England; Battle of Las Navas de Tolosa; accession of Hugh Capet to the French throne; accession of Philip Augustus; Battle of Legnano; signing of Magna Carta; death of Philip IV ("the Fair"); Henry IV's humiliation at Canossa; first European windmills

_____

_____

_____

_____

_____

_____

_____

_____

IDENTIFICATIONS

You should be familiar with the following terms:

three-field system
tandem harnessing
journeyman
national monarchy
"Holy Roman Empire"

Hohenstaufen
communes (Italian)
baron
Ile-de-France
Capetian dynasty

And the following people:

Eleanor of Aquitaine
Blanche of Castille
Otto the Great
Gregory VII

Frederick Barbarossa
Frederick II
Thomas Becket
St. Louis (France)

In the space provided after each, define the following terms:

manorialism _____

_____

_____

vassal _____

_____

_____

knight _____

_____

_____

fief _____

_____

_____

craft guild _____

_____

_____

merchant guild _____

_____

_____

itinerant judges _____

_____

_____

serf _____

_____

_____

baillis _____

_____

_____

lord's demesne _____

_____

_____

STUDY QUESTIONS

1. What were the causes of the "agricultural revolution" in northern and western Europe? Why did it not occur earlier than the High Middle Ages?
2. Summarize the prerequisites for the agricultural revolution that were found in Europe.
3. What specific advantages did the new agricultural techniques have over the old Roman farming methods?
4. What technological developments allowed horses to replace oxen as farm animals? What were the advantages of the shift to horses?
5. How did the greater use of iron help increase agricultural productivity?
6. What effects did a stable food supply have on European history?
7. Explain the origin of the medieval European manor. How did it differ from the old Roman landed estate?
8. Explain this statement: "The entire manorial system emphasized communal enterprise and solidarity."
9. What were the causes of the decline of serfdom in the thirteenth century?
10. How did the nobles benefit from the agricultural revolution, even after the emancipation of their serfs?
11. Explain the origin of the code of chivalry. What was expected of a chivalric lord?
12. How did the life-style and social attitudes of the nobility change during the High Middle Ages?
13. "Whereas the Romans were really only interested in land *communications*, medieval people, starting in the eleventh century, concentrated on land *transport*." Explain this statement.
14. Explain the growth of European towns in the twelfth and thirteenth centuries. What were its major causes? How was this growth related to changes in agriculture?
15. How did medieval guilds differ from modern trade unions?
16. What functions did medieval guilds serve in addition to purely professional ones?
17. How did the growth of a merchant class affect prevailing attitudes toward moneylending and profit?
18. Summarize the effects of the revival of trade in western Europe.
19. In 1050, Germany was the most centralized European territory. By 1300 it was the most fragmented. Explain how this came about.
20. How did the emperor Frederick II, in spite of his brilliance and energy, contribute to the misfortunes of both Italy and Germany?
21. Define political feudalism as it existed in medieval Western Europe. In view of its decentralized character, how could it nevertheless contribute to the growth of stable governments?
22. How did William the Conqueror aid the development of a national monarchy in England?
23. What developments in the judiciary mark the reign of Henry II as one of the most momentous in all of English history?
24. What were the consequences of the disagreement between Henry II and Thomas Becket?
25. Explain why Magna Carta was basically a feudal document rather than a "charter of liberties for the common people." What principles of value did it embody for the future?
26. In response to what needs did a trained officialdom develop in England?
27. What was the origin of the English Parliament? How did its composition change and its importance grow under Edward I?
28. Why did the Capetians have more difficulty in strengthening the monarchy in France than did the Norman rulers in England? How were they able to overcome these difficulties?

PROBLEMS

1. Investigate further any of the following:
   a. The development of agricultural technology during the High Middle Ages
   b. The social and domestic life of the feudal nobility

c. The personality and deeds of Frederick II of Hohenstaufen

d. The thirteenth-century origins of the English Parliament

e. Medieval craft guilds

2. Compare the life of the medieval peasant with that of the modern working person. In what ways was the life of the former superior? In what ways was it inferior?

3. Describe the chief differences between feudalism as a system of government and the modern state.

4. What factors operated during the High Middle Ages to bring the nation-state into existence?

5. Trace the development of Anglo-American democratic institutions in the high-medieval age.

6. Discuss the effects on civilization of the growth of cities.

7. Debate—pro or con—this proposition: The rise of national monarchies was essential to the development of modern civilization.

AIDS TO AN UNDERSTANDING OF THE HIGH MIDDLE AGES: ECONOMIC, SOCIAL, AND POLITICAL INSTITUTIONS

CEREMONIAL RELATIONSHIP BETWEEN LORD AND VASSAL

Through the whole remaining part of the day those who had been previously enfeoffed by the most pious Count Charles did homage to the [new] count, taking up now again their fiefs and offices and whatever they had before rightfully and legitimately obtained. On Thursday, the seventh of April, homages were again made to the count, being completed in the following order of faith and security.

First they did their homage thus. The count asked the vassal if he were willing to become completely his man, and the other replied, "I am willing"; and with hands clasped, placed between the hands of the count, they were bound together by a kiss. Secondly, he who had done homage gave his fealty to the representative of the count in these words, "I promise on my faith that I will in future be faithful to Count William, and will observe my homage to him completely against all persons, in good faith and without deceit." And, thirdly, he took his oath to this upon the relics of the saints. Afterward the count, with a little rod which he held in his hand, gave investitures to all who by this agreement had given their security and accompanying oath.

From J. H. Robinson, *Readings in European History*, Vol. I.

THE EMANCIPATION OF A SERF

To all the faithful of Christ to whom the present writing shall come, Richard, by the divine permission abbot of Peterborough and of the Convent of the same place, eternal greeting in the Lord:

Let all know that we have manumitted and liberated from all yoke of servitude William, the son of Richard of Wythington, whom previously we have held as our born bondman, with his whole progeny and all his chattels, so that neither we nor our successors shall be able to require or exact any right or claim in the said William, his progeny, or his chattels. But the same William, with his whole progeny and all his chattels, shall remain free and quit and without disturbance, exaction, or any claim on the part of us or our successors by reason of any servitude forever.

We will, moreover, and concede that he and his heirs shall hold the messuages, land, rents, and meadows in Wythington which his ancestors held from us and our predecessors, by giving and performing the fine which is called *merchet* for giving his daughter in marriage, and tallage from year to year according to our will—that he shall have and hold these for the future from us and our successors freely, quietly, peacefully, and hereditarily, by paying to us and our successors yearly 40s. sterling, at the four terms of the year, namely: at St. John the Baptist's day 10s., at Michaelmas 10s., at Christmas 10s., and at Easter 10s., for all service, exaction, custom, and secular demand; saving to us, nevertheless, attendance at our court of Castre every three weeks, wardship, and relief, and outside service of our lord the king, when they shall happen.

And if it shall happen that the said William or his heirs shall die at any time without an heir, the said messuage, land, rents, and meadows with their appurtenances shall return fully and completely to us and our successors. Nor will it be allowed to the said William or his heirs to give, sell, alienate, mortgage, or encumber in any way, the said messuage, land, rents, meadows, or any part of them, by which the said messuage, land, rents, and meadows should not return to us and our successors in the form declared above. And if this should occur later, their deed shall be declared null, and what is thus alienated shall come to us and our successors. . . .

Given at Borough, for the love of Lord Robert of good memory, once abbot, our predecessor and maternal uncle of the said William, and at the instance of the good man, Brother Hugh of Mutton, relative of the said abbot Robert, A.D. 1278, on the eve of Pentecost.

From J. H. Robinson, *Readings in European History*, Vol. I.

SIGNIFICANT PROVISIONS OF MAGNA CARTA

No *scutage* or aid shall be imposed in our kingdom, unless by the common council of our kingdom, except to redeem our person, and to make our eldest son a knight, and once to marry our eldest daughter; and for this there shall only be paid a reasonable aid.

And the city of London shall have all its ancient liberties and free customs, as well by land as by water.

Furthermore, we will and grant that all other cities and boroughs, and towns, and ports, shall have all their liberties and free customs; and shall have the common council of the kingdom concerning the assessment of their aids, except in the three cases aforesaid.

And for the assessing of scutages we shall cause to be summoned the archbishops, bishops, abbots, earls, and great barons of the realm, singly by our letters.

And furthermore, we shall cause to be summoned in general by our sheriffs and bailiffs, all others who hold of us in chief, at a certain day, that is to say, forty days (before their meeting) at least, to a certain place; and in all letters of such summons, we will declare the cause of the summons.

And summons being thus made, the business shall proceed on the day appointed, according to the advice of such as shall be present, although all that were summoned come not.

We will not for the future grant to any one, that he may take aid of his own free-tenants, unless to redeem his body; and to make his eldest son a knight, and once to marry his eldest daughter; and for this there shall only be paid a reasonable aid.

• • •

A free man shall not be amerced for a small fault, but according to the degree of the fault; and for a great crime, in proportion to the heinousness of it, saving to him his contentment, and after the same manner a merchant, saving to him his merchandise.

And a villain shall be amerced after the same manner, saving to him his wainage, if he falls under our mercy; and none of the aforesaid amerciaments shall be assessed, but by the oath of honest men of the neighbourhood.

• • •

No constable or bailiff of ours shall take corn or other chattels of any man, unless he presently gives him money for it, or hath respite of payment from the seller.

No constables shall distrein any knight to give money for castle-guard, if he himself shall do it in his own person, or by another able man, in case he shall be hindered by any reasonable cause.

And if we shall lead him, or if we shall send him into the army, he shall be free from castle-guard, for the time he shall be in the army, by our command.

No sheriff or bailiff of ours, or any other, shall take horses or carts of any for carriage.

Neither shall We or our officers or others, take any man's timber for our castles, or other uses, unless by the consent of the owner of the timber.

• • •

No freeman shall be taken, or imprisoned, or disscis'd, or outlaw'd, or banished, or any ways destroyed; nor will we pass upon him, or commit him to prison, unless by the legal judgment of his peers, or by the law of the land.

We will sell to no man, we will deny no man, nor defer right or justice.

All merchants shall have safe and secure conduct to go out of, and come into England; and to stay there, and to pass, as well by land as by water; to buy and sell by the ancient and allowed customs, without any evil tolls, except in time of war, or when they shall be of any nation in war with us.

And if there shall be found any such in our land in the beginning of a war, they shall be attached, without damage to their bodies or goods, until it may be known unto us, or our chief justiciary, how our merchants be treated in the nation at war with us, and if ours be safe there, they shall be safe in our land.

• • •

If any one hath been dispossessed, or deprived by us without the legal judgment of his peers, of his lands, castles, liberties or right, we will forthwith restore them to him; and if any dispute arises upon this head, let the matter be decided by the five and twenty barons hereafter mentioned, for the preservation of the peace.

As for those things, of which any person has, without the legal judgment of his peers, been dispossessed or deprived, either by King Henry our father or our brother King Richard, and which we have in our hands, or are possessed by others, and we are bound to warrant and make good, we shall have a respite, till the term usually allowed the croises; excepting those things about which there is a suit depending, or whereof an inquest hath been made by our order, before we undertook the crusade. But when we return from our pilgrimage, or if we do not perform it, we will immediately cause full justice to be administered therein.

• • •

And whereas, for the honour of God, and the amendment of our kingdom, and for quieting the discord that has arisen between Us and our barons, we have granted all the things aforesaid; willing to render them firm and lasting, we do given and grant our subjects the following security; namely, that the barons may choose five and twenty barons of the kingdom, whom they think convenient, who shall take care, with all their might, to hold and observe, and cause to be observed, the peace and liberties we have granted them, and by this our present Charter confirmed. . . .

From John Fairburn ed., *Magna Charta, the Bill of Rights; with the Petition of Right . . .*

LIFE IN A MEDIEVAL BURGHER'S HOME
Joseph and Frances Gies

In a thirteenth-century city the houses of rich and poor look more or less alike from the outside. Except for a few of stone, they are all tall timber post-and-beam structures, with a tendency to sag and lean as they get older. In the poor quarters several families inhabit one house. A weaver's family may be crowded into a single room, where they huddle around a fireplace, hardly better off than the peasants and serfs of the countryside.

A well-to-do burgher family, on the other hand, occupies all four stories of its house, with business premises on the ground floor, living quarters on the second and third, servants' quarters in the attic, stables and storehouses in the rear. From cellar to attic, the emphasis is on comfort, but it is thirteenth-century comfort, which leaves something to be desired even for the master and mistress.

Entering the door of such a house, a visitor finds himself in an anteroom. One door leads to a workshop or counting room, a second to a steep flight of stairs. The greater part of the second floor is occupied by the hall, or solar, which serves as both living and dining room. A hearth fire blazes under the hood of a huge chimney. Even in daytime the fire supplies much of the house's illumination, because the narrow windows are fitted with oiled parchment. Suspended by a chain from the wall is an oil lamp, usually not lighted until full darkness. A housewife also economizes on candles, saving fat for the chandler to convert into a smoky, pungent but serviceable product. Beeswax candles are limited to church and ceremonial use.

The large low-ceilinged room is bare and chilly. Walls are hung with panels of linen cloth, which may be dyed or decorated with embroidery; the day of tapestry will come in another fifty years. Carpets are extremely rare in thirteenth-century Europe; floors are covered with rushes. Furniture consists of benches, a long trestle table which is dismantled after meals, a big wooden cupboard displaying plate and silver, and a low buffet for the pottery and tinware used every day. Cupboards and chests are built on posts, with planks nailed lengthwise to form the sides. In spite of iron bindings, and linen and leather glued inside or out, the planks crack, split and warp. It will be two centuries before someone thinks of joining panels by tongue and groove, or mortise and tenon, so that the wood can expand and contract.

If furniture is drab, costume is not. A burgher and his wife wear linen and wool in bright reds, greens, blues, and yellows, trimmed and lined with fur. Though their garments are similar, differentiation is taking place. A century ago both sexes wore long, loose-fitting tunics and robes that were almost identical. Now men's clothes are shorter and tighter than women's, and a man wears an invention of the Middle Ages that has already become a byword for masculinity: trousers, in the form of hose, a tight-fitting combination of breeches and stockings. Over them he wears a long-sleeved tunic, which may be lined with fur, then a sleeveless belted surcoat of fine wool, sometimes with a hood. For outdoors, he wears a mantle fastened at the shoulder with a clasp or chain; although buttons are sometimes used for decoration, the buttonhole has not been invented. (It will be by the end of the century.) His clothes have no pockets, and he must carry money and other belongings in a pouch or purse slung from his belt, or in his sleeves. On his feet are boots with high tops of soft leather.

A woman may wear a tunic with sleeves laced from wrist to elbow, topped by a surcoat caught in at the waist by a belt, with full sleeves that reveal those of the tunic underneath. Her shoes are soft leather, with thin soles. Both sexes wear under-clothes—women long linen chemises, men linen undershirts and underdrawers with a cloth belt.

Hair is invariably parted in the middle, a woman's in two long plaits, which she covers with a white linen wimple, a man's worn jaw-long, sometimes with bangs, and often topped with a soft cap. Men's faces are stubbly. Only a rough shave can be achieved with available instruments, and a burgher may visit the barber only once a week.

At mealtime a very broad cloth is laid on the trestle table in the solar. To facilitate service, places are set along one side only. On that side the cloth falls to the floor, doubling as a communal napkin. At a festive dinner it sometimes gets changed between courses. Places are set with knives, spoons, and thick slices of day-old bread, which serve as plates for meat. There are several kinds of knives—for cutting meat, slicing bread, opening oysters and nuts—but no forks. Between each two places stands a two-handled bowl, or *écuelle*, which is filled with soup or stew. Two neighbors share the *écuelle*, as well as a winecup and spoon. A large pottery receptacle is used for waste liquids, and a thick chunk of bread with a hole in the middle serves as a salt shaker.

When supper is prepared, a servant blows a horn. Napkins, basins, and pitchers are ready; everyone washes his hands without the aid of soap. Courtesy requires sharing a basin with one's neighbor.

If there is no clergyman present, the youngest member of the family says grace. The guests join in the responses and the amen.

Supper may begin with a capon brewet, half soup, half stew, with the meat served in the bottom of the *écuelle*, broth poured over, and spices dusted on top. The second course is perhaps a porray, a soup of leeks, onions, chitterlings, and ham, cooked in milk, with stock and bread crumbs added. A civet of hare may follow—the meat grilled, then cut up and cooked with onions, vinegar, wine, and spices, again thickened with bread crumbs. Each course is washed down with wine from an earthenware jug. At a really elaborate meal roast meats and other stews and fish dishes follow. The meal may conclude with frumenty (a kind of custard), figs and nuts, wafers and spiced wine.

• • •

Ceaseless war is carried on against fleas, bedbugs, and other insects. Strategies vary. One practice is to fold coverlets, furs, and clothes so tightly in a chest that the fleas will suffocate. A housewife may spread birdlime or turpentine on trenchers of bread, with a lighted candle in the middle. More simply, she may cover a straw mattress with a white sheepskin so that the enemy can be seen and crushed. Netting is used in summer against flies and mosquitoes, and insect traps have been devised, of which the simplest is a rag dipped in honey.

Even for a well-to-do city family, making life comfortable is a problem. But arriving at a point where comfort becomes a problem for a fair number of people is a sign of advancing civilization.

From Joseph and Frances Gies, *Life in a Medieval City*. pp. 34, 37–39. Thomas Y. Crowell Company, New York, 1969.

ANALYSIS AND INTERPRETATION
OF THE READINGS

1. What improvement in status did manumission bring to a serf?
2. Do you get the impression that William had been in abject poverty during his period of serfdom?
3. What particular abuses or unjust practices did King John promise to renounce?
4. Did Magna Carta offer any benefits to the non-feudal elements of the population? If so, in which clauses?
5. Study carefully the first seven clauses quoted from Magna Carta. Just what financial limitations did they put upon the king? Did these clauses really incorporate the principle of "no taxation without representation," as was alleged in later times?
6. How is the life of a medieval burgher similar to, and different from, your own?

CHAPTER 14 | The High Middle Ages (1050–1300): Religious and Intellectual Developments

CHRONOLOGY

Write the correct date or dates in the blank after each of the following events:

Founding of monastery of Cluny _____

Council of Clermont _____

Concordat of Worms _____

Death of St. Bernard of Clairvaux _____

Pontificate of Innocent III _____

Fourth Lateran Council _____

Death of Emperor Frederick II of Hohenstaufen _____

Completion of the *Romance of the Rose*
   by John of Meun _____

Fall of the last of the Crusaders' holdings
   in the Holy Land _____

First papal jubilee in Rome _____

Death of Dante _____

IDENTIFICATIONS

In the blanks below, write the correct terms taken from the following list:

lay investiture	Fourth Lateran Council
minnesingers	Scholasticism
Cistercians	*Sic et Non*
Papal States	Albigensians
fabliaux	primogeniture
Goliards	Waldensians
canon law	simony
Sicilian Vespers	

1. _____ was the product of a centralized system of Church courts which both enhanced papal prestige and improved legal standards.

2. _____ was the ceremony whereby a churchman had the symbols of office conferred on him by the king or a noble.

3. The _____ were territories near Rome over which popes attempted to establish direct sovereignty.

4. The _____ of 1282 led to a fierce struggle involving the pope, the French king, and the Spanish house of Aragon.

5. _____ was a rule of inheritance that disadvantaged younger sons.

6. The _____ were a monastic order founded about 1100 who strikingly demonstrated an intensified religious zeal.

7. The _____ decreed that sacraments administered by the Church were indispensable for salvation.

8. The _____ claimed to be Christians but subscribed to extreme religious dualism.

9. _____ was the buying and selling of Church positions.

10. In _____ Abelard attempted to subject theology to the tools of logic.

11. The _____ were a heretical group originating in southern France who strove for literal imitation of the life of Christ.

12. _____ was a highly intellectual worldview that attempted to reconcile classical pagan philosophy with the Christian faith.

13. The Latin lyrics of the _____ flouted the ascetic ideals of Christianity.

14. The _____ were coarse but entertaining prose stories written in the vernacular.

15. The _____ were the German equivalent of French troubadours.

Circle the name of the appropriate individual in the following statements. If none of those listed is the appropriate person, write the correct name in the blank space at (d).

1. A pope who for his reforming zeal and challenging of secular rulers was called a "Holy Satan" was: (a) Boniface VIII; (b) Gregory I; (c) Gregory VII; (d) _____

2. The founder of the order of friars to which St. Thomas Aquinas belonged was: (a) St. Dominic; (b) St. Augustine; (c) St. Francis of Assisi; (d) _____

3. The pope who forced King John to acknowledge England as a papal fief was: (a) Innocent III; (b) Nicholas I; (c) Innocent IV; (d) _____

4. The first pope to preach a Crusade was: (a) Gregory VII; (b) Gregory the Great; (c) Urban II; (d) _____

5. The leader of a unique Crusade that succeeded through peaceful diplomacy was: (a) Frederick Barbarossa; (b) Frederick II; (c) Richard the Lionhearted; (d) _____

6. The ruler who declared: "As every knee is bowed to Jesus, so all men should obey his Vicar" was: (a) Innocent III; (b) Frederick II; (c) John XII; (d) _____

7. The Byzantine emperor who appealed to the pope for aid against the Seljuk Turks was: (a) Leo III, Isaurian; (b) Saladin; (c) Alexius Comnenus; (d) _____

8. The greatest of the Scholastic philosophers and long-time professor at the University of Paris was: (a) Robert Grosseteste; (b) William of Lorris; (c) Gottfried von Strassburg; (d) _____

9. The translator of Aristotle's *Ethics* and a pioneer in mathematics, astronomy, and optics was: (a) Roger Bacon; (b) Peter Abelard; (c) Robert Grosseteste; (d) _____

10. A gifted, challenging, but highly controversial teacher who clashed with the Church and was convicted of heresy was: (a) Héloise; (b) Peter Lombard; (c) Peter Abelard; (d) _____

11. A leader of the Cluny reform movement who was elected Pope in 1073 took the name: (a) Boniface VIII; (b) Innocent III; (c) Pius IV; (d) _____

STUDY QUESTIONS

1. Define *papal monarchy*. Summarize its significance in European political and religious developments.
2. Why did the founding of the monastery of Cluny represent an important step toward the development of papal power?
3. Explain the significance of the decree on papal elections issued in 1059.
4. What were the contributions of Pope Gregory VII to the rise of the papal monarchy? What was Gregory's conception of "right order in the world"?
5. The investiture struggle was seemingly a quarrel over symbols and ceremony. What were the real underlying issues? How were they settled?
6. What were the goals of Pope Innocent III? To what extent did he attain them?
7. Explain the assertion that, for all of its accomplishments, the reign of Innocent III "sowed some of the seeds of future ruin" for the papal monarchy.
8. How did the clash between the popes and various monarchs in the thirteenth and fourteenth centuries ultimately weaken the power of the papacy?
9. What were Urban II's motives in calling the First Crusade? What did the First Crusade accomplish?
10. What were the religious causes of the Crusades?
11. "While the crusading idea helped build up the papal monarchy, it also helped destroy it." Explain how.
12. Estimate the positive and negative effects of the Crusades on European society and economy.
13. What change in religious beliefs is indicated by the twelfth-century cult of the Virgin Mary? How did this change affect social attitudes and artistic expression?
14. How do you account for the rise of popular heretical movements in the late twelfth century?
15. How did the emergence of new orders of friars fit into Innocent III's larger reform objectives?
16. Describe the nature and effects of the "high-medieval educational boom."
17. What was the relationship between cathedral schools and high-medieval universities?
18. Show how the great medieval universities set the pattern for higher education in the modern Western world. In what ways were they different from modern institutions?
19. How did the lives of medieval students differ from those of their modern descendants?
20. To what extent were Robert Grosseteste and Roger Bacon forerunners of modern science?
21. What was St. Thomas Aquinas attempting in writing his *Summaries*? In what way, if any, did his thought differ from that of the early Church father St. Augustine?
22. What were the main types of secular literature in the High Middle Ages? Give examples of each type.
23. How do the ideas and attitudes expressed in the *Divine Comedy* contrast with those of the early Middle Ages?

24. Dante's *Divine Comedy* has been described as a synthesis of high-medieval knowledge and beliefs. In what ways does it also show originality?
25. Point out the differences between the Romanesque and Gothic styles of architecture.
26. In addition to their religious function, what aspects of high-medieval culture are reflected in the great Gothic cathedrals?

PROBLEMS

1. Investigate further any of the following:
   a. The Cluniac reform movement
   b. St. Francis of Assisi
   c. One of the first four Crusades
   d. Medieval science
   e. The Goliard poets
   f. A major Gothic cathedral (e.g., Chartres, Notre Dame of Paris, Amiens, Lincoln, Canterbury, or Cologne)

2. Compare modern universities with their medieval prototypes.
3. Read the chapter titled "The Virgin and the Dynamo" in Henry Adams' *The Education of Henry Adams* and decide whether or not it expresses accurately the medieval religious temper.
4. To what extent was medieval Scholasticism a "rationalist" philosophy? Was it an example of rationalism in the modern sense?
5. Which, in your opinion, was a better summation of late medieval ideals and attitudes: Gothic architecture or vernacular literature?
6. Read the *Song of Roland* and explain how it illustrates the interests and ideals of high-medieval civilization.
7. The Scholastics "had extraordinary faith in the powers of human reason—probably more than we do today." Do you agree or disagree? Substantiate your argument.
8. Examine the High Middle Ages as an "age of faith." What made it so? What were its tangible results?

AIDS TO AN UNDERSTANDING OF THE HIGH MIDDLE AGES: RELIGIOUS AND INTELLECTUAL DEVELOPMENTS

THE STRUGGLE BETWEEN SECULAR AND SPIRITUAL AUTHORITIES: Gregory VII's Conception of the Pope's Prerogatives

Among the letters and decrees of Gregory VII a list of propositions is found which briefly summarizes the claims of the papacy. The purpose of this so-called *Dictatus* is unknown; it was probably drawn up shortly after Gregory's accession and no doubt gives an official statement of the powers which he believed that he rightly possessed. The more important of the twenty-seven propositions contained in the *Dictatus* are given below.

The Roman church was founded by God alone.
The Roman bishop alone is properly called universal.
He alone may depose bishops and reinstate them.
His legate, though of inferior grade, takes precedence, in a council, of all bishops and may render a decision of deposition against them.
He alone may use the insignia of empire.
The pope is the only person whose feet are kissed by all princes.
His title is unique in the world.
He may depose emperors.
No council may be regarded as a general one without his consent.
No book or chapter may be regarded as canonical without his authority.

A decree of his may be annulled by no one; he alone may annul the decrees of all.
He may be judged by no one.
No one shall dare to condemn one who appeals to the papal see.
The Roman church has never erred, nor ever, by the witness of Scripture, shall err to all eternity.
He may not be considered Catholic who does not agree with the Roman church.
The pope may absolve the subjects of the unjust from their allegiance.

From J. H. Robinson, *Readings in European History*, Vol. I.

THE CRUSADES: Pope Urban II's Speech at the Council of Clermont

Although, O sons of God, you have promised more firmly than ever to keep the peace among yourselves and to preserve the rights of the church, there remains still an important work for you to do. Freshly quickened by the divine correction, you must apply the strength of your righteousness to another matter which concerns you as well as God. For your brethren who live in the east are in urgent need of your help, and you must hasten to give them the aid which has often been promised them. For, as the most of you have heard, the Turks and Arabs have attacked them and have conquered the territory of Romania [the Greek empire] as far west as the shore of the Mediterranean and the Hellespont, which is called the Arm of St. George. They have occupied more and more of the lands of those Christians, and have overcome them in seven battles. They have killed and captured many, and have destroyed the churches and devastated the empire. If you permit them to continue thus for awhile with impunity, the faithful of God will be much more widely attacked by them. On this account I, or rather the Lord, beseech you as Christ's heralds to publish this everywhere and to persuade all people of whatever rank, foot-soldiers and knights, poor and rich, to carry aid promptly to those Christians and to destroy that vile race from the lands of our friends. I say this to those who are present, it is meant also for those who are absent. Moreover, Christ commands it.

All who die by the way, whether by land or by sea, or in battle against the pagans, shall have immediate remission of sins. This I grant them through the power of God with which I am invested. O what a disgrace if such a despised and base race, which worships demons, should conquer a people which has the faith of omnipotent God and is made glorious with the name of Christ! With what reproaches will the Lord overwhelm us if you do not aid those who, with us, profess the Christian religion! Let those who have been accustomed unjustly to wage private warfare against the faithful now go against the infidels and end with victory this war which should have been begun long ago. Let those who, for a long time, have been robbers, now become knights. Let those who have been fighting against their brothers and relatives now fight in a proper way against the barbarians. Let those who have been serving as mercenaries for small pay now obtain the eternal reward. Let those who have been wearing themselves out in both body and soul now work for a double honor. Behold! on this side will be the sorrowful and poor, on that, the rich; on this side, the enemies of the Lord, on that, his friends. Let those who go not put off the journey, but rent their lands and collect money for their expenses; and as soon as winter is over and spring comes, let them eagerly set out on the way with God as their guide.

From O. J. Thatcher and E. J. McNeal, *A Source Book for Medieval History.*

Late Medieval Philosophy: The Rationalism of St. Thomas Aquinas

Now though the aforesaid truth of the Christian faith surpasses the ability of human reason, nevertheless those things which are naturally instilled in human reason cannot be opposed to this truth. For it is clear that those things which are implanted in reason by nature, are most true, so much so that it is impossible to think them to be false. Nor is it lawful to deem false that which is held by faith, since it is so evidently confirmed by God. Seeing then that the false alone is opposed to the true, as evidently appears if we examine their definitions, it is impossible for the aforesaid truth of faith to be contrary to those principles which reason knows naturally.

Again. The same thing which the disciple's mind receives from its teacher is contained in the knowledge of the teacher, unless he teach insincerely, which it were wicked to say of God. Now the knowledge of naturally known principles is instilled into us by God, since God Himself is the author of our nature. Therefore the divine Wisdom also contains these principles. Consequently whatever is contrary to these principles, is contrary to the divine Wisdom; wherefore it cannot be from God. Therefore those things which are received by faith from divine revelation cannot be contrary to our natural knowledge.

Of God

Having shown then that it is not futile to endeavour to prove the existence of God, we may proceed to set forth the reasons whereby both philosophers and Catholic doctors have proved that there is a God. In the first place we shall give the arguments by which Aristotle sets out to prove God's existence: and he aims at proving this from the point of view of movement, in two ways.

The *first way* is as follows. Whatever is in motion is moved by another: and it is clear to the sense that something, the sun for instance, is in motion. Therefore it is set in motion by something else moving. Now that which moves it is itself either moved or not. If it be not moved, then the point is proved that we must needs postulate an immovable mover, and this we call God. If, however, it be moved, it is moved by another mover. Either, therefore, we must proceed to infinity, or we must come to an immovable mover. But it is not possible to proceed to infinity. Therefore it is necessary to postulate an immovable mover. . . .

The Philosopher proceeds in a *different way* in *2 Metaph.* to show that it is impossible to proceed to infinity in efficient causes, and that we must come to one first cause, and this we call God. This is how he proceeds. In all efficient causes following in order, the first is the cause of the intermediate cause, and the intermediate is the cause of the ultimate, whether the intermediate be one or several. Now if the cause be removed, that which it causes is removed. Therefore if we remove the first the intermediate cannot be a cause. But if we go on to infinity in efficient causes, no cause will be first. Therefore all the others which are intermediate will be removed. Now this is clearly false. Therefore we must suppose *the existence of a first efficient cause*: and this is God. . . .

Another argument in support of this conclusion is adduced by Damascene from the government of things: and the same reasoning is indicated by the Commentator in *2 Phys.* It runs as follows. It is impossible for contrary and discordant things to accord in one order always or frequently except by someone's governance, whereby each and all are made to tend to a definite end. Now we see that in the world things of different natures accord in one order, not seldom and fortuitously, but always or for the most part. Therefore it follows that there is *someone by whose providence the world is governed.* And this we call God.

From St. Thomas Aquinas, *Summa contra Gentiles,* trans. by the English Dominican Fathers, Vol I. Copyright 1924 by Burns, Oates and Washbourne Ltd. Reprinted by permission of Burns & Oates Ltd and Benzinger Brothers.

LATE MEDIEVAL SCIENCE: The Empiricism of Roger Bacon, from *Opus Majus*

Having laid down fundamental principles of the wisdom of the Latins so far as they are found in language, mathematics, and optics, I now wish to unfold the principles of experimental science, since without experience nothing can be sufficiently known. For there are two modes of acquiring knowledge, namely, by reasoning and experience. Reasoning draws a conclusion and makes us grant the conclusion, but does not make the conclusion certain, nor does it remove doubt so that the mind may rest on the intuition of truth, unless the mind discovers it by the path of experience; since many have the arguments relating to what can be known, but because they lack experience they neglect the arguments, and neither avoid what is harmful nor follow what is good. For if a man who has never seen fire should prove by adequate reasoning that fire burns and injures things and destroys them, his mind would not be satisfied thereby, nor would he avoid fire, until he placed his hand or some combustible substance in the fire, so that he might prove by experience that which reasoning taught. But when he has had actual experience of combustion his mind is made certain and rests in the full light of truth. Therefore reasoning does not suffice, but experience does. . . .

He therefore who wishes to rejoice without doubt in regard to the truths underlying phenomena must know how to devote himself to experiment. For authors write many statements, and people believe them through reasoning which they formulate without experience. Their reasoning is wholly false. For it is generally believed that the diamond cannot be broken except by goat's blood, and philosophers and theologians misuse this idea. But fracture by means of blood of this kind has never been verified, although the effort has been made; and without that blood it can be broken easily. For I have seen this with my own eyes, and this is necessary, because gems cannot be carved except by fragments of this stone. . . . Moreover, it is generally believed that hot water freezes more quickly than cold water in vessels, and the argument in support of this is advanced that contrary is excited by contrary, just like enemies meeting each other. But it is certain that cold water freezes more quickly for any one who makes the experiment. . . .

But experience is of two kinds; one is gained through our external senses, and in this way we gain our experience of those things that are in the heavens by instruments made for this purpose, and of those things here below by means attested by our vision. Things that do not belong in our part of the world we know through other scientists who have had experience of them. As, for example, Aristotle on the authority of Alexander sent two thousand men through different parts of the world to gain experimental knowledge of all things that are on the surface of the earth, as Pliny bears witness in his Natural History. This experience is both human and philosophical, as far as man can act in accordance with the grace given him; but this experience does not suffice him, because it does not give full attestation in regard to things corporeal owing to its difficulty, and does not touch at all on things spiritual. It is necessary, therefore, that the intellect of man should be otherwise aided, and for this reason the holy patriarchs and prophets, who first gave sciences to the world, received illumination within and were not dependent on sense alone. The same is true of many believers since the time of Christ. For the grace of faith illuminates greatly, as also do divine inspirations, not only in things spiritual, but in things corporeal and in the sciences of philosophy; as Ptolemy states in the Centilogium, namely, that there are two roads by which we arrive at the knowledge of facts, one through the experience of philosophy, the other through divine inspiration, which is far the better way, as he says.

From Roger Bacon, *Opus Majus*, R. B. Burke trans. University of Pennsylvania Press. Reprinted by permission of the publisher.

ANALYSIS AND INTERPRETATION OF THE READINGS

1. Did Pope Gregory claim the powers of an absolute monarch over the whole earth? Explain.
2. Pope Urban II's speech at the Council of Clermont has been described as one of the most effective in the history of oratory. Can you explain why? What varied motives did he appeal to in attempting to arouse his hearers to action?
3. Do you detect any weaknesses in the empiricism of Roger Bacon? Explain.

CHAPTER 15 | The Later Middle Ages (1300–1500)

CHRONOLOGY

Using the blanks below, arrange the following events in their proper chronological order: union of Aragon and Castile; outbreak of the Black Death in Europe; Battle of Crécy; beginning of the "Babylonian Captivity" of the papacy; accession of the Tudor king Henry VII; death of Boccaccio; the Jacquerie; end of the Great Schism; burning of John Hus; death of Ivan the Great; fall of Constantinople; Mongol invasion of the Kievan state

_____

_____

_____

_____

_____

_____

_____

_____

_____

_____

_____

_____

IDENTIFICATIONS

You should know the meaning and importance of the following terms:

Hanseatic League	*Imitation of Christ*
double-entry bookkeeping	Lollards
"book transfers"	Wars of the Roses
Ciompi	Tudors
Knights of the Garter	Khanate of the Golden Horde
flagellation	Grand Duchy of Moscow
Council of Constance	nominalism
heretics of the Free Spirit	*Canterbury Tales*

You should be able to identify the following persons:

Richard II	Master Eckhart
Wat Tyler	John Hus
Gregory XI	Joan of Arc
Urban VI	Henry VII
Clement VII	Giotto
Martin V	Jan van Eyck

STUDY QUESTIONS

1. What were the causes of the economic depression that lasted roughly a century and a half in the later Middle Ages?
2. Summarize the effects of the Black Death on the following:
   a. Demographic trends
   b. The condition of agriculture
   c. The role of towns and cities
3. What new business techniques came into operation during the fourteenth and fifteenth centuries?

4. How do you account for the rash of lower-class revolts in the later Middle Ages?

5. How did the English Peasants' Revolt of 1381 differ from the French Jacquerie of two decades earlier? In what ways was the *Ciompi* uprising in Florence, in spite of its failure, still more significant for future history?

6. "Religion in the Later Middle Ages was a more effective rallying ground for large numbers of people than political, economic, and social demands." What are the reasons for this?

7. How do you explain the aristocracy's obsession with luxury and extravagant display during the later Middle Ages?

8. What did the papacy gain in power and why did it at the same time lose respect during the period of residence at Avignon?

9. What caused the Great Schism of 1378–1417? How was it ended?

10. What were the objectives of the conciliar movement within the Church and by what means did the popes defeat it?

11. What was the connection between the increase in literacy and the decline of clerical prestige during the Middle Ages?

12. How do you explain the later-medieval "hunger for the divine"? What forms did it take?

13. Explain the "practical mysticism" of the religious handbook attributed to Thomas à Kempis.

14. Why did John Wyclif's teachings win support among the English aristocracy? In what way did his work anticipate the later Protestant Reformation?

15. Name the major political divisions of Italy around 1450.

16. What were the causes of the Hundred Years' War? How do you explain the spectacular victories of the English armies and also their ultimate defeat?

17. How did the results of the Hundred Years' War strengthen the French monarchy and also promote national unity in England in spite of internal conflict there?

18. Account for the expansion of the Kingdom of Poland in the fourteenth and fifteenth centuries. What factors eventually checked this expansion?

19. List the principal stages in the evolution of the Russian state in the later Middle Ages. What circumstances led to Russia's separation from Western Europe?

20. What were the contributions of Ivan III ("the Great") to the Russian imperial tradition?

21. How does William of Ockham's philosophy represent a significant departure from that of St. Thomas Aquinas? Are the differences related to changes in the condition of society during the fourteenth century?

22. If Ockham rejected Aquinas's confidence in human reason, how could he have contributed to the rise of the scientific method?

23. What qualities entitle Boccaccio's *Decameron* to rank as a landmark in the evolution of European literature?

24. How is naturalism illustrated in late-medieval art?

25. Summarize the technological advances made during the later Middle Ages. Which do you consider the most important? Why?

PROBLEMS

1. Investigate further any of the following:
   a. Changes in the techniques of warfare between 1300 and 1500
   b. The English Wars of the Roses
   c. The effects of the Black Death
   d. The conciliar reform movement
   e. The teachings and influence of John Wyclif or of John Hus
   f. The nominalism of William of Ockham
   g. Byzantine influence upon Russian culture and institutions

2. Read George Bernard Shaw's play *Saint Joan* and evaluate it as an exposition of political trends and concepts in the later Middle Ages.

3. Compare the *Decameron* and the *Canterbury Tales* as commentaries upon human nature and society.

4. Read Jean Froissart's *Chronicles* for his account of the period of the Hundred Years' War. Note what he chooses to emphasize. Assess the historical and literary value of this document.

5. Read the *Imitation of Christ* by Thomas à Kempis. What in this book helps explain why it has been second only to the Bible in popularity among Christians?

AIDS TO AN UNDERSTANDING OF THE LATER MIDDLE AGES

NATURALISM AS SEEN IN BOCCACCIO'S *Decameron*

In the year then of our Lord 1348, there happened at Florence, the finest city in all Italy, a most terrible plague; which, whether owing to the influence of the planets, or that it was sent from God as a just punishment for our sins, had broken out some years before in the Levant; and after passing from place to place, and making incredible havoc all the way, had now reached the west; where, spite of all the means that human foresight could suggest, as keeping the city clear from filth, and excluding all suspected persons; notwithstanding frequent consultations what else was to be done; nor omitting prayers to God in frequent processions: in the spring of the foregoing year, it began to show itself in a sad and wonderful manner; and, different from what it had been in the east, where bleeding from the nose is the fatal prognostic, here there appeared certain tumours in the groin, or under the armpits, some as big as a small apple, others as an egg; and afterwards purple spots in most parts of the body: in some cases large and but few in number, in others less and more numerous, both sorts the usual messengers of death. To the cure of this malady, neither medical knowledge nor the power of drugs was of any effect; whether because the disease was in its own nature mortal, or that the physicians (the number of whom, taking quacks and women pretenders into account, was grown very great) could form no just idea of the cause, nor consequently ground a true method of cure; whichever was the reason, few or none escaped; but they generally died the third day from the first appearance of the symptoms, without a fever or other bad circumstance attending. And the disease, by being communicated from the sick to the well, seemed daily to get ahead, and to rage the more, as fire will do by laying on fresh combustibles. . . ..

But I am weary of recounting our late miseries; therefore, passing by everything that I can well omit, I shall only observe, that the city being left almost without inhabitants, it happened one Tuesday in the evening as I was informed by persons of good credit, that seven ladies all in deep mourning, as most proper for that time, had been attending Divine service (being the whole congregation), in new St. Mary's Church: who, as united by the ties either of friendship or relation, and of suitable years, viz., the youngest not less than eighteen, nor the eldest exceeding twenty-eight; so were they all discreet, nobly descended, and perfectly accomplished, both in person and behaviour I do not mention their names, lest they should be displeased with some things said to have passed in conversation, there being a greater restraint on those diversions now. . . . And that I may relate therefore all that occurred without confusion, I shall affix names to every one bearing some resemblance to the quality of the person. The eldest then I call Pampinea, the next to her Flammetta, the third Philomena, the fourth Emilia, the fifth Lauretta, the sixth Neiphile, the youngest Eliza: who being got together by chance rather than any appointment, into a corner of the church, and there seated in a ring; and leaving off their devotions, and falling into some discourse together concerning the nature of the times; in a little while Pampinea thus began:

"My dear girls, you have often heard as well as I, that no one is injured, where we only make an honest use of our own reason: now reason tells us that we are to preserve our lives by all possible means and, in some cases, at the expense of the lives of others. And if the laws which regard the good of the community allow this, may not we much rather (and all that mean honestly as we do), without giving offence to any, use the means now in our power for our own preservation. . . . We stay here for no other purpose that I can see, but to observe what numbers come to be buried, or to listen if the monks, who are now reduced to a very few, sing their services at the proper times, or else to show by our habits the greatness of our distress. And if we go from hence, we are saluted with numbers of the dead and sick carried along the streets; or with persons who had been outlawed for their villainies, now facing it out publicly, in defiance of the laws. Or we see the scum of the city enriched with the public calamity, and insulting us with reproachful ballads. Nor is anything talked of but that such an one is dead or dying; and, were any left to mourn, we should hear nothing but lamentations. . . .

"Therefore the case is the same, whether we stay here, depart hence, or go home; especially as there are few who are able to go, and have a place to go to, left but ourselves. And those few, I am told, fall into all sorts of debauchery; and even the religious and ladies shut up in monasteries, supposing themselves entitled to equal liberties with others, are as bad as the worst. . . . Wherefore, lest through our own wilfulness or neglect, this calamity, which might have been prevented, should befall us, I should think it best (and I hope you will join with me) for us to quit the town, and avoiding, as we would death itself, the bad example of others, to choose some place of retirement, of which every one of us has more than one, where we may make ourselves innocently merry, without offering the least violence to the dictates of reason and our own consciences. There will our ears be entertained with the warbling of the birds, and our eyes with the verdure of the hills and valleys; with the waving of corn-fields like the sea itself; with trees of a thousand different kinds, and a more open and serene sky which, however overcast, yet affords a far more agreeable prospect than these desolate walls. The air also is pleasanter, and there is greater plenty of everything, attended with fewer inconveniences: for, though people die there as well as here, yet we shall have fewer such objects before us, as the inhabitants are less in number; and on the other part, if I judge right, we desert nobody, but are rather ourselves forsaken. For all our friends, either by death, or endeavouring to avoid it, have left us, as if we in no way belonged to them. As no blame then can ensue by following this advice, and perhaps sickness and death by not doing so, I would have us take our maids, and everything we may be supposed to want, and to remove every day to a different place, taking all the diversions in the meantime which the seasons will permit; and there continue, unless death should interpose, till we see what end Providence designs for these things."

[And so the ladies, in company with some gentlemen bent upon the same purpose, took refuge in a villa outside Florence, where they amused themselves by telling tales—the tales which make up the remainder of *The Decameron*.]

————

From Giovanni Boccaccio, *The Decameron*, Albert and Charles Boni, 1926.

The Late Medieval Vision of Death
J. Huizinga

No other epoch has laid so much stress as the expiring Middle Ages on the thought of death. An everlasting call of memento mori resounds through life. Denis the Carthusian, in his *Directory of the Life of Nobles*, exhorts them: "And when going to bed at night, he should consider how, just as he now lies down himself, soon strange hands will lay his body in the grave." In earlier times, too, religion had insisted on the constant thought of death, but the pious treatises of these ages only reached those who had already turned away from the world. Since the thirteenth century, the popular preaching of the mendicant orders had made the eternal admonition to remember death swell into a sombre chorus ringing throughout the world. Towards the fifteenth century, a new means of inculcating the awful thought into all minds was added to the words of the preacher, namely, the popular woodcut. Now these two means of expression, sermons and woodcuts, both addressing themselves to the multitude and limited to crude effects, could only represent death in a simple and striking form. All that the meditations on death of the monks of yore had produced, was now condensed into a very primitive image. This vivid image, continually impressed upon all minds, had hardly assimilated more than a single element of the great complex of ideas relating to death, namely, the sense of the perishable nature of all things. It would seem, at times, as if the soul of the declining Middle Ages only succeeded in seeing death under this aspect.

The endless complaint of the frailty of all earthly glory was sung to various melodies. Three motifs may be distinguished. The first is expressed by the question: where are now all those who once filled the world with their splendour? The second motif swells on the frightful spectacle of human beauty gone to decay. The third is the death-dance: death dragging along men of all conditions and ages.

At the close of the Middle Ages the whole vision of death may be summed up in the word *macabre*, in its modern meaning. Of course, this meaning is the outcome of a long process. But the sentiment it embodies, of something gruesome and dismal, is precisely the conception of death which arose during the last centuries of the Middle Ages. This bizarre word appeared in French in the fourteenth century, under the form *macabré*, and, whatever may be its etymology, as a proper name. A line of the poet Jean Le Fèvre, "Je fis de Macabré la dance," which may be dated 1376, remains the birth-certificate of the word for us.

Towards 1400 the conception of death in art and literature took a spectral and fantastic shape. A new and vivid shudder was added to the great primitive horror of death. The macabre vision arose from deep psychological strata of fear; religious thought at once reduced it to a means of moral exhortation. As such it was a great cultural idea, till in its turn it went out of fashion, lingering on in epitaphs and symbols in village cemeteries.

The idea of the death-dance is the central point of a whole group of connected conceptions. The priority belongs to the motif of the three dead and three living men, which is found in French literature from the thirteenth century onward. Three young noblemen suddenly meet three hideous dead men, who tell them of their past grandeur and warn them of their own near end. Art soon took hold of this suggestive theme. We can see it still in the striking frescoes of the *Campo santo* of Pisa. The sculpture of the portal of the church of the Innocents at Paris, which the duke of Berry had carved in 1408, but which has not been preserved, represented the same subject. Miniature painting and woodcuts spread it broadcast.

The theme of the three dead and three living men connects the horrible motif of putrefaction with that of the death-dance. This theme, too, seems to have originated in France, but it is unknown whether the pictorial representation preceded the scenic or the reverse. The thesis of Monsieur Emile Mâle, according to which the sculptural and pictorial motifs of the fifteenth century were supposed as a rule to be derived from dramatic representations, has not been able to keep its ground, on critical examination. It may be, however, that we should make an exception in favour of the death-dance. Anyhow, the Dance of the Dead has been acted as well as painted and engraved. The duke of Burgundy had it performed in his mansion at Bruges in 1449. If we could form an idea of the effect produced by such a dance, with vague lights and shadows gliding over the moving figures, we should no doubt be better able to understand the horror inspired by the subject, than we are by the aid of the pictures of Guyot Marchant or Holbein.

The woodcuts with which the Parisian printer, Guyot Marchant, ornamented the first edition of the *Danse Macabré* in 1485 were, very probably, imitated from the most celebrated of these painted death-dances, namely, that which, since 1424, covered the walls of the cloister of the churchyard of the Innocents at Paris. The stanzas printed by Marchant were those written under these mural paintings; perhaps they even hail back to the lost poetry of Jean Le Fèvre, who in his turn seems to have followed a Latin model. The woodcuts of 1485 can give but a feeble impression of the paintings of the Innocents, of which they are not exact copies, as the costumes prove. To have a notion of the effect of these frescoes, one should rather look at the mural paintings of the church of La Chaise-Dieu, where the unfinished condition of the work heightens the spectral effect.

The dancing person whom we see coming back forty times to lead away the living, originally does not represent Death itself, but a corpse: the living man such as he will presently be. In the stanzas the dancer is called "the dead man" or "the dead woman." It is a dance of the dead and not of Death; the researches of Monsieur Gédéon Huet have made it probable that the primitive subject was a roundabout dance of dead people, come forth from their graves, a theme which Goethe revived in his *Totentanz*. The indefatigable dancer is the living man himself in his future shape, a frightful double of his person. "It is yourself," said the horrible vision to each of the spectators. It is only towards the end of the century that the figure of the great dancer, of a corpse with hollow and fleshless body, becomes a skeleton, as Holbein depicts it. Death in person has then replaced the individual dead man.

While it reminded the spectators of the frailty and the vanity of earthly things, the death-dance at the same time preached social equality as the Middle Ages understood it, Death levelling the various ranks and professions. At first only men appeared in the picture. The success of his publication, however, suggested to Guyot the idea of a dance macabre of women. Martial d'Auvergne wrote the poetry; an unknown artist, without equalling his model, completed the pictures by a series of feminine figures dragged along by a corpse. Now it was impossible to enumerate forty dignities and professions of women. After the queen, the abbess, the nun, the saleswoman, the nurse, and a few others, it was necessary to fall back on the different states of feminine life: the virgin, the beloved, the bride, the woman newly married, the woman with child. And here the sensual note reappears, to which we referred above. In lamenting the frailty of the lives of women, it is still the briefness of joy that is deplored, and with the grave tone of the *memento mori* is mixed the regret for lost beauty.

From J Huizinga, *The Waning of the Middle Ages*, New York St. Martin's Press, 1949, London: Edward Arnold Ltd., 1924. Reprinted by permission of the publishers.

CLOISTERED WOMEN: Nuns in the Middle Ages
Caroline Walker Bynum

Being a nun was almost the only specialized religious role available to women in the early Middle Ages. (Canonesses, who appeared in the Carolingian period, were similar to nuns but took less strict vows of poverty.) The history of early medieval nuns is a complex one, and recent research suggests that there was more variation over time than earlier historians noticed, both in the influence of nunneries (and abbesses) on the surrounding society and in society's respect for the piety of married laywomen. But however powerful certain early medieval ladies may have been either as abbesses or as saintly queens, specialized religious roles for women were usually restricted to the high aristocracy. In the tenth and early eleventh centuries—a grim period of war and hardship for western Europe—few female monasteries were founded, and religious leaders showed little concern for encouraging women's religiosity. The major monastic reform of the period, Cluny, founded scores of male monasteries but only one house for nuns before 1100, and its purpose was to provide a retreat for women whose husbands wished to become Cluniac monks. Although we have no idea what proportion of the population of medieval Europe belonged to religious houses (or, indeed, what the size of the European population was) we are certain that before 1200, monks vastly outnumbered nuns. Over the course of the twelfth and thirteenth centuries, especially in the Rhineland and Low Countries, this ratio began to change.

The proliferation in the late eleventh and twelfth centuries of wandering preachers who attracted bands of followers determined to "imitate the apostolic life" in poverty and penitence had such a significant impact on women that contemporary chroniclers commented on the phenomenon, with as much trepidation as admiration. Women flocked after wandering evangelists such as Norbert of Xanten (d. 1134) and Robert of Arbrissel (d. 1116–1117), and these preachers—ambivalent about itinerant preaching even for themselves and clearly hostile to it as a form of female piety—founded monasteries for them. So-called double monasteries (i.e., communities with both male and female houses, often side by side) emerged again in England, where there was also a significant increase in the number of female recluses (women who vowed themselves to a life of withdrawal in little cells attached to churches). On the continent, two of the most prestigious new orders of the twelfth century, the Premonstratensians and the Cistercians, found the number of women's houses in their ranks growing at an alarming rate. The story of female enthusiasm institutionalized as strict monasticism repeated itself in the early thirteenth century, when Clare of Assisi (d. 1253) tried to follow Francis in the mendicant (i.e., begging) life but was forced to accept a strictly cloistered role.

Women were not only followers, manipulated and circumscribed in their religious ideals by powerful clerics, they were also leaders and reformers. In the thirteenth century, when Benedictine monasticism for men was eclipsed by the mendicant movement (i.e., the friars), an Italian woman, Santuccia Carabotti, founded a convent near Gubbio, enforced a strict interpretation of the Benedictine Rule there, and later reformed and supervised twenty-four other monasteries, taking them under her direction. In the early fifteenth century Colette of Corbie (d. 1447), who began her religious life as a hermit, reformed many convents of Poor Clares in France and Flanders and founded others.

The rapid growth of women's houses strained the resources of the new orders, which had to provide clergy for the women's spiritual direction and sacramental needs. The Premonstratensians were the first to pass legislation curtailing women's monasteries; the Cistercians followed. As R. W. Southern has made us aware, misogyny—a male fear of female sexuality that was a projection of male fear of male sexuality—was sometimes the articulated motive for such repression. The notorious opinion, attributed to the Premonstratensian abbot Conrad of Marchtal, that "the wickedness of women is greater than all other wickedness of the world and . . . the poison of asps and dragons is more curable and less dangerous to men than the familiarity of women" may be spurious. But a number of twelfth-century monastic leaders feared that celibate males would be contaminated by women and were willing to limit women's religious opportunities in order to protect fragile male virtue. Bernard of Clairvaux (d. 1153) warned his monks: "To be always with a woman and not to have sexual relations with her is more difficult than to raise the dead. You cannot do the less difficult; do you think I will believe that you can do what is more difficult?"

Recent research has, however, shown that male reluctance and opposition did little to slow the growth of women's religious life. In eastern areas (such as Franconia and Bavaria), women even continued to attach themselves to the Premonstratensian

order. The Cistercian decree of 1228 forbidding the incorpora-
tion of any more convents remained a dead letter, and throughout the thirteenth century Cistercian nunneries proliferated (often
with support from local Dominicans) in the Low Countries and
the lower Rhineland. Although some monks, canons, and friars
did resist taking responsibility for the pastoral care of nuns,
some religious authorities, from popes to local clergy, and some
prominent laymen supported and endowed women's houses.
Both Santuccia and Colette received significant support from
popes and papal legates. In the thirteenth and early fourteenth
centuries, these women's monasteries formed influential spiritual networks among themselves and produced collections of
the sisters' lives and visions that were often read in both female
and male houses as a form of spiritual instruction. In some parts
of Europe, where male houses declined fairly steadily both in
economic base and in religious fervor, nuns were a majority of
the cloistered religious by the fifteenth century. . . .

––––––––

From Caroline Walker Bynum, *Holy Feast and Holy Fast.* pp. 15–16. University of
California Press, 1987.

ANALYSIS AND INTERPRETATION
OF THE READINGS

1. How does the attitude toward death expressed in Boccaccio's *The Decameron* differ from that typified by the
   death-dance as described by Huizinga? Considering the
   year to which *The Decameron* was attributed, how do
   you account for this difference?
2. What opportunities did becoming a nun provide for a
   woman of the Middle Ages?

CHAPTER 16 | Centuries of Turmoil and Grandeur in Asia

CHRONOLOGY

Select the appropriate date for each of the six events from Indian history listed below:

c. 1000   1206–1290
1398–1399   1565
1489   1347–1489

_____ Timur's raid of northern India

_____ Destruction of the Hindu city of Vijayanagar

_____ "Slave Dynasty" of Delhi

_____ Founding of the Bijapur kingdom

_____ Beginning of Muslim invasions of India

_____ Bahmani kingdom

Put the following items in correct chronological order by writing in the blank to the left of each item the order in which it appeared in Japanese history:

_____ Founding of the Shogunate by Minamoto family

_____ Introduction of Zen Buddhism

_____ Flourishing of *No* drama

_____ Ascendancy of Fujiwara family and rise of feudalism

_____ Sengoku period of war

_____ Attempt of Emperor Go-Daigo to recover real power

Select the correct dates for each of the dynasties from Chinese history listed below:

960–1127   1279–1368
1127–1279   1368–1644

_____ Southern Song

_____ Ming

_____ Yuan

_____ Northern Song

IDENTIFICATIONS

You should be able to identify each of the following and explain their importance:

Delhi Sultanate   Wang Yangming
Rajputs   Zheng Ho
Ala-ud-din   Fujiwara family
purdah   samurai
Qidan (Khitan)   Minamoto family
Ruzhen   Shogun
Mongols   "Tent Government"
Kublai Khan   daimyo
Forbidden City

Supply the name of the person who fits each of the following descriptions:

1. Invoking the authority of Confucian principles, this Chinese scholar-official of the eleventh century proposed agrarian reforms that shocked the conservative landowning class and resulted in a backlash against him.

_____

2. Poet, painter, calligrapher, and philosopher, this government official demonstrated the multifaceted intellectual and artistic accomplishments of the Song period.

_____

3. A great synthesizer of a variety of philosophical and religious ideas, he was responsible for a new interpretation of Confucianism that became standard for centuries in China and beyond.

_____

4. His late-fourteenth-century invasion of India severely weakened the Delhi Sultanate and added to his reputation as an unstoppable marauder.

_____

5. This woman ruled the Delhi Sultanate capably and vigorously until her death by assassination, after which the throne fell into more ruthless hands.

_____

6. This scholarly, pious ruler forced the inhabitants of Delhi to migrate to a new capital.

_____

7. Once a Buddhist monk, later a bandit leader, this man of low birth became the founding emperor of the Ming dynasty.

_____

Match the dynasty on the left with the characterization that fits best from the list on the right:

Song   cosmopolitan
Yuan   inward-look
Ming   cultural high point

STUDY QUESTIONS

1. Why might the Muslim conquests of northern India be seen as less favorable to cultural progress than the expansion of Islam in the Mediterranean area?
2. "Islam stood at the opposite pole from the religions of India." Explain this statement.
3. What problems were created by, and what were the results of, the Islamic impact upon Hinduism?
4. What changes in Indian society can be noted during the years of the Muslim kingdoms?
5. What were the similarities between the *bhakti* and *sufi* religious movements?
6. How did Sufism help implant Islam in India?
7. Who was Sankara, and what were his contributions?

8. Why was Buddhism disappearing from India while it was thriving in other Asian countries? Why did Hinduism survive in India?
9. In what sense did the Song period mark a watershed in the evolution of Chinese civilization?
10. Compare the traditional position of women in India with that in China. What changes can you identify in women's position in these two civilizations? How do you account for any changes you see?
11. Trace the role of the state in Chinese civilization from the Song through the Ming dynasties.
12. Why did non-Chinese regimes adopt Chinese-style dynastic titles and many aspects of Chinese governance?
13. Trace the process of consolidation of power in the person of the Chinese emperor from the Song to the Ming dynasty.
14. What were the reasons for the remarkable growth in the Chinese economy from the Song to the Ming periods?
15. What concrete factors contributed to either the improvement or the decline in the position of women in China during the Song-Ming period?
16. Why did the Ming dynasty collapse?
17. In what ways were the Mongols effective rulers of China? In what ways were they ineffective?
18. "In the end the greatest weakness of the Mongols was in ideology." Explain this statement, and discuss what it tells us about Chinese civilization.
19. What important cultural developments took place under the Yuan and Ming dynasties?
20. Explain the statement that Zhu Xi's neo-Confucianism "bridged the gap" between the traditional concerns of Confucianism and the concerns of Buddhism and Daoism.
21. What aspects of feudalism developed in Japan?
22. Explain the dual system of government that developed in Japan beginning in the late twelfth century. How was it related to Japanese feudalism? Why did the Shoguns not abolish the office of emperor?
23. How was the character of Japanese feudalism changing in the fourteenth and fifteenth centuries?
24. Trace the essential aspects of economic change in sixteenth-century Japan.

PROBLEMS

1. Read Marco Polo's account of conditions in China in the late thirteenth century. From other sources, try to determine the accuracy and reliability of his account.
2. Henry Wallace, Unites States Secretary of State under President Franklin Roosevelt, is said to have derived some of his ideas from the Chinese reformer Wang Anshi. Compare Wang's proposals with the "New Deal" agricultural program of the 1930s.

3. Investigate the "New-Confucianism" of Zhu Xi and compare it with the scholastic philosophy which was developing in western Europe at approximately the same time.

4. Sankara, Zhu Xi, and Thomas Aquinas (among others) have all been described as synthesizers. Explore the motivations behind their endeavors, and the results that stemmed from them. How do you account for the urge on the part of some thinkers to create a coherent synthesis out of numerous existing strands of thought?

5. Investigate further any of the following: a) the origin and characteristics of the Rajputs in India; b) the career of Timur; c) Zen Buddhism; d) the *No* drama; e) the Chinese theatre; f) Chinese landscape painting; g) the Hindu empire of Vijayanagar; h) Chinese navigation under the Ming; i) the development of printing in China; j) the code of the samurai.

6. Describe the "profound transformation" in Chinese society during the Song period.

7. Investigate conflicting views of the effects of the Mongol conquest of China. (For an example of a negative judgment, see C. P. Fitzgerald, *China: A Short Cultural History*.)

8. Read Arthur Waldron's *The Great Wall of China*. Pay particular attention to the stages in the building of the wall, the wall's purpose, and the extent to which it accomplished its purpose.

9. Analyze the similarities and differences between developments in China and Japan from the tenth to the seventeenth century.

10. For all of its great technological innovations, China did not experience a "scientific revolution" as occurred in the West. Explore the reasons for this.

11. It is known that China possessed great skill in navigation, and had ships capable of long voyages. Study the question of why China did not engage in extensive exploration and colonization comparable to that undertaken by countries in the West.

12. Read *Journey to the West* and analyze its allegorical nature. Compare this with works of allegory in Western literature, such as Dante's *Divine Comedy* or John Bunyan's *Pilgrim's Progress*.

13. Some scholars have suggested that austerity is a trait that *No* drama, Zen Buddhism, and warrior rule all have in common. Come to your own conclusions as to whether or not this is true. What dominant characteristics can you identify in Japanese culture through the fifteenth century?

14. Why did feudalism develop in some places, but not in others? For background information, consult Peter Duus, *Feudalism in Japan*, and Rushton Coulborn, ed., *Feudalism in History*.

AIDS TO AN UNDERSTANDING OF CENTURIES OF TURMOIL AND GRANDEUR IN ASIA

THE CHARACTER OF THE MUSLIM CONQUESTS IN INDIA AS INTERPRETED BY A MODERN MUSLIM SCHOLAR
S. M. Ikram

For a long time it was held by Western writers that Islam was spread by the sword in India. This view, has, however, now been abandoned in responsible circles, as apart from lack of evidence in its favour, the very distribution of Muslim population in the subcontinent does not support it. If the spread of Islam in the subcontinent [had] been due to the might of the Muslim kings, one would naturally expect the largest proportion of Muslims in those areas which were the centres of Muslim political power. This, however, is not the case. The percentage of Muslims is at its lowest around Delhi, Lucknow, Ahmedabad, Ahmednagar, and Bijapur, which were the principal seats of Muslim political power. Even in the case of Mysore, where Sultan Tipu is said to have forcibly converted people to Islam, the ineffectiveness of royal proselytism may be measured by the fact that Muslims are hardly five per cent of the total population of the state. On the other hand, Islam was never a political power in Malabar, but today, Muslims form nearly thirty per cent of its total population, and European observers like Arnold have estimated that if in the sixteenth century, the Portuguese had not put an end to the peaceful spread of Islam in this tract, all its inhabitants would have become Muslims. . . .

In [the] Indo-Pakistan subcontinent, the heaviest concentration of Muslims is in the two areas which now form West and East Pakistan, and the spread of Islam in these areas has been studied by two eminent non-Muslim scholars. Both of them have come to the conclusion that the spread of Islam in these areas was the work of Muslim Sufis, and in the western areas the process was greatly facilitated by the fact that in the Thirteenth Century thousands of Muslim theologians, saints and missionaries migrated to India to escape the Mongol terror. . . .

But the phenomenal spread of Islam in Bengal was not entirely due to the ability and efforts of the Sufi missionaries. It was greatly facilitated by certain local developments. In Bengal, the main factor in the spread of Islam "was a reaction of the lower classes against the strict Hinduism enforced by the Senas. It will be recalled that the indigenous Pala dynasty which ruled from the eighth to the twelfth century had been devoted to Buddhism, a faith under which the lower classes enjoyed practical freedom. In the twelfth century the Senas entering Bengal from the south, brought with them the severe rules of Hinduism, under which the lower classes were subjected to many onerous restrictions; and at the end of the same century, before these restrictions had become customary, Islam arrived, preaching freedom and culture for all, even if the equality was not always apparent in practice. In these circumstances, a mass movement towards the new creed is so inherently probable that it is unnecessary to seek further afield for other hypothetical causes." . . .

It is interesting to record that Islam gained its greatest success in areas on the eastern and western fringes of the Indo-Pakistan subcontinent, where Buddhism had not yet been completely wiped out by the revival of Brahminism, and the steel-frame of caste system had not yet gained its hold over society. . . .

There was considerable interaction of Islam and Hinduism, but as pointed out by Prof. Mazumdar, it touched merely the fringe and the external elements of life and even as such, the influence was confined to a small section of Hindus and Muslims of India taken as a whole . . . there was no rapprochement in respect of popular or national traditions, and those social and religious ideas, beliefs, practices, and institutions which touch the deeper chord of life and give it a distinctive form, tone, and vigour. In short, the reciprocal influences were too superficial in character to affect materially the fundamental differences between the two communities in respect of almost everything that is deep-seated in human nature and makes life worth living. So the two great communities, although they lived side by side, moved each in its own orbit, and there was as yet no sign that the "twain shall ever meet."

From S. M. Ikram, *Muslim Civilization in India and Pakistan*, Columbia University Press, 1964. Reprinted by permission of the publisher.

An Essay on Ming-Era Merchants
Chang Han

Money and profit are of great importance to men. They seek profit, then suffer by it, yet they cannot forget it. They exhaust their bodies and spirits, run day and night, yet they still regard what they have gained as insufficient. . . .

Those who become merchants eat fine food and wear elegant clothes. They ride on beautifully caparisoned, double-harnessed horses—dust flying as they race through the streets and the horses' precious sweat falling like rain. Opportunistic persons attracted by their wealth offer to serve them. Pretty girls in beautiful long-sleeved dresses and delicate slippers play string and wind instruments for them and compete to please them.

Merchants boast that their wisdom and ability are such as to give them a free hand in affairs. They believe that they know all the possible transformations in the universe and therefore can calculate all the changes in the human world, and that the rise and fall of prices are under their command. They are confident that they will not make one mistake in a hundred in their calculations. These merchants do not know how insignificant their wisdom and ability really are. As the *Chuang Tzu* says: "Great understanding is broad and unhurried; little understanding is cramped and busy."

Because I have traveled to many places during my career as an official, I am familiar with commercial activities and business conditions in various places. The capital is located in an area with mountains at its back and a great plain stretching in front. The region is rich in millet, grain, donkeys, horses, fruit, and vegetables, and has become a center where goods from distant places are brought. Those who engage in commerce, including the foot peddler, the cart peddler, and the shopkeeper, display not only clothing and fresh foods from the fields but also numerous luxury items such as priceless jade from K'un-lun, pearls from the island of Hai-nan, gold from Yunnan, and coral from Vietnam. These precious items, coming from the mountains or the sea, are not found in central China. But people in remote areas and in other countries, unafraid of the dangers and difficulties of travel, transport these items step by step to the capital, making it the most prosperous place in the empire. . . .

South of the capital is the province of Honan, which is the center of the empire. Going from K'ai-feng, its capital, northwards to Wei-chung, one can reach the Yangtze and Han rivers. Thus, K'ai-feng is a great transportation center; one can travel by either boat or carriage from this spot to all other places, which makes it a favorite gathering place for merchants. The area is rich in lacquer, hemp, sackcloth, fine linen, fine gloss silk, wax, and leather. In antiquity, the Chou dynasty had its capital here. The land is broad and flat, the people are rich and prosperous, and the customs are refined and frugal. . . .

In general, in the Southeast area the greatest profits are to be had from fine gauze, thin silk, cheap silk, and sackcloth. San-wu in particular is famous for them. My ancestors' fortunes were based solely on such textile businesses. At the present time, a great many people in San-wu have become wealthy from the textile industry.

In the nation's Northwest, profits are greatest in wool, coarse woolen serge, felt, and fur garments. Kuan-chung is especially famous for these items. There is a family named Chang in that area which has engaged in the animal-breeding business generation after generation. They claim to have 10,000 sheep. Their animal-breeding enterprise is the largest in the Northwest and has made them the richest family in the area. In the surrounding areas of Yen, Chou, Ch'i, and Chin, many other people have also become rich from animal breeding. From there, merchants seeking great profits go west to Szechwan and south to Kwang-tung. Because of the nature of the special products from the latter area—fine and second-grade pearls, gold, jade, and precious woods—profits can be five- or ten-fold or more.

The profits from the tea and salt trades are especially great but only large-scale merchants can undertake these businesses. Furthermore, there are government regulations on their distribution, which prohibit the sale of tea in the Northwest and salt in the Southeast. Since tea is produced primarily in the Southeast, prohibiting its sale to the non-Chinese on the northern border is wise and can be enforced. Selling privately produced salt where it is manufactured is also prohibited. This law is rigidly applied to all areas where salt was produced during the Ming dynasty. Yet there are so many private salt producers there now that the regulation seems too rigid and is hard to enforce.

Profits from selling tea and the officials' income from the tea tax are usually ten to twenty percent of the original investment. By contrast, merchants' profits from selling salt and the officials' income from the salt tax can reach seventy to eighty percent of the original invested capital. In either case, the more the invested capital, the greater the profit; the less the invested capital, the less the profit. The profits from selling tea and salt enrich the nation as well as the merchants. Skillful merchants can make great profits for themselves while the inept ones suffer losses. This is the present state of the tea and salt business.

In our Chekiang province it appears that most of the rich gain their wealth from engaging in salt trade. But the Chia family in Wu-ling became rich from selling tea and have sustained their prosperity for generations. The "Book of Chou" says: "If farmers do not work, there will be an insufficiency of food; if craftsmen do not work, there will be an insufficiency of tools; if merchants do not work, circulation of the three necessities will be cut off, which will cause food and materials to be insufficient."

As to the foreign trade on the northwestern frontier and the foreign sea trade in the Southeast, if we compare their advantages and disadvantages with respect to our nation's wealth and the people's well-being, we will discover that they are as different as black and white. But those who are in charge of state economic matters know only the benefits of the Northwest trade, ignoring the benefits of the sea trade. How can they be so blind?...

From *Classics of Eastern Thought*, Lynn H. Nelson and Patrick Peebles, eds. pp. 295–96, 298. Harcourt Brace Jovanovich, 1991.

THE JAPANESE WARRIOR ETHIC:
The Death of Atsumori
The Tale of Heike

Kumagae no Jirō Naozane walked his horse toward the beach after the defeat of the Heike. "The Taira nobles will be fleeing to the water's edge in the hope of boarding rescue vessels," he thought. "Ah, how I would like to grapple with a high-ranking Commander-in-Chief!" Just then, he saw a lone rider splash into the sea, headed toward a vessel in the offing. The other was attired in a crane-embroidered *nerinuki* silk *hitatare*, a suit of armor with shaded green lacing, and a horned helmet. At his waist, he wore a sword with gilt bronze fittings; on his back, there rode a quiver containing arrows fledged with black-banded white eagle feathers. He grasped a rattan-wrapped bow and bestrode a white-dappled reddish horse with a gold-edged saddle. When his mount had swum out about a

hundred and fifty or two hundred feet, Naozane beckoned him with his fan.

"I see that you are a Commander-in-Chief. It is dishonorable to show your back to an enemy. Return!"

The warrior came back. As he was leaving the water, Naozane rode up alongside him, gripped him with all his strength, crashed with him to the ground, held him motionless, and pushed aside his helmet to cut off his head. He was sixteen or seventeen years old, with a lightly powdered face and blackened teeth—a boy just the age of Naozane's own son Kojirō Naoie, and so handsome that Naozane could not find a place to strike.

"Who are you? Announce your name. I will spare you," Naozane said.

"Who are you?" the youth asked.

"Nobody of any importance: Kumagae no Jirō Naozane, a resident of Musashi Province."

"Then it is unnecessary to give you my name. I am a desirable opponent for you. Ask about me after you take my head. Someone will recognize me, even if I don't tell you."

"Indeed, he must be a Commander-in-Chief," Naozane thought. "Killing this one person will not change defeat into victory, nor will sparing him change victory into defeat. When I think of how I grieved when Kojirō suffered a minor wound, it is easy to imagine the sorrow of this young lord's father if he were to hear that the boy had been slain. Ah, I would like to spare him!" Casting a swift glance to the rear, he discovered Sanehira and Kagetoki coming along behind him with fifty riders.

"I would like to spare you," he said, restraining his tears, "but there are Genji warriors everywhere. You cannot possibly escape. It will be better if I kill you than if someone else does it, because I will offer prayers on your behalf."

"Just take my head and be quick about it."

Overwhelmed by compassion, Naozane could not find a place to strike. His senses reeled, his wits forsook him, and he was scarcely conscious of his surroundings. But matters could not go on like that forever: in tears, he took the head.

"Alas! No lot is as hard as a warrior's. I would never have suffered such a dreadful experience if I had not been born into a military house. How cruel I was to kill him!" He pressed his sleeve to his face and shed floods of tears.

Presently, since matters could not go on like that forever, he started to remove the youth's armor *hitatare* so that he might wrap it around the head. A brocade bag containing a flute was tucked in at the waist. "Ah, how pitiful! He must have been one of the people I heard making music inside the stronghold just before dawn. There are tens of thousands of riders in our eastern armies, but I am sure none of them has brought a flute to the battlefield. Those court nobles are refined men!"

When Naozane's trophies were presented for Yoshitsune's inspection, they drew tears from the eyes of all the beholders. It was learned later that the slain youth was Tayū Atsumori, aged seventeen, a son of Tsunemori, the Master of the Palace Repairs Office.

After that, Naozane thought increasingly of becoming a monk.

The flute in question is said to have been given by Retired Emperor Toba to Atsumori's grandfather Tadamori, who was a skilled musician. I believe I have heard that Tsunemori, who inherited it, turned it over to Atsumori because of his son's proficiency as a flautist. Saeda [Little Branch] was its name. It is deeply moving that music, a profane entertainment, should have led a warrior to the religious life.

————

From *The Tale of Heike*. Helen Craig McCullough, trans. pp. 316–317. Stanford University Press, 1988.

ANALYSIS AND INTERPRETATION OF THE READINGS

1. How can the emphasis on wealth in the passage on Ming merchants be reconciled with the Confucian disdain for profit?
2. "The Death of Atsumori" is one of the most famous passages in Japanese literature. What traits do the warriors display that might help account for its endurance?

| The Americas and Africa Before the Age of European Overseas Expansion

CHRONOLOGY

The two columns below, labeled "Andean" and "Mesoamerican," indicate two of the major regions discussed in this chapter. Write in the proper column, and in correct chronological order, the names of each of the following cultures or societies. Approximate dates are given for four of them. Indicate which.

Tiahuanacan, Teotihuacán, Maya-Toltec, Moche, Olmec, Maya, Inca, Aztec, Chavin

(1) 1000–500 B.C.E.   (3) 950–1500 C.E.
(2) 1250–1150 B.C.E.   (4) 1100–1500 C.E.

ANDEAN   MESOAMERICAN

IDENTIFICATIONS

You should be able to explain the meaning or importance of the following:

"Pyramid of the Sun"   Sunjata
Toltecs   Mansa Musa
Quetzalcoatl   "Askia"
Chichén Itzá   *Swahili*
Bantu   animism

Complete each of the following statements by circling the correct letter:

1. In the Americas agriculture began first in: (a) Canada; (b) New Mexico; (c) Mexico; (d) the Amazon valley.

2. The cliff dwellers' culture of New Mexico flourished about: (a) 900–1200; (b) 700–500 B.C.E.; (c) 1500–1750; (d) c. 1000 B.C.E.

3. The site of the earliest advanced civilization in the Americas was: (a) the Gulf Coast of Mexico; (b) Guatemala; (c) the Mississippi delta; (d) the western slopes of the Andes.

4. The most massive architecture in the Western Hemisphere was produced by the: (a) Olmecs; (b) Aztecs; (c) Tiahuanacans; (d) Incas.

5. The Toltecs, who dominated central Mexico by 950 C.E.: (a) completely destroyed Teotihuacán civilization; (b) surpassed the Mayas as artists; (c) embellished the plumed-serpent cult; (d) were the first people to practice human sacrifice.

STUDY QUESTIONS

1. How have recent archaeological discoveries modified long-standing theories about the origins of New World civilization?

2. What do you consider some of the most remarkable features of the ancient Andean civilization? What did it lack?

3. Explain why the political organization of the Inca civilization is described as a confederation.

4. What were the unique features of the Mayan calendar?

5. Compare the religious practices and beliefs of the Mayas, Aztecs, and Incas.

6. How do you account for the rigid structure of Inca society? What were its advantages and disadvantages?

7. What is meant by "stateless societies" when describing Africa of this period? What kept these stateless societies together?

8. What factors contributed to the rise of larger and more powerful empires in Africa during this period?
9. Explain Mansa Musa's role in the growth of Islam in Africa.
10. How do you explain Muhammad Touré's success in building an expansive empire in West Africa?
11. What were the major teachings of al-Maghili?
12. What changes can you identify in the respective role of men and women in African societies?
13. Outline the process of the emergence of Swahili civilization.
14. What part did slavery and the slave trade play in Africa during this period?
15. How did Madagascar's location affect its history?
16. When did the Ethiopian kingdom reach its height, and what were the causes of its decline?

PROBLEMS

1. Study the practice and significance of human sacrifice in the early American civilizations.
2. Investigate the development of the calendar in Mesoamerican cultures and the unique features of the Mayan calendar.
3. Try to determine the contributions of the Olmecs to succeeding cultures.
4. Compare the impact of Islam in Africa with its impact in India.
5. Explore the reasons for the decline of western Sudanic civilization after the fall of the Songhay empire in 1591.
6. Compare and contrast al-Maghili's *Obligation of Princes* with Niccolò Machiavelli's *Prince*.
7. Explore the similarities and contrasts between the architecture of the early American civilizations and that of ancient Egypt. Consider not only architectural styles, but functions as well.

AIDS TO AN UNDERSTANDING OF THE AMERICAS AND AFRICA BEFORE THE AGE OF EUROPEAN OVERSEAS EXPANSION

AZTEC MYTHOLOGY: The Creation of Humans

And thereupon the gods conferred and said:
'Who now shall be alive?
Heaven is founded, earth is founded,
who now shall be alive, oh gods?'
They were sorrowful:
Star Skirt and Milky Way,
and (with them) the Bridger, the Emerger,
the Earth-firmer, the Tiller;
Quetzalcoatl whom we serve.
And then Quetzalcoatl goes to Mictlan, the Dead Land.
He approached the Lord and Lady of Mictlan and said:
'What I have come for is the precious bones which you possess;
I have come to fetch them.'
And he was asked:
'What do you want to do with them, Quetzalcoatl?'
And he answered:
'What worries the gods is who shall live on earth.'
And the Lord of Mictlan then said:
'All right. Blow this conch and carry the bones four times round my jade circle.'
But the conch is totally blocked up.
Quetzalcoatl summons the worms, they hollow it out.
The large and the small bees force their way through.
He blows it; the sound reaches the Lord of Mictlan.

And the Lord of Mictlan next said to him:
'All right, take them.'
But to his vassals, the Micteca, he said:

'Tell him, oh gods, he should leave them here.'
But Quetzalcoatl answered:
'No: I'm taking them with me.'
And then his nahual said to him:
'Just tell them: "I've left them here."'
And so he said, he shouted to them:
'I have left them here.'
But then he really went back up, clutching the precious bones,
male bones on one side, female on the other.
He took them and wrapped them up, and took them with him.
And the Lord of Mictlan again spoke to his vassals:
'Oh gods, is Quetzalcoatl really taking the bones? Dig him a pit.'
They dug him one; he stumbled and fell in.
And Quails menaced him and he fainted.
He dropped the precious bones and the Quails tore and pecked at them.
And then Quetzalcoatl came to and weeps and says to his nahual:
'Oh my nahual, what now?'
And the reply came:
'What now? Things went badly; let it be.'

And then he gathered the bits, took them and wrapped them in a bundle
which he took to Tamoanchan.
When he had brought it there it was ground up by the
woman named Quilzatli, that is, Cihuacohuatl.
Then she placed the meal in a jade bowl and Quetzalcoatl dropped blood on it by piercing his member.
Then all the gods named here did penance like

the Bridger, the Tiller
the Emerger, the Earth-firmer,
the Plunger, the Shooter:
Quetzalcoatl.
And they said:
'The servants of the gods are born'. For indeed they did
    penance for us.
Then they said:
'What shall they eat? The gods must find food'.
And the ant fetched
the maize kernels from the heart of the Food Mountain.

———

History of the Kingdoms, §§ 141–1440

———

From Gordon Brotherston. *Image of the New World*, London Thames and Hudson, 1979, pp 158–159. Reprinted by permission of Thames and Hudson Ltd

KANEM: THE COMING OF ISLAM

In the name of God, the Merciful, the Compassionate. May God bless our Lord Muhammad, his relations and friends. Peace from King Umme to my children who will succeed me, be they Emirs or Officers or Chiefs, or [Men of Learning], or others. Peace be upon you. Hear and understand, and receive good tidings.

The first country in the Sudan which Islam entered was the land of Bornu. It came through Muhammad ibn Māni, who lived in Bornu for five years in the time of King Bulu, six years in the time of King Arki, four years in the time of King Kadai Hawami, fourteen years in the time of King Umme.

Then he summoned Bornu to Islam by the grace of King Umme. . . .

Mai Umme read secretly from the [Koran] and gave Māni one hundred camels, one hundred pieces of gold, one hundred pieces of silver, and one hundred slaves, all because of the reading and instruction he derived from him.

. . . Mai Umme and Muhammad ibn Māni spread abroad Islam to last till the day of judgment.

The goods of Muhammad ibn Māni the First are taboo till the day of judgment, to the Beni Umme or any besides. He who disobeys the command of the King, and transgresses, and sins, may God not give him heaven, but may he fill his belly with the fire of hell. He who follows my command, may God order his wellbeing both in this life and the next.

Says the Sultan Umme, the noble—"Their goods and blood from time of Muhammad ibn Māni are in the keeping of the Beni Umme, and all others; I consider them as the flesh of swine, or the flesh of the dog, or the flesh of a monkey or ass. . . .

"He among them who does a wrong let the matter be left to their chief; there is no other way than this. This is the command of the Sultan; change it not nor alter it, and oppress not the children of Muhammad ibn Māni, for ever.

"I make their land *hubus*, let them be ennobled in their faith.

"Change not this injunction, for he who after hearing it changes it, his lot is that of those who innovate; for God will note his action. Spread abroad Islam in Bornu and strive to keep the posterity of Muhammad ibn Māni *harām*." King Umme says to his children— "I make the children of Muhammad ibn Māni hubus to you, and I exempt them from the obligation to entertain your men in the dry season or to pay *diya* and all forms of tribute, to the time of my children's children, and to the day of judgment.

"He who puts forth his hand against them, may God not bless him, for he transgresseth my behest."

King Umme spread abroad Islam; on that day he was a victor.

———

From Thomas Hodgkin, ed., *Nigerian Perspectives: An Historical Anthology*, Oxford University Press, 1960.

CONVERSION TO ISLAM IN ORAL TRADITION
The Epic of Askia Mohammed

237 Now, Mamar came to sit down.
238 He ruled then, he ruled, he ruled, he ruled, he converted.
239 Throughout Mamar's reign, what he did was to convert people.
240 Any village that he hears is trying to resist,
241 That is not going to submit,
242 He gets up and destroys the village.
243 If the village accepts, he makes them pray.
244 If they resist, he conquers the village, he burns the village.
245 Mamar made them convert, Mamar made them convert, Mamar made them convert.
246 Until, until, until, until, until, until he got up and said he would go to Mecca.
247 Thus he started off and went as far, as far, as far as the Red Sea.
248 He said he wants to cross.
249 They told him, "There is no path.
250 "Anyone who has killed an ancestor does not have the right to cross to Mecca.
251 "But there are two ways, three ways, so look for one you can take.
252 "Now you will return home.
253 "You must find a hen who has just produced chicks, and drive them from home.
254 "You will drive a hen who has just produced chicks and its little ones to the Red Sea.
255 "Then you can cross to go on the pilgrimage."
256 They said, "Either you go home,
257 "Or You go into the distant, uncleared bush.
258 "You clear it with your own hands.
259 "You don't let anyone help with it.
260 "You sow by your own hand without the help of anybody.
261 "You cultivate it and you recultivate it, and you leave the millet so that the birds and the wild animals may eat it.
262 "If you do that, and if you come, you can cross to go on the pilgrimage.
263 "Or you go home to start a holy war.

264 "So that you can make them submit until you reach the Red Sea.

265 "You will cross."

266 He said that he would be able to carry out the holy war.

267 Mamar went home to Gao.

268 It is at this time that he gathered together all the horses.

269 He took all the horses.

270 He began by the west.

271 You have heard that among the Mossi, there are descendants of Mamar.

272 They say that it is during this conquest that he continued to father them.

273 You have heard that they say the pure Bargantché.

274 In each ethnic group you hear about, people say there are descendants of Mamar.

275 Well, from that area where he started,

276 In each village where he stopped during the day, for example, this place,

277 If he arrives in midafternoon, he stops there and spends the night.

278 Early in the morning, they pillage and they go on to the next village, for example, Liboré.

279 The cavalier who goes there,

280 He traces on the ground for the people the plan for the mosque.

281 Once the plan for the foundation is traced,

282 The people build the mosque.

283 It is at the time,

284 Mamar Kassaye comes to dismount from his horse.

285 He makes the people—

286 They teach them verses from the Koran relating to prayer.

287 They teach them prayers from the Koran.

288 Any villages that refuse, he destroys the village, burns it, and moves on.

289 In each village where he arrives,

290 The village that he leaves in the morning,

291 The horses ride ahead.

292 They build a mosque before his arrival.

293 When he arrives, he and his people,

294 He teaches the villagers prayers from the Koran.

295 He makes them pray.

296 They—they learn how to pray.

297 After that, in the morning, he continues on.

298 Every village that follows his orders, that accepts his wishes,

299 He conquers them, he moves on.

300 Every village that refuses his demand,

301 He conquers it, he burns it, he moves on.

302 Until the day—Mamar did that until, until, until, until the day he arrived at the Red Sea.

303 It is on that day that they gave him the right to cross.

304 Before arriving at the Red Sea,

305 All the horsemen, those who died, those who were tired, returned.

306 Except for Modi Baja, Modi Baja and the *jeseré*, his cousin, who stayed with him.

307 It is they alone who remained at his side.

308 He made the crossing in their company.

309 So they arrived in Mecca.

310 He made the pilgrimage and he said then that he would like to see the tomb of Our Lord's Messenger.

311 In those days they had not built it yet.

312 He came, they told him, he said he wanted to see the tomb of Our Lord's Messenger.

313 They replied to him, "By Allah truly, the tomb, you won't see it.

314 "Because if you peek into this tomb,

315 "The thing that is in there will keep you from getting out."

316 He asked that they let him peek into it.

317 They said, "Fine, on one condition.

318 "Now have them go off to get large pieces of iron chain,

319 "To tie around his waist.

320 "Some strong men should stay behind him and hold on tightly to the chains.

321 "He too should come to the edge of the hole to peek into it."

322 He said that he would accept that.

323 They brought the iron chains, they attached them to him well.

324 The strong men stood behind and braced themselves to hold onto the chains.

325 He came to the edge of the hole.

326 He peeked into it.

327 What he found there at the bottom of that tomb,

328 It resembled young onion shoots, and it looked very soft, very soft, very soft, very soft, very soft.

From *The Epic of Askia Mohammed*, Thomas A. Hale, trans. lines 237–328; pp. 24–27. Indiana University Press, 1996.

ANALYSIS AND INTERPRETATION OF THE READINGS

1. Does anything in the Aztec myth suggest a familiarity with bloody sacrifice?

2. What were the necessary preconditions to the rise of Islam in West Africa?

Expansion of Islam, 1301–1566

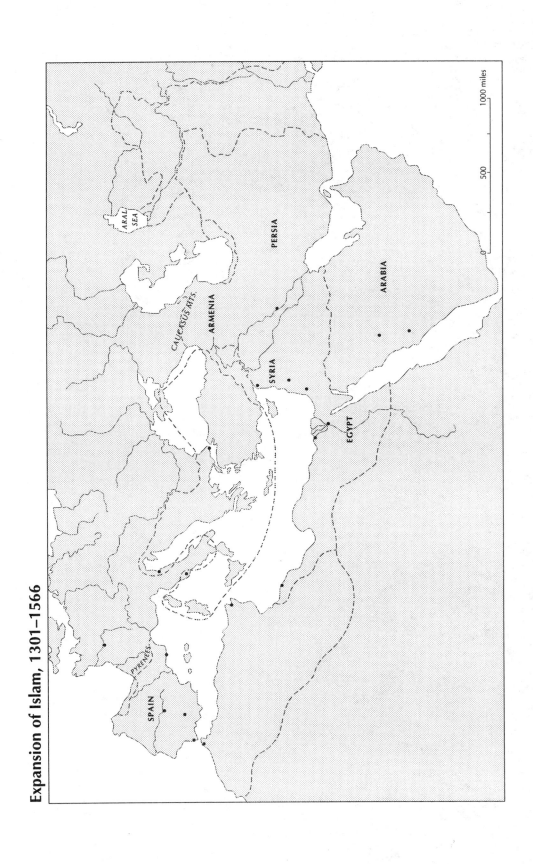

Ottoman Rise

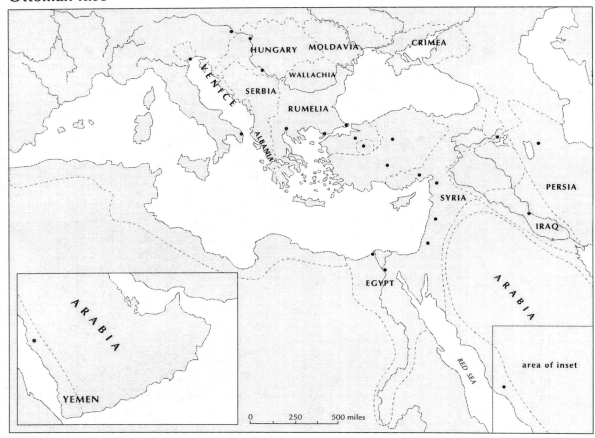

HUNGARY
MOLDAVIA
CRIMEA
VENICE
SERBIA
WALLACHIA
RUMELIA
ALBANIA
PERSIA
SYRIA
IRAQ
EGYPT
ARABIA
RED SEA

ARABIA

YEMEN

area of inset

0   250   500 miles

Expansion of Islam (1301–1566) and the Ottoman Rise *(Chapters 12–17)*

EXPANSION OF ISLAM

1. On the "Expansion of Islam" map (see page 101), label the Mediterranean Sea, Black Sea, Atlantic Ocean, Caspian Sea, Aegean Sea, Adriatic Sea, Red Sea, and Persian Gulf. Locate and label the locations that control passage between the Atlantic Ocean and the Mediterranean Sea, and between the Mediterranean Sea and the Black Sea.

2. Locate the following cities:

Medina	Venice
Mecca	Naples
Baghdad	Rome
Jerusalem	Constantinople
Damascus	Cordova
Antioch	Cologne
Alexandria	Paris
Tunis	

3. Show the extent of Islamic rule at the death of Muhammad, and at its greatest extent.

4. Show the areas occupied by the Franks, the West Goths, and the Berbers. Indicate the location of the empire of Charlemagne.

5. Mark the following locations:

Rivers: Nile, Danube, Tigris, Euphrates, Oder, Rhine, Seine
Islands: Sicily, Corsica, Crete, Sardinia, Cyprus

OTTOMAN RISE

1. On the "Ottoman Rise" map (see page 102, opposite), label the following seas: Mediterranean, Red, Black.

2. Label the following locations: Istanbul (Constantinople), Manzikert, Jerusalem, Mecca.

3. Shade in the area where the Ottoman Empire began its growth. Using different shading, show the extent of the Ottoman Empire by the middle of the sixteenth century.

CHAPTER 18 | The Civilization of the Renaissance (c. 1350–c.1550)

CHRONOLOGY

Rather than memorizing a list of dates, you should be able to distinguish between the early Renaissance and the High Renaissance and the leading figures of each. Before each of the following names, indicate the half-century in which the individual was active (e.g., 1450–1500, Pico della Mirandola). Dates for some of the individuals will not fall neatly into a half-century period, but you should attempt to indicate the period during which they made their most significant contributions, keeping in mind that the purpose of the exercise is not to compile an exact chronology.

_____ Ariosto

_____ Raphael

_____ Petrarch

_____ Botticelli

_____ Masaccio

_____ Pico della Mirandola

_____ Michelangelo

_____ Albrecht Dürer

_____ Leonardo da Vinci

_____ Erasmus

_____ Giovanni da Palestrina

_____ Michael Servetus

IDENTIFICATIONS

In each of the blanks write the correct name selected from the list below:

Lorenzo de Medici	Cesare Borgia
Botticelli	Copernicus
Marsilio Ficino	Baldassare Castiglione
Leonardo da Vinci	Galileo
Petrarch	Andreas Vesalius
Raphael	Johann Kepler
Ludovico Ariosto	Giordano Bruno
Michelangelo	Lorenzo Valla
Niccolò Machiavelli	Masaccio
Donatello	

1. This Neoplatonic philosopher was condemned by the Inquisition and burned at the stake in 1600 for his belief in the plurality of worlds.

_____

2. A superb and sensitive Florentine painter, he is famed for his *Allegory of Spring* and *Birth of Venus*, which reflect Neoplatonic concepts.

_____

3. Noted for his statue of David triumphant over Goliath, this sculptor executed the first monumental bronze equestrian statue since the Romans.

_____

4. A short-lived, early master of the High Renaissance, perhaps the most popular of all Renaissance painters, he portrayed human beings as temperate, wise, and dignified.

_____

5. Although he was the first Italian humanist, he upheld the medieval Christian ideal. His famous sonnets to Laura were written in the style of the troubadours.

_____

6. Styled the Magnificent, this Florentine ruler and patron of art was for a time the patron of Leonardo da Vinci.

_____

7. His astronomical observations helped prove the heliocentric theory, and his experiments in physics established the law of falling bodies.

_____

8. His *Orlando Furioso* incorporated medieval legends but in its point of view differed sharply from the typical medieval epic.

_____

9. This giant of the High Renaissance was both a great painter and a great sculptor as his paintings in the Sistine Chapel and his tomb figures show.

_____

10. Author of *Discourses on Livy* and *The Prince*, he is best known for his realistic views of the nature of politics and the duties of heads of state.

_____

11. Architect, musician, inventor, and painter, he created in the *Last Supper* and the *Mona Lisa* two of the most famous paintings in the Western world.

_____

12. Inspired by Neoplatonic teachings, this Polish astronomer attempted to prove the validity of the heliocentric theory.

_____

13. One of the earliest prominent Florentine painters, a remarkable naturalist, he died at the age of twenty-seven.

_____

14. A leading member of the Platonic Academy in Florence, he translated Plato's works into Latin.

_____

15. The shrewd and ruthless statecraft of this son of a pope provided a fascinating study for Machiavelli.

_____

16. This diplomat wrote a book depicting the ideal Renaissance man.

_____

17. This mystical but indefatigable thinker discovered the elliptical orbits of the planets.

_____

18. A native of Brussels, he is considered the father of the science of anatomy.

_____

19. A skilled grammarian who exposed the fraudulent "Donation of Constantine," he applied vigorous critical scholarship to his *Notes on the New Testament*.

_____

Below are listed a number of famous Renaissance works, including paintings, writings, and sculpture. In the blank after each, put the name of the artist or author selected from the following list:

Ulrich von Hutten	Edmund Spenser
Raphael	Erasmus
Albrecht Dürer	Pico della Mirandola
François Rabelais	Copernicus
Hans Holbein	Leon Battista Alberti
Sir Thomas More	Andreas Vesalius
Johann Kepler	Michelangelo

On the Structure of the Human Body _____

On the Family _____

Gargantua and Pantagruel _____

Oration on the Dignity of Man _____

Utopia _____

The Faërie Queen _____

Praise of Folly _____

School of Athens _____

Moses _____

Portraits of Erasmus and More _____

Knight, Death, and Devil _____

On the Revolutions of the Heavenly Spheres _____

STUDY QUESTIONS

1. When did the idea of a "Renaissance period" originate? In what ways does the long-popular concept of a "Renaissance period" need to be modified? To what aspects of the two centuries considered in this chapter can the term "Renaissance" be most usefully applied?
2. How did Renaissance knowledge and interpretation of ancient classical literature differ from that exhibited by medieval scholars?

3. Explain the meanings of humanism—in both specific and general senses—as applied to the Renaissance.
4. Why did the Renaissance begin in Italy?
5. How do you explain the growing aversion to medieval Scholasticism? Was it based purely on intellectual considerations?
6. What were the objectives of the civic humanists?
7. In spite of the differences between the two groups, what did the Neoplatonists have in common with the "civic humanists"?
8. What was Machiavelli's contribution to political philosophy?
9. What technical improvements between 1300 and 1500 made possible the full flowering of Italian painting?
10. What was Leonardo da Vinci's conception of painting? What relationship did he see between art and science?
11. "If Leonardo was a naturalist, Michelangelo was an idealist." Show how this is exemplified in the works of these two supreme artists.
12. In what directions did Michelangelo deviate from naturalism during his career?
13. What developments help explain the decline of the Italian Renaissance?
14. Point out the chief differences between the Renaissance in Italy and that in northern and western Europe. How do you explain these differences?
15. Erasmus is generally regarded as "the prince of the Christian humanists." Show how his writings entitle him to such a distinction.
16. What did Erasmus mean by the "philosophy of Christ"?
17. Compare "Christian humanism" with other varieties of humanism. Why did Christian humanism fade after the early sixteenth century?
18. How does Thomas More's *Utopia* illustrate the ideals of humanism?
19. How are the manifestations of the Renaissance in Germany illustrated by the *Letters of Obscure Men*?
20. Compare the effects of the Counter-Reformation and of the rise of Protestantism on Renaissance culture.
21. How do the writings of Rabelais contrast with those of Erasmus as examples of Renaissance humanism?
22. How were developments in music related to other aspects of the Renaissance?
23. Why was Renaissance humanism less of a stimulus to scientific progress than was the mystical philosophy of Neoplatonism?
24. What factors besides Neoplatonism aided in the development of science?
25. What is meant by a "mechanistic" interpretation of the universe?
26. Trace the steps in the achievement of the "Copernican revolution."

PROBLEMS

1. If the instability of political life in Italy contributed to the ending of the Renaissance there after 1550, why did the political instability of the preceding 250 years not prevent a Renaissance in the first place?
2. Investigate the causes of the waning of the Italian Renaissance.
3. Investigate further any of the following:
   a. The Florence of the Medicis
   b. Petrarch's sonnets
   c. Leonardo da Vinci's inventions
   d. Galileo's discoveries
   e. the Renaissance papacy
4. Read Machiavelli's *Prince*. Which of its principles do you see in practice today? Are there any of its principles you would *like* to see implemented?
5. Was the Renaissance more medieval than modern? Support your answer with evidence.
6. Compare Florentine and Venetian painting.
7. Read in one of the literary masterpieces of the Renaissance, such as *Praise of Folly*, *The Faërie Queen*, or *Orlando Furioso*.
8. Read Castiglione's *Book of the Courtier*. Critique his view of the respective roles of men and women.
9. Read More's *Utopia*. What aspects of humanism does it illustrate? What aspects of More's vision have been attempted since his time?
10. Explore further the sources, meaning, and contributions of Neoplatonism.

AIDS TO AN UNDERSTANDING OF THE CIVILIZATION OF THE RENAISSANCE

The Realism of Leonardo da Vinci: As Described in His *Notebooks*

The Painter's Need for Alertness

The mind of the painter should be like a mirror which always takes the color of the thing that it reflects, and which is filled by as many images as there are things placed before it. Knowing therefore that you cannot be a good master unless you have a universal power of representing by your art all the varieties of the forms which nature produces—which indeed you will not know how to do unless you see them and retain them in your mind—look to it. O Painter, that when you go into the fields you give your attention to the various objects, and look carefully in turn first at one thing and then at another, making a bundle of different things selected and chosen from among those of less value. And do not after the manner of some painters who when tired by imaginative work, lay aside their task and take exercise by walking, in order to find relaxation, keeping, however, such weariness of mind as prevents them either seeing or being conscious of different objects.

Of the Way to Fix in Your Mind the Form of a Face

If you desire to acquire facility in keeping in your mind the expression of a face, first learn by heart the various different kinds of heads, eyes, noses, mouths, chins, throats, and also necks and shoulders. Take as an instance noses, they are of ten types: straight, bulbous, hollow, prominent either above or below the centre, aquiline, regular, simian, round, and pointed. These divisions hold good as regards profile. Seen from in front, noses are of twelve types: thick in the middle, thin in the middle, with the tip broad, and narrow at the base, and narrow at the tip, and broad at the base, with nostrils broad or narrow, or high or low, and with the openings either visible or hidden by the tip. And similarly you will find variety in the other features; of which things you ought to make studies from nature and so fix them in your mind. Or when you have to draw a face from memory, carry with you a small notebook in which you have noted down such features, and then when you have cast a glance at the face of the person whom you wish to draw you can look privately and see which nose or mouth has a resemblance to it, and make a tiny mark against it in order to recognise it again at home. Of abnormal faces I here say nothing, for they are kept in mind without difficulty.

How It Is Necessary for the Painter to Know the Inner Structure of Man

The painter who has acquired a knowledge of the nature of the sinews, muscles, and tendons will know exactly in the movement of any limb how many and which of the sinews are the cause of it, and which muscle by its swelling is the cause of the sinew's contracting, and which sinews having been changed into most delicate cartilage surround and contain the said muscle. So he will be able in divers ways and universally to indicate the various muscles by means of the different attitudes of his figures; and he will not do like many who in different actions always make the same things appear in the arm, the back, the breast, and the legs; for such things as these ought not to rank in the category of minor faults.

Of The Conformity of The Limbs

Further I remind you to pay great attention in giving limbs to your figures, so that they may not merely appear to harmonize with the size of the body but also with its age. So the limbs of youths should have few muscles and veins, and have a soft surface and be rounded and pleasing in color; in men they should be sinewy and full of muscles; in old men the surface should be wrinkled, and rough, and covered with veins, and with the sinews greatly protruding.

From Edward MacCurdy. *The Notebooks of Leonardo do Vinci*, Vol II. Reynal & Hitchcock, Inc., 1938. Reprinted by permission of Harcourt, Brace & World, Inc.

Philosophy and Science: The Cynicism and Realism of Machiavelli

From hence arises a dispute, whether it is better to be belov'd or feard: I answer, a man would wish he might be the one and the other: but because hardly can they subsist both together, it is much safer to be feard, than be loved; being that one of the two must needs fail; for touching men, we may say this in general, they are unthankful, unconstant, dissemblers, they avoyd dangers, and are covetous of gain; and whilest thou doest them good, they are wholly thine; their blood, their fortunes, lives and children are at thy service, as is said before, when the danger is remote; but when it approaches, they revolt. And that Prince who wholly relies upon their words, unfurnished of all other preparations, goes to wrack: for the friendships that are gotten with rewards, and not by the magnificence and worth of the mind, are dearly bought indeed; but they will neither keep long, nor serve well in time of need: and men do less regard to offend one that is supported by love, than fear. For love is held by a certainty of obligation, which because men are mischievous, is broken upon any occasion of their own profit. But fear restrains with a dread of punishment which never forsakes a man. Yet ought a Prince cause himself to be belov'd in such a manner, that if he gains not love, he may avoid hatred: for it may well stand together, that a man may be feard and not hated; which shall never fail, if he abstain from his subjects goods, and their wives; and whensoever he should be forc'd to proceed against any of their lives, do it when it is to be done upon a just cause, and apparent conviction; but above all things forbeare to lay his hands on other mens goods; for men forget sooner the death of their father, than the loss of their patrimony. Moreover the occasions of taking from men their goods, do never fail: and alwaies he that begins to live by rapine, finds occasion to lay hold upon other mens goods: but against mens lives, they are seldome found, and sooner fail.

• • •

For a people in command, if it be duly restrained, will have the same prudence and the same gratitude as a prince has, or even more, however wise he may be reckoned; and a prince on the other hand, if freed from the control of the laws, will be more ungrateful, fickle, and short-sighted than a people. And further, I say that any difference in their methods of acting results not from any difference in their nature, that being the same in both, or, if there be advantage on either side, the advantage resting with the people, but from their having more or less respect for the laws under which each lives. And whosoever attentively considers the history of the Roman people, may see that for four hundred years they never relaxed in their hatred of the regal name, and were constantly devoted to the glory and welfare of their country, and will find numberless proofs given by them of their consistency in both particulars. And should any allege against me the ingratitude they showed to Scipio, I reply by what has already been said at length on that head, where I proved that peoples are less ungrateful than princes. But as for prudence and stability of purpose, I affirm that a people is more prudent, more stable, and of better judgment than a prince. Nor is it without reason that the voice of the people has been likened to the voice of God; for we see that wide-spread beliefs fulfil themselves, and bring about marvellous results, so as to have the appearance of presaging by some occult quality either weal or woe. Again, as to the justice of their opinions on public affairs, we seldom find that after hearing two speakers of equal ability urging them in opposite directions, they do not adopt the sounder view, or are unable to decide on the truth of what they hear. And if, as I have said, a people errs in adopting courses which appear to it bold and advantageous, princes will likewise err when their passions are touched, as is far oftener the case with them than with a people.

We see, too, that in the choice of magistrates a people will choose far more honestly than a prince; so that while you shall never persuade a people that it is advantageous to confer dignities on the infamous and profligate, a prince may readily, and in a thousand ways, be drawn to do so. Again, it may be seen that a people, when once they have come to hold a thing in abhorrence, remain for many ages of the same mind; which we do not find happen with princes.

• • •

Nor would I have it thought that anything our historian may have affirmed in the passage cited, or elsewhere, controverts these may opinions. For if all the glories and all the defects both of peoples and of princes be carefully weighed, it will appear that both for goodness and for glory a people is to be preferred. And if princes surpass peoples in the work of legislation, in shaping civil institutions, in moulding statutes, and framing new ordinances, so far do the latter surpass the former in maintaining what has once been established, as to merit no less praise than they.

And to state the sum of the whole matter shortly. I say that popular governments have endured for long periods in the same way as the governments of princes, and that both have need to be regulated by the laws; because the prince who can do what he pleases is a madman, and the people which can do as it pleases is never wise. If, then, we assume the case of a prince bound, and of a people chained down by the laws, greater virtue will appear in the people than in the prince, while if we assume the case of each of them freed from all control, it will be seen that the people commits fewer errors than the prince, and less serious errors, and such as admit of readier cure. For a turbulent and unruly people may be spoken to by a good man, and readily brought back to good ways; but none can speak to a wicked prince, nor any remedy be found against him but by the sword.

• • •

. . . when the entire safety of our country is at stake, no consideration of what is just or unjust, merciful or cruel, praiseworthy or shameful, must intervene. On the contrary, every other consideration being set aside, that course alone must be taken which preserves the existence of the country and maintains its liberty.

From Niccolò Machiavelli, *The Prince* and *Discourses on the First Ten Books of Titus Livius*, E. Dacres trans.

THE SATIRICAL HUMANISM OF ERASMUS: *The Praise of Folly*

The merchants, however, are the biggest fools of all. They carry on the most sordid business and by the most corrupt methods. Whenever it is necessary, they will lie, perjure themselves, steal, cheat, and mislead the public. Nevertheless, they are highly respected because of their money. There is no lack of flattering friars to kowtow to them. . . . [because] they are after some of the loot.

• • •

After the lawyers come the philosophers, who are reverenced for their beards and the fur on their gowns. They announce that they alone are wise, and that the rest of men are only passing shadows. Their folly is a pleasant one. They frame countless worlds and measure the sun, moon, stars, and spheres as with thumb and line. They unhesitatingly explain the causes of lightning, winds, eclipses, and other inexplicable things. One would think that they had access to the secrets of nature, who is the maker of all things, or that they had just come from a council of the gods. Actually, nature laughs uproariously at them all the time. The fact that they can never explain why they constantly disagree with each other is sufficient proof that they do not know the truth about anything. They know nothing at all, yet profess to know everything. They are ignorant even of themselves, and are often too absent-minded or near-sighted to see the ditch or stone in front of them. At the same time, they assert that they can see ideas, universals, pure forms, original matter, and essences—things so shadowy that I doubt if Lynceus could perceive them. They show their scorn of the layman whenever they produce their triangles, quadrangles, circles, and other mathematical forms, lay one on another or entangle them into a labyrinth, then maneuver letters as if in battle formation, and presently reverse the arrangement. It is all designed to fool the uninitiated. Among these philosophers are some who predict future events by consulting the stars, and others who promise even greater wonders. And these fortunate fellows find people to believe them.

Perhaps it would be wise to pass over the theologians in silence. That short-tempered and supercilious crew is as unpleasant to deal with as Lake Camarina or *Anagyris foetida*. They may attack me with an army of six hundred syllogisms; and if I do not recant, they will proclaim me a heretic. With this thunderbolt they terrify the people they don't like. They are extremely reluctant to acknowledge my benefits to them, which are nevertheless considerable. Their opinion of themselves is so great that they behave as if they were already in heaven; they look down pityingly on other men as so many worms. A wall of imposing definitions, conclusions, corollaries, and explicit and implicit propositions protects them. They have so many hideouts that even Vulcan could not catch them with his net. They escape through distinctions, and cut knots as easily as with a double-bitted axe from Tenedos. They are full of big words and newly-invented terms.

They explain (to suit themselves) the most difficult mysteries: how the world was created and set in order; through what channels original sin has passed to successive generations; by what means, in what form, and for how long the perfect Christ was in the womb of the Virgin; and how accidents subsist in the Eucharist without their subject. But these are nothing. Here are questions worthy of these great and reputedly illuminated theologians. If they encounter these questions they will have to extend themselves. Was divine generation at a particular instant? Are there several son-ships in Christ? Is this a possible proposition: God the Father hates the Son? Could God have assumed the form of a woman, a devil, an ass, a gourd, a stone? If so, how could the gourd have preached, performed miracles, and been crucified? What would Peter have consecrated if he had administered the sacrament when Christ's body hung on the Cross? And was Christ at that moment a man? After the resurrection will it be forbidden to eat and drink? (They are providing now against hunger and thirst!) These subtleties are countless, and include even more refined propositions dealing with instants of time, opinions, relations, accidents, quiddities, entities, which no one can discern unless, like Lynceus, he can see in blackest darkness things that are not there.

There are in addition those moral maxims, or rather, contradictions, that make the so-called Stoic paradoxes seem like child's play. For example: it is less of a sin to cut the throats of a thousand men than to stitch a poor man's shoe on Sunday; it is better to commit the whole world to destruction than to tell a single lie, even a white one. These subtlest of subtleties are made more subtle by the methods of the scholastic philosophers. It is easier to escape from a maze than from the tangles of Realists, Nominalists, Thomists, Albertists, Occamists, and Scotists, to name the chief ones only. There is so much erudition and obscurity in the various schools that I imagine the apostles themselves would need some other spiritual assistance if they were to argue these topics with modern theologians. . . .

―――――

From Desiderius Erasmus, *The Praise of Folly*, Leonard F. Dean trans. Copyright © 1946 by Hendricks House, Inc. New York. Reprinted 1959. Selection reprinted by permission.

THE HUMANISM OF SIR THOMAS MORE: *Utopia*

OF WARFARE

War or battle as a thing very beastly, and yet to no kind of beasts in so much use as to man, they [the Utopians] do detest and abhor. And contrary to the custom almost of all other nations, they count nothing so much against glory, as glory gotten in war. And therefore though they do daily practise and exercise themselves in the discipline of war, and not only the men, but also the women upon certain appointed days, lest they should be to seek in the feat of arms, if need should require, yet they never go to battle, but either in the defence of their own country, or to drive out of their friend's land the enemies that have invaded it, or by their power to deliver from the yoke of bondage of tyranny some people, that be therewith oppressed. Which thing they do of mere pity and compassion. Howbeit they send help to their friends; not ever in their defence, but sometimes also to requite and revenge injuries before to them done. But this they do not unless their counsel and advice in the matter be asked, whiles it is yet new and fresh.

―――――

From Sir Thomas More, *Utopia*, Maurice Adams ed.

ANALYSIS AND INTERPRETATION OF THE READINGS

1. Are there evidences of democracy in the political theory of Machiavelli? Explain.
2. Do you think Sir Thomas More could be classified as a pacifist? Why or why not?

CHAPTER 19 | Europe Expands and Divides: Overseas Discoveries and Protestant Reformation

CHRONOLOGY

In the blanks write the correct dates selected from the list below:

1415	1517	1545–1563
1460	1519–1521	1546–1547
1488	1525	1549
1502	1534	1564
1513	1540	1580

Council of Trent _____

Death of Henry the Navigator_____

Index of Prohibited Books _____

Founding of the Jesuit Order_____

Peasants' Revolt in Germany _____

Balboa's discovery of the Pacific Ocean_____

Cortés's conquest of the Aztec empire _____

Posting of the Ninety-Five Theses _____

Founding of the University of Wittenberg _____

Bartholomew Dias rounds the southern tip of Africa _____

IDENTIFICATIONS

In the blank before each statement write the letter identifying the correct completion:

_____1. The voyages of overseas discovery can best be accounted for by: (a) the Renaissance interest in science; (b) the pursuit of late medieval economic goals; (c) the need for emigration from overpopulated European countries; (d) knowledge of the New World acquired by the Vikings.

_____2. Early leadership in overseas discovery and trade was taken by: (a) France; (b) England; (c) Spain; (d) Portugal.

_____3. A factor that delayed discovery of the New World until the end of the fifteenth century was: (a) belief that the earth was flat; (b) the profitability of African trade; (c) the lack of ships capable of crossing the Atlantic; (d) papal prohibition of intercourse with heathen lands.

_____4. Vasco da Gama's exploits extended Portuguese trade to: (a) India; (b) Africa; (c) the West Indies; (d) the East Indies.

_____5. Christopher Columbus: (a) advanced the novel theory of the earth's sphericity; (b) was the first European to land on the American continent; (c) greatly underestimated the earth's circumference; (d) was bitterly disappointed by his failure to reach Asia.

_____6. The *conquistadors* obtained for Spain: (a) a direct water route to India; (b) raw materials that stimulated industrial development; (c) the eastern seaboard of North America; (d) control of Central and South America except for Brazil.

You should know what the following are and what their importance was in relation to the Reformation.

dispensation	justification by faith
indulgences	Lollards
"Treasury of Merits"	Elizabethan compromise
Augustinianism	Anabaptists
predestination	Mennonites
transubstantiation	Calvin's Institutes
Eucharist	Council of Trent
"good works"	

In the blanks, write the appropriate names from the following list:

Charles V	Martin Luther
Henry VIII	Cardinal Ximenes
Elector Frederick the Wise	John of Leyden
Thomas Cranmer	Paul III
Julius II	Ulrich Zwingli
Mary I	Elizabeth I
Leo X	John Calvin
John Knox	Ignatius Loyola

1. A German prince who protected Luther from arrest by Catholic authorities.

_____

2. An Anabaptist leader who declared himself successor of David and king of the New Jerusalem of Münster.

_____

3. An archbishop of Canterbury who with the dukes of Somerset and Northumberland made the Church of England more decidedly Protestant during the reign of Edward VI.

_____

4. A Protestant Reformer who is said to have reduced church service to "four bare walls and a sermon."

_____

5. A Spanish nobleman and ex-soldier who founded a militant religious order in the sixteenth century.

_____

6. A pope whose authorization of the sale of indulgences in Germany incensed Luther.

_____

7. The Holy Roman emperor who summoned a Diet that condemned Luther.

_____

8. A pope of the Counter-Reformation who convoked the Council of Trent.

_____

9. An English queen whose determined efforts to restore Catholicism to her country ended in failure.

_____

10. A Swiss reformer who converted much of northern Switzerland to Protestantism.

_____

STUDY QUESTIONS

1. "Just when Europe was expanding it was also dividing." Explain this statement. Why did the rupture of European unity not prevent the extension of European power and influence?
2. What is meant by referring to Europe as a "Community of Christendom"?
3. Explain the reasons for European voyages of discovery.
4. What were the major results of European expansion and colonization?
5. What were the causes of the dramatic decline in native population in the Spanish colonies?
6. Among the causes of the Protestant Reformation, abuses within the Roman Catholic Church were one important factor. What were some of the characteristic abuses on the eve of the Lutheran upheaval?
7. "Luther preferred a rigorously Augustinian system of theology to a medieval Thomistic one." Explain the terms "Augustinian" and "Thomistic."
8. How did Luther's private objections to Church practices turn into a public cause?
9. Explain why German political authorities supported Luther's cause and why their support was essential to its success.
10. What were the important changes that Luther brought about in the Church in Germany?
11. If their political objectives were similar to those of the German princes, why did the kings of Spain and France not likewise break with the Catholic Church?
12. How did King Henry VIII's marital difficulties lead to a break with Rome? What elements of Catholicism did Henry retain in the Church of England?
13. Why did Henry VIII's break with Rome have the support of so many people in England?
14. Trace the fortunes of Catholicism and Protestantism in England from Henry VIII to Elizabeth I.
15. What is meant by the Elizabethan compromise?
16. What were the chief emphases in the creed of the Anabaptists? Why were they almost entirely suppressed?
17. How did Calvin's religious ideas differ from those of Luther? Is it possible to say that one of them was more medieval in his outlook? (In answering this question, be sure to explain how you are interpreting the word "medieval.")
18. Describe the work and the importance of the Council of Trent.
19. How did the Jesuits differ from previous monastic orders? Why was their organization so peculiarly fit to serve the Catholic Reformation?
20. What was the relationship of the Protestant Reformation to the Renaissance? What were the differences between the two movements?
21. Point out the effects of the Protestant Reformation upon the following:

a. The theory and practice of state sovereignty
b. The growth of nationalism
c. The position of women in European society

22. Compare and contrast the effects of the Catholic Reformation (Counter-Reformation) in these same respects.

PROBLEMS

1. Explore how Spanish and Portuguese colonization in the Americas differed from later colonization by the British.
2. How can you explain the ability of the *conquistadors* Cortés and Pizarro to defeat the Aztec and Inca empires with a relatively small number of soldiers?
3. Study the administration and economy of the Spanish colonies in the Americas. How did the Spanish combine elements of despotism and paternalism?
4. Assess the role of the Catholic Church both in Spain's subjugation of indigenous American populations and in efforts to protect them from exploitation.
5. How did Lutheranism penetrate Scandinavia?
6. How did the Jesuits go about reconverting much of central Europe to Roman Catholicism?
7. In order to further your understanding of the Reformation, investigate any of the following:

a. Martin Luther and the German Bible
b. John Calvin's rule in Geneva
c. Henry VIII and the confiscation of monastic lands
d. The career of Ignatius Loyola
e. The Anabaptists
f. The career of Ulrich Zwingli
g. The role of the Jesuits in South American colonies

8. Explain the conflict between the Augustinian and Scholastic systems of theology. What was the significance of this conflict?
9. How did capitalism relate to the Protestant Reformation? You may wish to consult R. H. Tawney's *Religion and the Rise of Capitalism.*
10. What relationship can you show between the Lutheran movement and the later history of Germany?
11. Read Luther's *Address to the Christian Nobility of the German Nation.* What sorts of arguments does he use in urging resistance to the papacy?
12. To what extent was the Catholic Reformation a Counter-Reformation?
13. Make an argument for or against the proposition that the Reformation was a great milestone on the road of progress.
14. What is the justification for considering European overseas expansion and the Protestant Reformation as related movements in spite of the fundamental difference between them?

AIDS TO AN UNDERSTANDING OF OVERSEAS DISCOVERIES AND PROTESTANT REFORMATION

CHRISTOPHER COLUMBUS' REPORT OF HIS FIRST VOYAGE

LETTER FROM COLUMBUS TO LOUIS DE SANTANGEL, 1493

Sir,—Believing that you will take pleasure in hearing of the great success which our Lord has granted me in my voyage. I write you this letter, whereby you will learn how in thirty-three day's time I reached the Indies with the fleet which the most illustrious King and Queen, our Sovereigns, gave to me, where I found very many islands thickly peopled, of all which I took possession without resistance for their Highnesses by proclamation made and with the royal standard unfurled. To the first island that I found I gave the name of *San Salvador*, in remembrance of His High Majesty, who hath marvelously brought all these things to pass; the Indians call it *Guanaham*. To the second Island I gave the name of *Santa-Maria de Concepción*; the third I called *Fernandina*, the fourth, *Isabella*; the fifth, *Juana*; and so to each one I gave a new name. When I reached *Juana*, I followed its coast to the westward, and found it so large that I thought it must be the mainland—the province of Cathay; and, as I found neither towns nor villages on the sea-coast, but only a few hamlets, with the inhabitants of which I could not hold conversation, because they all immediately fled, I kept on the same route, thinking that I could not fail to light upon some large cities and towns. At length . . . [having] learned from some . . . Indians whom I had seized, that this land was certainly an island . . . I followed the coast eastward for a distance of one hundred and seven leagues, where it ended in a cape. From this cape, I saw another island to the eastward at a distance of eighteen leagues from the former, to which I gave the name of *La Española* [Hispaniola]. Thither I went, and followed its northern coast to the eastward . . . one hundred and seventy-eight full leagues due east. This island, like all the others, is extraordinarily large. . . . The lands are high, and there are many very lofty mountains . . . covered with trees of a thousand kinds of such great height that they seemed to reach the skies. Some were in bloom, others bearing fruit. . . . The nightingale was singing . . . and that, in November. . . . In the interior there are many mines of metals and a population innumerable. *Española* is a wonder. Its mountains and plains, and meadows, and fields, are so beautiful and rich for planting and sowing, and rearing cattle of all kinds, and for building towns and villages. The harbours on the coast, and the number and size and wholesomeness of the rivers, most of them bearing gold, surpass anything that would be believed by one who has not seen them. There is a great difference between the trees, fruits, and plants of this island and those of *Juana*. In this island there are many spices and extensive mines of gold and other metals. The inhabitants of this and of all the other islands I have found or gained intelligence of, both men and women, go as naked as they were born, with the exception that some of the women cover one part only with a single leaf of grass or with a piece of cotton, made for that purpose. They have neither iron, nor steel, nor arms, nor are they competent to use them, not that they are not well-formed and of handsome stature, but because they are timid to a surprising degree. . . . It is true that when they are reassured and have thrown off this fear, they are guileless. . . . They never refuse anything that they possess when it is asked of them, on the contrary, they offer it themselves . . . and, whether it be something of value or of little worth that is offered to them, they are satisfied. . . . They are not acquainted with any kind of worship, and are not idolators; but believe that all power and, indeed, all good things are in heaven, and they are firmly convinced that I, with my vessels and crews, came from heaven, and with this belief received me at every place at which I touched, after they had overcome their apprehension. . . . On my reaching the Indies, I took by force . . . some of these natives, that they might learn our language and give me information in regard to what existed in these parts; . . . [they] are still with me, and, from repeated conversations . . . I find that they still believe that I come from heaven. . . . Although I have taken possession of all these islands in the name of their Highnesses, and they are all more abundant in wealth than I am able to express, and although I hold them all for their Highnesses, so that they can dispose of them quite as absolutely as they can of the kingdoms of Castile, yet there was one large town in *Española* of which especially I took possession, situated in a locality well adapted for the working of the gold mines, and for all kinds of commerce, either with the mainland on this side, or with that beyond which is the land of the great Khan, with which there will be vast commerce and great profit. To that city I gave the name of *Villa de Navidad*, and fortified it with a fortress, which by this time will be quite completed, and I have left in it a sufficient number of men with arms, artillery, and provisions for more than a year, a barge, and a sailing master skilful in the arts necessary for building others I have also established the greatest friendship with the king of that country, so much so that he took pride in calling me his brother, and treating me as such. Even should these people change their intentions towards us and become hostile, they do not know what arms are, but, as I have said, go naked, and are the most timid people in the world; so that the men I have left could, alone, destroy the whole country, and this island has no danger for them, if they only know how to conduct themselves. . . . Finally, and speaking only of what has taken place in this voyage, which has been so hasty, their Highnesses may see that I shall give them all the gold they require, if they will give me but a very little assistance; spices also, and cotton, as much as their Highnesses shall command to be shipped; and mastic, hitherto found only in Greece, in the island of Chios . . . slaves, as many of these idolators as their Highnesses shall command to be shipped. I think also I have found rhubarb and cinnamon, and I shall find a thousand other valuable things by means of the men that I have left behind me, for I tarried at no point so long as the wind allowed me to proceed. . . . Much more I would have done if my vessels had been in as good a condition as by rights they ought to have been. This is much, and praised be the eternal God, our Lord, who gives to all those who walk in his ways victory over things which seem impossible; . . . although others may have spoken or written concerning these countries, no one could say that he had seen them. . . . But our Redeemer hath granted this victory to our illustrious King and Queen and their kingdoms, which have acquired great fame by an event of such high importance, in which all Christendom ought to rejoice, and which it ought to celebrate with great festivals and the offering of solemn thanks to the Holy Trinity with many solemn prayers, both for the great exaltation which may accrue to them in turning so many nations to our holy faith, and also for the temporal benefits which will bring great refreshment and gain, not only to Spain, but to all Christians. This, thus briefly, in accordance with the events.

Done on board the caravel, off the Canary Islands, on the fifteenth of February, fourteen hundred and ninety-three.

At your orders.

The Admiral

From R. H. Major ed., *Select Letters of Christopher Columbus.*

The Theology of the Protestant Revolution: Luther's Idea of Good Works and Justification by Faith

The first and highest, the most precious of all good works is faith in Christ, as He says, John vi. When the Jews asked Him; "What shall we do that we may work the works of God?" He answered: "This is the work of God, that ye believe on Him Whom He hath sent." When we hear or preach this word, we hasten over it and deem it a very little thing and easy to do, whereas we ought here to pause a long time and to ponder it well. For in this work all good works must be done and receive from it the inflow of their goodness, like a loan. This we must put bluntly, that men may understand it.

We find many who pray, fast, establish endowments, do this or that, lead a good life before men, and yet if you should ask them whether they are sure that what they do pleases God, they say, "No"; they do not know, or they doubt. And there are some very learned men, who mislead them, and say that it is not necessary to be sure of this; and yet, on the other hand, these same men do nothing else but teach good works. Now all these works are done outside of faith, therefore they are nothing and altogether dead. For as their conscience stands toward God and as it believes, so also are the works which grow out of it. Now they have no faith, no good conscience toward God, therefore the works lack their head, and all their life and goodness is nothing. Hence it comes that when I exalt faith and reject such works done without faith, they accuse me of forbidding good works, when in truth I am trying hard to teach real good works of faith.

From Martin Luther. "Treatise on Good Works." in *Collected Works of Martin Luther*, A. J. Holman Co., 1915–, Vol. I. pp. 187–188. Reprinted by permission of United Lutheran Publication House.

ON REBELLION AGAINST RULERS
Martin Luther

Here stands the law, and says, "No one shall fight or make war against his overlord; for a man owes his overlord obedience, honor and fear" (Romans xiii). If one chops over one's head, the chips fall in one's eyes, and as Solomon says, "He who throws stones in the air, upon his head they fall." That is the law in a nutshell. God Himself has instituted it and men have accepted it, for it does not fit together that men shall both obey and resist, be subject and not put up with their lords.

But we have already said that justice ought to be mistress of law, and where circumstances demand, guide the law, or even command and permit men to act against it. Therefore the question here is whether it can be just, i.e., whether a case can arise in which one can act against this law, be disobedient to rulers and fight against them, depose them or put them in bonds. . . .

The peasants in their rebellion alleged that the lords would not allow the Gospel to be preached and robbed the poor people, and, therefore that they must be overthrown; but I have answered this by saying that although the lords did wrong in this, it would not therefore be just or right to do wrong in return, that is, to be disobedient and destroy God's ordinance, which is not ours. On the contrary, we ought to suffer wrong and if prince or lord will not tolerate the Gospel, then we ought to go into another princedom where the Gospel is preached, as Christ says in Matthew X, "If they persecute you in one city flee into another."

It is just, to be sure, that if a prince, king, or lord goes crazy, he should be deposed and put under restraint, for he is not to be considered a man since his reason is gone. Yes, you say a raving tyrant is crazy, too, or is to be considered even worse than a madman, for he does much more harm. That answer puts me in a tight place, for such a statement makes a great appearance and seems to be in accord with justice. Nevertheless, it is my opinion that the cases of madmen and tyrants are not the same; for a madman can neither do nor tolerate anything reasonable, nor is there any hope for him because the light of reason has gone out. But a tyrant, however much of this kind of thing he does, knows that he does wrong. He has his conscience and his knowledge, and there is hope that he may do better, allow himself to be instructed, and learn, and follow advice, none of which things can be hoped for in a crazy man, who is like a clod or a stone. . . .

Here you will say, perhaps, "Yes, if everything is to be endured from the tyrants, you give them too much and their wickedness only becomes stronger and greater by such teaching. Is it to be endured then that every man's wife and child, body and goods, are to be in danger? Who can start any good thing if that is the way we are to live?" I reply: My teaching is not for you, if you will to do whatever you think good and whatever pleases you. Follow your own notion and slay all your lords, and see what good it does you. My teaching is only for those who would like to do right. To these I say that rulers are not to be opposed with violence and rebellion, as the Romans, the Greeks, the Swiss and the Danes have done; but there are other ways of dealing with them.

In the first place, if they see that the rulers think so little of their soul's salvation that they rage and do wrong, of what importance is it that they ruin your property, body, wife and child? They cannot hurt your soul, and they do themselves more harm than they do you, because they damn their own souls and the ruin of body and property must then follow. Do you think that you are not already sufficiently revenged upon them?

In the second place, what would you do if these rulers of yours were at war and not only your goods and wives and children, but you yourself must be broken, imprisoned, burned and slain for your lord's sake? Would you for that reason slay your lord? . . .

In the third place, if the rulers are bad, what of it? God is there, and He has fire, water, iron, stone and numberless ways of killing. How quickly He has slain a tyrant! He would do it, too, but our sins do not permit it; for He says in Job, "He letteth a knave rule because of the people's sins." It is easy enough to see that a knave rules, but no one is willing to see that he is ruling not because of his knavery, but because of the people's sin. The people do not look at their own sin, and think that the tyrant rules because of his knavery; so blinded, perverse and mad is the world! That is why things go as they went with the peasants in the revolt. They wanted to punish the sins of the rulers, just as though they were themselves pure and guiltless; therefore, God had to show them the beam in their eye in order to make them forget another's splinter.

In the fourth place, the tyrants run the risk that, by God's decree, their subjects may rise up, as has been said, and slay them or drive them out. For we are here giving instruction to those who want to do what is right, and they are very few; the great multitude remain heathen, godless, and unchristian, and these, if God so decrees, set themselves wrongfully against the rules and create disaster, as the Jews and Greeks and Romans often did. Therefore you have no right to complain that by our doctrine the tyrants and rulers gain security to do evil; nay, they are certainly not secure. . . .

In the fifth place, God has still another way to punish rulers, so that you have no need to revenge yourself. He can raise up foreign rulers, like the Goths against the Romans, the Assyrians against the Jews, etc., so that there is vengeance, punishment, and danger enough hanging over tyrants and rulers, and God does not allow them to be wicked and have peace and joy; He is right behind them, and has them between spurs and under bridle. This agrees, also, with the natural law that Christ teaches, in Matthew vii, "What ye would that people do to you, that do you to them." No father would be driven out by his own family, slain, or ruined because of his misdeeds (especially if the family did it out of disregard of authority and love of violence, in order to revenge themselves and be judges in their own case) without previous complaint to a higher authority. It ought to be just as wrong for any subject to act against his tyrant.

———

From Martin Luther, *A Compendium of Luther's Theology,* Hugh Thomson Kerr, Jr., ed.

THE THEOLOGY OF THE PROTESTANT REVOLUTION: Calvin's Doctrine of Predestination
John Calvin

In conformity, therefore, to the clear doctrine of the Scripture, we assert, that by an eternal and immutable counsel, God has once for all determined, both whom he would admit to salvation, and whom he would condemn to destruction. We affirm that this counsel, as far as concerns the elect, is founded on his gratuitous mercy, totally irrespective of human merit; but that to those whom he devotes to condemnation, the gate of life is closed by a just and irreprehensible, but incomprehensible, judgment. In the elect, we consider calling as an evidence of election, and justification as another token of its manifestation, till they arrive in glory, which constitutes its completion. As God seals his elect by vocation and justification, so by excluding the reprobate from the knowledge of his name and the sanctification of his Spirit, he affords an indication of the judgment that awaits them.

———

From John Calvin, *Institutes of the Christian Religion,* John Allen trans.

ON CIVIL GOVERNMENT
John Calvin

And for private men, who have no authority to deliberate on the regulation of any public affairs, it would surely be a vain occupation to dispute which would be the best form of government in the place where they live. Besides, this could not be simply determined, as an abstract question, without great impropriety, since the principle to guide the decision must depend on circumstances. And even if we compare the different forms together, without their circumstances, their advantages are so nearly equal, that it will not be easy to discover of which the utility preponderates. The forms of civil government are considered to be of three kinds: Monarchy, which is the dominion of one person, whether called a king, or a duke, or any other title; Aristocracy, or the dominion of the principal persons of a nation; and Democracy, or popular government, in which the power resides in the people at large. It is true that the transition is easy from monarchy to despotism; it is not much more difficult from aristocracy to oligarchy, or the faction of a few; but it is most easy of all from democracy to sedition. Indeed, if these three forms of government, which are stated by philosophers, be considered in themselves, I shall by no means deny, that either aristocracy, or a mixture of aristocracy and democracy, far excels all others; and that indeed not of itself, but because it very rarely happens that kings regulate themselves so that their will is never at variance with justice and rectitude; or, in the next place, that are they endued with such penetration and prudence, as in all cases to discover what is best. The vice or imperfection of men therefore renders it safer and more tolerable for the government to be in the hands of many, that they may afford each other mutual assistance and admonition, and that if any one arrogate to himself more than is right, the many may act as censors and masters to restrain his ambition. This has always been proved by experience, and the Lord confirmed it by his authority, when he established a government of this kind among the people of Israel, with a view to preserve them in the most desirable condition, till he exhibited in David a type of Christ. And as I readily acknowledge that no kind of government is more happy than this, where liberty is regulated with becoming moderation, and properly established on a durable basis, so also I consider those as the most happy people, who are permitted to enjoy such a condition; and if they exert their strenuous and constant efforts for its preservation and retention, I admit that they act in perfect consistence with their duty. And to this object the magistrates likewise ought to apply their greatest diligence, that they suffer not the liberty, of which they are constituted guardians, to be in any respect diminished, much less to be violated: if they are inactive and unconcerned about this, they are perfidious to their office, and traitors to their country. But if those, to whom the will of God has assigned another form of government, transfer this to themselves so as to be tempted to desire a revolution, the very thought will be not only foolish and useless, but altogether criminal. If we limit not our views to one city, but look round and take a comprehensive survey of the whole world, or at least extend our observations to distant lands, we shall certainly find it to be a wise arrangement of Divine Providence that various countries are governed by different forms of civil polity; or they are admirably held together with a certain inequality, as the elements are combined in very unequal proportions. All these remarks, however, will be unnecessary to those who are satisfied with the will of the Lord. For if it be his pleasure to appoint kings over kingdoms, and senators or other magistrates over free cities, it is our duty to be obedient to any governors whom God has established over the places in which we reside.

———

From John Calvin, *Institutes of the Christian Religion,* John Allen trans.

ANALYSIS AND INTERPRETATION OF THE READINGS

1. To what extent was Columbus guilty of exaggeration in describing the new lands he had discovered?
2. Explain Luther's interpretation of "good works."
3. In relation to the theory of predestination, what does Calvin mean by the statement, "We consider calling as an evidence of election"?
4. What differences do you detect between Luther and Calvin in their views of government and the role of the people under government?

CHAPTER 20 | A Century of Crisis for Early-Modern Europe (c. 1560–c. 1660)

CHRONOLOGY

1555	1588	1648
1562	1598	1649
1572	1609	1659

From the list above, select the correct date for each of the following:

Massacre of St. Bartholomew's Day_____

Peace of the Pyrenees _____

Edict of Nantes _____

Defeat of the Spanish Armada _____

Recognition of independent Dutch Republic _____

Execution of Charles I _____

Religious Peace of Augsburg _____

Peace of Westphalia _____

Outbreak of civil war in France _____

IDENTIFICATIONS

In the blank below each description write the correct name selected from the list below:

Gustavus Adolphus   Cardinal Richelieu
Oliver Cromwell   Emperor Charles V
Pope Innocent VIII   Henry of Navarre
William the Silent   James I

1. Although he was a deadly foe of the Stuarts and their abuses, he ended by exercising more arbitrary power than any Stuart ever knew.

_____

2. This king of Scotland and England was, in the opinion of a French contemporary, "the wisest fool in Christendom."

_____

3. This seventeenth-century prince of the church was instrumental in making his country the most powerful in Europe and in leading it far along the road to royal despotism.

_____

4. A convert from Catholicism, this wealthy nobleman led the Dutch struggle against the rule of Philip II of Spain.

_____

5. Although a Lutheran, this Scandinavian ruler fought in Germany as an ally of Catholic France.

_____

6. This king who converted to Catholicism for political reasons gave France one of the most benevolent and progressive reigns in the country's history.

_____

Select the appropriate letter to complete each of the following:

_____1. Montaigne's *Essays* are characterized by: (a) mystical pietism; (b) rationalism and materialism; (c) carefully disguised atheism; (d) skepticism and tolerance.

117

_____2. The author of *Six Books on the Commonwealth* was: (a) Jean Bodin; (b) Oliver Cromwell; (c) Thomas Hobbes; (d) the duke of Sully.

_____3. The most radical political and economic theories in seventeenth-century England were those advanced by: (a) the Puritans; (b) the Presbyterians; (c) the Diggers; (d) the Levellers.

_____4. The political philosopher Thomas Hobbes: (a) upheld the right of revolution; (b) viewed the ideal state as a theocracy; (c) regarded the state of nature as a condition of war; (d) stressed the inherent goodness of human nature.

_____5. Blaise Pascal, the author of *Pensées*: (a) was a French Lutheran; (b) persecuted the Huguenots; (c) upheld the supremacy of reason; (d) believed that faith alone could save man from his wretched state.

_____6. A common characteristic of the works of the great Elizabethan dramatists was: (a) an exuberant national pride; (b) unmitigated optimism; (c) glorification of royal absolutism; (d) weariness and disillusionment.

_____7. John Milton: (a) was the author of a major poem, classical in form, Christian in content; (b) was a classical scholar who wrote a great Latin epic; (c) protested against the execution of Charles I; (d) was a Puritan zealot who advocated censorship of the press.

_____8. The colonnade in front of St. Peter's basilica was the work of: (a) Michelangelo; (b) El Greco; (c) Bernini; (d) Byzantine sculptors.

Explain the meaning of each of the following (if a literary or artistic work, name the author or artist):

Huguenots	Cavaliers and Roundheads
"Invincible Armada"	Commonwealth
intendants	*Leviathan*
the *Fronde*	*Volpone*
"No bishop, no king"	*The Tempest*
Petition of Right	*Paradise Lost*
ship money	Baroque
prerogative courts	*Massacre of the Innocents*

STUDY QUESTIONS

1. What other period or periods of history that you have already studied offer parallels to Europe's "iron century"? What difference do you detect between the problems of the fourteenth century and those of the period 1560–1660?

2. What were the causes of the "price revolution"? Why was inflation harder on the poor than on the rich?

3. What was the impact of the price revolution on governments?

4. Assess the validity of this statement about Europe's "iron century": "Given prevalent attitudes, newly arisen religious rivalries made wars inevitable."

5. What made the religious wars of the latter half of the sixteenth century more brutal than those previously fought by Europeans, including the medieval crusades?

6. What was the importance of the Peace of Augsburg? What were its weaknesses?

7. Summarize the provisions of Henry IV's Edict of Nantes. In what ways did it advance religious freedom? In what ways was religious freedom still limited?

8. Explain why antagonisms between Catholics and Protestants in the Netherlands led to a revolt against Spanish rule.

9. Why was the defeat of the Spanish Armada "one of the most decisive battles of Western history"?

10. How did religious disputes contribute to the outbreak of the Thirty Years' War? Why did religion become subordinated to other issues in the course of the conflict?

11. Explain why access to huge quantities of American silver failed to prevent Spain's economic decline.

12. What did each of the following contribute to the development of strong central government in France: Henry IV, the duke of Sully, Cardinal Richelieu?

13. Why did the revolt known as the Fronde fail to check the growth of centralized absolutism in France?

14. Louis XIV was "the most effective royal absolutist in all of French history." What made him so?

15. "Compared to the civil disturbances of the 1640s in Spain and France, those in England proved the most momentous in their results for the history of limited government." Explain this statement.

16. What were the reasons for the unpopularity of King James I with his English subjects? Did he fully deserve this unpopularity?

17. Describe the part played by each of the following in causing the English Civil War: the Puritan religious movement, the Crown's struggle for increased revenue, the Stuart rulers' political doctrines, the Scottish war of 1640.

18. The period of the Commonwealth and Protectorate constitutes England's only experiment with a republican form of government. Why was the experiment abandoned? Was it a complete failure?

19. To what extent was the witchcraft hysteria of the period 1560–1660 a religious phenomenon? What other factors help account for it?

20. Compare the political theories of Jean Bodin and Thomas Hobbes. Which of them was more absolutist in his point of view? Why was Hobbes generally unpopular with royalists in spite of his championing of absolutism?

21. What is the social and psychological significance of Cervantes' greatest work?

22. Describe briefly the characteristics of Shakespeare's plays from each of the three periods that mark his career as a dramatist.

23. Both the Mannerist and the Baroque styles of painting reflected the influence of religion. What were the differences between the two styles?
24. What Baroque characteristics are found in the work of Rubens?
25. What is the justification for claiming Rembrandt as the greatest of all Netherlandish painters?

PROBLEMS

1. Why did absolutism decline in England at a time when it was rising on the Continent?
2. Compare the political role of the Huguenots in France with that of the Puritans in England.
3. Investigate further any of the following:
   a. The Huguenot communities in southern France
   b. The witchcraft hysteria
   c. The impact of the price revolution of the late sixteenth century
   d. The French court under the cardinals Richelieu and Mazarin
   e. The Dutch struggle for independence
   f. The reign of Henry IV of France
   g. The influence of the Puritans on English thought and English politics in the seventeenth century
   h. The career of Oliver Cromwell
4. Explore the waxing and waning of Habsburg influence in Europe.
5. Read several of Montaigne's *Essays* to discover what light they throw on the character of the age in which he wrote.
6. How does the Baroque style in painting, sculpture, or architecture reflect the dominant interests, ideals, or passions of the period? Illustrate your judgments by citing specific works.

AIDS TO AN UNDERSTANDING OF A CENTURY OF CRISIS FOR EARLY-MODERN EUROPE

KING JAMES I's Conception of the Divine Right of Kings

The state of monarchy is the supremes thing upon earth; for kings are not only God's lieutenants upon earth, and sit upon God's throne, but even by God himself are called gods. There be three principal similitudes that illustrate the state of monarchy: one taken out of the word of God; and the two other out of the grounds of policy and philosophy. In the Scriptures kings are called gods, and so their power after a certain relation compared to the divine power. Kings are also compared to fathers of families: for a king is truly *Parens patriae*, the politique father of his people. And lastly, kings are compared to the head of this microcosm of the body of man.

Kings are justly called gods, for that they exercise a manner or resemblance of divine power upon earth: for if you will consider the attributes to God, you shall see how they agree in the person of a king. God hath power to create or destroy, make or unmake at his pleasure, to give life or send death, to judge all and to be judged nor accountable to none; to raise low things and to make high things low at his pleasure, and to God are both souls and body due. And the like power have kings: they make and unmake their subjects, they have power of raising and casting down, of life and of death, judges over all their subjects and in all causes and yet accountable to none but God only. . . .

I conclude then this point touching the power of kings with this axiom of divinity, That as to dispute what God may do is blasphemy. . . . so is it sedition in subjects to dispute what a king may do in the height of his power. But just kings will ever be willing to declare what they will do, if they will not incur the curse of God. I will not be content that my power be disputed upon; but I shall ever be willing to make the reason appear of all my doings, and rule my actions according to my laws. . . . I would wish you to be careful to avoid three things in the matter of grievances:

First, that you do not meddle with the main points of government, that is my craft . . . to meddle with that were to lesson me. . . . I must not be taught my office.

Secondly, I would not have you meddle with such ancient rights of mine as I have received from my predecessors. . . . All novelties are dangerous as well in a politic as in a natural body, and therefore I would be loath to be quarreled in my ancient rights and possessions; for that were to judge me unworthy of that which my predecessors had and left me.

And lastly, I pray you beware to exhibit for grievance anything that is established by a settled law, and whereunto . . . you know I will never give a plausible answer; for it is an undutiful part in subjects to press their king, wherein they know beforehand he will refuse them.

From King James I, *Works* (1609).

REPLY OF THE HOUSE OF COMMONS TO KING JAMES I, 1604

Most Gracious Sovereign:

. . . With all humble and due respect to your Majesty, our sovereign lord and head, against these misinformations we most truly avouch, first, that our privileges and liberties are our right and due inheritance, no less than our very lands and goods. Secondly, that they cannot be withheld from us, denied, or impaired, but with apparent wrong to the whole state of the realm. Thirdly, that our making of request in the entrance of parliament to enjoy our privilege is an act only of manners, and doth weaken our right no more than our suing to the king for our lands by petition, which form, though new and more decent than the old by *praecipe*, yet the subject's right is no less than of old. Fourthly, we avouch also that our House is a court of record, and so ever esteemed. Fifthly, that there is not the highest standing court in this land that ought to enter into competency either for dignity or authority with this high court of parliament, which with your Majesty's royal assent gives laws to other courts, but from other courts receives neither laws or orders.

Sixthly, and lastly, we avouch that the House of Commons is the sole proper judge of return of all such writs, and of the election of all such members as belong unto it, without which the freedom of election were not entire; and that the chancery, though a standing court under your majesty, be to send out those writs and receive the returns and to preserve them, yet the same is done only for the use of the parliament; over which neither the chancery nor any other court ever had or ought to have any manner of jurisdiction.

The rights and liberties of the Commons of England consisteth chiefly of these three things: first, that the shires, cities, and boroughs of England, by representation to be present, have free choice of such persons as they shall put in trust to represent them; secondly, that the persons chosen, during the time of the parliament, as also of their access and recess, be free form restraint, arrest and imprisonment; thirdly, that in parliament they may speak freely their consciences without check and controlment, doing the same with due reverence to the sovereign court of parliament, that is, to your Majesty and both the Houses, who all in this case make but one politic body, whereof your Highness is the head. . . .

From *Journals of the House of Commons*, Vol. I, 1547–1629

AN ENGLISH JUSTIFICATION OF ABSOLUTISM
Thomas Hobbes

The only way to erect such a common power as may be able to defend them from the invasion of foreigners and the injuries of one another, and thereby to secure them in such sort as that by their own industry and by the fruits of the earth they may nourish themselves and live contentedly, is to confer all their power and strength upon one man, or upon one assembly of men, that may reduce all their wills by plurality of voices unto one will; which is as much to say, to appoint one man or assembly of men to bear their person; and every one to own and acknowledge himself to be author of whatsoever he that so beareth their person shall act, or cause to be acted, in those things which concern the common peace and safety; and therein to submit their wills, every one to his will, and their judgments to his judgment. This is more than consent or concord: it is a real unity of them all, in one and the same person,

made by covenant of every man with every man, in such manner as if every man should say to every man. 'I authorize and give up my right of governing myself to this man, or to this assembly of men, on this condition, that thou give up thy right to him and authorize all his actions in like manner.' This done, the multitude so united in one person is called a 'commonwealth,' in Latin *civitas*. This is the generation of that great 'leviathan,' or, rather, to speak more reverently, of that 'mortal god,' to which we owe under the 'immortal God,' our peace and defence. For by this authority, given him by every particular man in the commonwealth, he hath the use of so much power and strength conferred on him that by terror thereof he is enabled to perform the wills of them all, to peace at home and mutual aid against their enemies abroad. And in him consisteth the essence of the commonwealth; which, to define it, is 'one person, of whose acts a great multitude by mutual covenants one with another have made themselves every one the author, to the end he may use the strength and means of them all as he shall think expedient for their peace and common defence.'

And he that carrieth this person is called 'sovereign,' and said to have 'sovereign power'; and every one besides his 'subject.'

The attaining to this sovereign power is by two ways. One by natural force, as when a man maketh his children to submit themselves and their children to his government, as being able to destroy them if they refuse; or by war subdueth his enemies to his will, giving them their lives on that condition. The other is when men agree amongst themselves to submit to some man, or assembly of men, voluntarily, on confidence to be protected by him against all others. This latter may be called a political commonwealth, or commonwealth by 'institution'; and the former, a commonwealth by 'acquisition.'

From Thomas Hobbes, *Leviathan.*

THE THINKING REED: From *Pensées*
Blaise Pascal

Our intelligence occupies the same position in the realm of intelligible things as our body in the realm of nature.

Limited in every direction, this middle state between two extremes is characteristic of all our faculties. Our senses do not register extremes; too much noise deafens us; too much light dazzles us; too great or too short a distance impedes our view; too long or too short an address makes it obscure; too strong a dose of truth staggers us (I know people who cannot understand that four from nought leaves nought); first principles are too obvious for us; too much pleasure incommodes us; too many harmonies are displeasing in music, and too many benefactions are a source of irritation: we want the means to overpay the debt. We do not feel either extreme heat or extreme cold. Qualities which are excessive are inimical to us and not perceptible; we do not feel them; we suffer them. The extremes of youth and age stultify the mind, like too much or too little learning. In short, extremes do not exist for us, or we for them: they escape us, or we them.

That is our veritable condition. It is that which makes us incapable either of certain knowledge or of absolute ignorance.

We float over a vast expanse, always uncertain and drifting, tossed hither and thither. Whatever the point to which we seek to attach ourselves to consolidate our position, it shifts and leaves us; and if we follow it, it eludes our grasp, slips away and flies from us in unending flight. Nothing stops for us. It is the state which is natural to us, and at the same time the one most contrary to our inclinations; we burn with the desire to find a stable position, a solid base for building a tower which will rise to infinity; but our entire foundations crack; the earth opens like a vast abyss.

Therefore, let us not look for security and stability. Our reason is always cheated by deceitful appearances; nothing can stabilise the finite between the two infinites which enclose it, and fly from it.

Once this is clearly understood, I think that we can remain at peace in ourselves, each of us in the state to which nature has called him. Since the middle state which has fallen to our lot is always far from the extremes, what does it matter if one [man] has a little more understanding than another? If he has, it simply means that he is a little quicker in grasping them. Is he not always an infinite distance from the end, and is not the span of our life equally tiny in the bosom of eternity, whether or not it lasts another ten years?

In the sight of these infinites all finite things are equal; and I do not see why I should fix my imagination on one rather than on the other. The mere comparison between ourselves and the finite is painful to us.

If man studied himself first, he would see how incapable he is of going further. How could a part come to know a whole?— But he may perhaps try to get to know at least the parts when there is some proportion between him and them? But the parts of the world are so inter-related and their connection with one another such that I believe that it is impossible to know one without the other and without the whole.

There is, for example, a relation between man and everything that he knows. He needs space to contain him, time in which to exist, motion in order to live, warmth and food to nourish [him], air to breathe; he sees light; he feels bodies; in short, he has a relationship with everything. In order to know man, therefore, we must know why he needs air to breathe; and, to understand air, to understand why it plays the part it does in man's life, etc.

Flame cannot exist without air; thus in order to know one it is necessary to know the other.

It follows that as all things are caused and causing, supported and supporting, mediate and immediate, and all held together by a natural and imperceptible link which joins the most distant and diverse, I am convinced that it is impossible to know the parts without knowing the whole, any more than we can know the whole without a detailed knowledge of the parts.

[The eternity of things in itself or in God must still be a source of astonishment in our little life. The fixed and unchanging immobility of nature compared with the changes continually taking place in ourselves ought to produce on us the same effect.]

And what crowns our incapacity to know things is that they are simple in themselves and that we are composed of two opposite natures which are different in kind: soul and body. For it is impossible that the part of us which reasons should be other than spiritual; and if it were claimed that we were simply cor-poreal, it would exclude us all the more completely from the knowledge of things because there is nothing so inconceivable as saying that matter knows itself; it is not possible for us to say how it could know itself.

And so, if we [are] purely material we can know nothing at all, and if we are composed of spirit and matter, we cannot know simple things perfectly, whether spiritual or corporeal.

That is why almost all philosophers confuse the ideas of things, speaking in spiritual terms of material things, and in material terms of spiritual things. For they declare boldly that bodies fall, that they aspire towards their centre, that they flee destruction, that they fear the void, that [they have] inclinations, sympathies, antipathies, which are all attributes belonging only to minds. And in speaking of minds, they treat them as being localised in a particular place, and ascribe to them the faculty of moving from one place to another, which are qualities that belong only to bodies.

Instead of perceptions being received in their pure form, they are coloured by our own attributes, and we set the stamp [of] our composite being on all the simple things which confront us.

Who would not imagine, when he saw us endow everything with mind and body, that such a mixture would be perfectly comprehensible to us? It is nevertheless the thing that we understand least. In his own eyes, man is the most marvellous object in the world; for he cannot grasp what a body is, still less what a mind is, and least of all how a body can be joined to a mind. That is his supreme difficulty, and yet it is the essence of his being.

Finally, in order to complete the demonstration of our weakness, I will close by these two observations. . . . Man is only a reed, the feeblest thing in nature; but he is a thinking reed. It is not necessary for the entire universe to take up arms in order to crush him: a vapour, a drop of water is sufficient to kill him. But if the universe crushed him, man would still be nobler than the thing which destroys him because he knows that he is dying; and the universe which has him at its mercy, is unaware of it.

All our dignity therefore lies in thought. It is by thought that we must raise ourselves, and not by space or time, which we could never fill. Let us apply ourselves then to thinking well; that is the first principle of morality. . . .

From *Pascal's Pensées*, Martin Turnell, trans. pp. 218–21. Harvill Press, London, 1962.

ANALYSIS AND INTERPRETATION OF THE READINGS

1. What part did the rights of the people play in the struggle between James I and the English Parliament?
2. What was the real point at issue between king and parliament?
3. Upon what grounds does Thomas Hobbes justify absolute government?
4. What does Pascal mean when he writes that humanity is in a "middle state"? Why is thinking so important to Pascal that he describes it as "the first principle of morality"?

CHAPTER 21

India, East Asia, and Africa During the Early-Modern Era (c. 1500–1800)

CHRONOLOGY

Supply the date or dates for each of the following events bearing on the history of India:

1. Death of Babur, founder of the Mughal Dynasty

_____

2. Beginning of the reign of Akbar, "the Great Mughal"

_____

3. Chartering of the British East India Company

_____

4. Reign of Shah Jahan, builder of the Taj Mahal

_____

5. Acquisition of Bombay by the British

_____

6. Sack of Delhi by Nadir Shah

_____

Below is a list of events from the history of China, Japan, and Africa. For each item, write in the blank the number of the item from the India list to which it corresponds most closely in time.

_____ Beginning of Qing (Manchu) Dynasty

_____ Arrival of first Portuguese vessel at Guangzhou (Canton)

_____ Establishment of Portuguese settlement at Macao

_____ Establishment of Tokugawa Shogunate

_____ Suppression of Christianity in Japan and beginning of policy of isolation

_____ Beginning of reign of Kangxi

_____ Beginning of reign of Qianlong

_____ Portuguese lose enclaves in West Africa to the Dutch

_____ Chartering of Royal Africa Company

IDENTIFICATIONS

You should be able to define or explain the importance of each of the following:

Hamayun	Lord George Macartney
Shivaji	daimyo
Nanak	Hideyoshi
Urdu	samurai
Tulsi Das	"floating world"
Sultan Ibrahim II	Kabuki drama
Seven Years War	Oyo kingdom
Manchu	"New Christians"
Dorgon	jihad
banner units	*Asiento*
White Lotus Society	Boers
Six Records of a Floating Life	Ogboni Society

STUDY QUESTIONS

1. How did the Mughal Dynasty of India get its name? Was the title appropriate? Why or why not?
2. What significant changes in governmental policy were introduced by Akbar? To what extent were they beneficial?
3. What measures did Akbar take to win the allegiance of his Hindu subjects?

4. Describe Akbar's unique religious establishment. How successful was it?

5. In spite of impressive achievements, how did the long reign of Aurangzeb weaken the Mughal state?

6. How were the Sikhs and the Marathas, respectively, threats to Mughal power in the seventeenth and eighteenth centuries?

7. Cite specific examples to show that Indian culture of the Mughal period was eclectic and cosmopolitan.

8. What date would you assign to the final ascendancy of the British over the French in India?

9. What policies did the Qing emperors adopt to confirm their legitimacy as rulers of China? In what ways did the Chinese and Manchus remain separate?

10. What was at issue in the "War of the Three Feudatories"? What were its results?

11. Examine tax policies under Kangxi. What were the purposes behind his policies? What were the strengths and weaknesses of his taxation policies?

12. What problems were created by China's swelling population during the Qing period? How did the government deal with these problems?

13. In what respects did the position of women deteriorate during the Qing period? Are there any ways in which it improved?

14. What did the following Jesuits contribute to China: Matteo Ricci, Ferdinand Verbiest, Giuseppe Castiglione?

15. What was the Jesuit approach to missionary work in China? What were its advantages and disadvantages? How did it lead to conflict with other Catholic orders?

16. How did the "School of Han Learning" contribute to Chinese philosophy and learning? What was the contribution of Gu Yanwu?

17. What new problems were posed for the governments of both China and Japan by the coming of European traders to their ports? How did the two governments differ in their attempts to handle these problems?

18. Explain the key features of the government of Japan under the Tokugawa Shoguns. How effective was this government?

19. What specific measures did the Tokugawa Shoguns take to control the daimyo?

20. What important economic changes took place in Japan during the Tokugawa period? How did these changes threaten the survival of the Shogunate?

21. What intellectual and religious trends were at work in Japan that could also undermine the Shogun's position?

22. Describe the Japanese social hierarchy in theory and in practice. Why did theory and practice sometimes diverge?

23. Describe the importance of sugar in the African economy during this period. What was the role of sugar in the development of the Atlantic slave trade?

24. What were the effects of the slave trade on African societies? Give specific examples.

25. When did the shipment of slaves from Africa directly to the Americas begin, and why?

26. What were the Portuguese goals in Africa? How successful were the Portuguese in attaining these goals?

27. Compare the forms of government in the Oyo and Dahomean empires. In what ways were they similar? In what ways did they differ from one another?

28. What was the purpose of claims of divinity by African monarchs? How did this divinity manifest itself?

29. How did the nature of European involvement in Africa change after the opening of the sixteenth century?

30. How do you explain the flourishing of Asante civilization during the first half of the eighteenth century?

31. "History took another, more tragic, course in the extreme southwest corner of Africa." Explain this statement.

PROBLEMS

1. Every one of the Mughal rulers of India between 1526 and 1707 offers an interesting and colorful subject for study. Akbar was undoubtedly one of the most remarkable personalities ever to govern a state. Look into Akbar's intellectual and religious activities, his relations with Portuguese Jesuits, or his building program.

2. Examine the contrasts in character and personality among the first three Mughal rulers who succeeded Akbar.

3. Trace the evolution of the Indo-Muslim style of architecture.

4. Investigate the origins and development of the religion of the Sikhs.

5. Analyze the remarkable population growth in China under the Qing Dynasty and its probable causes.

6. Compare the background, personality, and governing style of Akbar and Kangxi. (For Kangxi, you might start with Jonathan Spence, *Emperor of China: Self-Portrait of K'ang Hsi.*)

7. Examine the writings of Voltaire or other leading exponents of the European Enlightenment for evidence of Western awareness of and reactions to Chinese civilization (actual or imagined).

8. Study the Chinese family system as reflected in the novel *Dream of the Red Chamber* (trans. C. C. Wang).

9. Investigate any of these aspects of Chinese culture during the Qing period: the "School of Han Learning"; scholars; painting; architecture; the drama; the cult of Confucius.

10. "Most specialists now believe that population growth in China had outstripped the carrying capacity of the land at the current level of technology in China by the end of Qianlong's reign." Examine the implications of this statement in light of the English economist Thomas Malthus's famous theory about population growth and resources.

11. Study the suppression of Christianity by the early Tokugawa Shoguns; the origins and development of Kabuki

drama; development of the Japanese wood-block print; or city life in Japan during the Tokugawa period.

12. Read Thomas C. Smith's *The Agrarian Origins of Modern Japan* and evaluate his argument about Tokugawa-period economic changes.

13. Examine African art from this period. Read William Bascom's *African Art in Cultural Perspective*. What does the art tell you about the societies that produced it?

14. Explore the role of the missionary impulse in Africa.

15. Explore in more detail the impact of European rivalries on African history.

16. Investigate the founding and activities of the Royal African Company.

17. Study African religious beliefs. How did these religious beliefs affect daily life? How did they affect art? How did they affect interaction with Europeans?

AIDS TO AN UNDERSTANDING OF INDIA, EAST ASIA, AND AFRICA DURING THE EARLY MODERN ERA

CHARACTER OF AKBAR THE GREAT MUGHAL
V. A. Smith

Akbar, as seen in middle life, was a man of moderate stature, perhaps five feet seven inches in height, strongly built, neither too slight nor too stout, broad-chested, narrow-waisted, and long-armed. His legs were somewhat bowed inwards from the effect of much riding in boyhood, and when walking he slightly dragged the left leg, as if he were lame, although the limb was sound. His head drooped a little towards the right shoulder. His forehead was broad and open. The nose was of moderate size, rather short, with a bony prominence in the middle, and nostrils dilated as if with anger. A small wart about half the size of a pea which connected the left nostril with the upper lip was considered to be a lucky mark. His black eyebrows were thin, and the Mongolian strain of blood in his veins was indicated by the narrow eyes characteristic of the Tartar, Chinese, and Japanese races. The eyes sparkled brightly and were "vibrant like the sea in sunshine." His complexion, sometimes described by the Indian term "wheat-coloured," was dark rather than fair. His face was clean shaven, except for a small, closely trimmed moustache worn in the fashion adopted by young Turks on the verge of manhood. His hair was allowed to grow, not being clipped close in the ancestral manner. His very loud voice was credited with "a peculiar richness." . . .

Akbar was extremely moderate in his diet, taking but one substantial meal in the day, which was served whenever he called for it, not at any fixed hour. The variety of dishes placed at his disposal was of course great, and they were presented with appropriate magnificence and elaborate precautions against poison. He cared little for flesh food, and gave up the use of it almost entirely in the later years of his life, when he came under Jain influence. . . .

He followed the practice of his family for many generations in consuming both strong drink and various preparations of opium, sometimes to excess. His drinking bouts, naturally, were more frequent while he was young than they were in his more mature years, but it is certain that tolerably often he was

"in his cups," as his son puts it. When he had drunk more than was good for him he performed various mad freaks, as when at Agra he galloped the elephant Hawai across the bridge of boats, and at Surat tried to fight his sword. . . .

He took special delight in the practice of mechanical arts with his own hands. We are told that "there is nothing that he does not know how to do, whether matters of war, or of administration, or of any mechanical art. Wherefore he takes particular pleasure in making guns and in founding and modelling cannon." Workshops were maintained on a large scale within the palace enclosure, and were frequently visited by him. He was credited with many inventions and improvements. That side of his character suggests a comparison with Peter the Great. . . .

"A monarch," he said, "should be ever intent on conquest, otherwise his neighbours rise in arms against him. The army should be exercised in warfare, lest from want of training they become self-indulgent." Accordingly he continued to be intent on conquest all his life and to keep his army in constant training. He never attained more than a part of the objective of his ambition, which included the conquest of every part of India besides Central Asia. . . .

In 1582 he resolved to attempt the impossible task of providing all sects in his empire with one universal eclectic religion to which he gave the name of Divine Monotheism. He persuaded himself that he was the vicegerent of the Almighty, empowered to rule the spiritual as well as the temporal concerns of his subjects. That audacious attempt was an utter failure, but Akbar never formally admitted the fact, and to the end of his life he persisted in maintaining the farce of the new religion. From the time he proclaimed that creed he was not a Muslim. The formula of initiation required the categorical apostasy from Islam of the person initiated.

His attitude towards religion expressed the queer mixture in his mind of mysticism, rationalism, superstition, and a profound belief in his own God-given powers. His actions at times gave substantial grounds for the reproach that he was not unwilling to be regarded as a God on earth.

From V. A. Smith, *Akbar the Great Mogul (1542–1605)*, Clarendon Press, 1919. Reprinted by permission of the publisher.

CONFUCIAN CLASSICS AND THE CHINESE EXAMINATION SYSTEM
Matteo Ricci

I think it will be as interesting as it is new to the reader to treat somewhat more fully of this phase of their studies. Confucius, called the Prince of Chinese Philosophers, compiled four volumes of the works of more ancient philosophers and wrote five books of his own. These five he entitled "The Doctrines," and they contain the ethical principles of right living, precepts governing the conduct of political life, customs, and examples of the ancients, their rites and sacrifices, and even samples of their poetry and other subjects of this nature. Besides these five books there is another one composed of the precepts of the great philosopher and of his disciples and compiled without particular arrangement. These are chiefly directions for proper moral proceedings, in the light of human reason, with a view to virtuous conduct on the part of the individual, of the family and of the kingdom in general. This volume, being a summary in excerpts from the four books mentioned, is called the Tetrabiblion. The nine books of Confucius, making up the most ancient of Chinese libraries, of which all others are a development, are written mostly in hieroglyphic characters, and present a collection of moral precepts for the future good and development of the kingdom.

There is a law in the land, handed down from ancient kings and confirmed by the custom of centuries, stating that he who wishes to be learned, and to be known as such, must draw his fundamental doctrine from these same books. In addition to this it is not sufficient for him to follow the general sense of the text, but what is far more difficult, he must be able to write aptly and exactly of every particular doctrine contained in these books. To this end he must commit the entire Tetrabiblion to memory, so as to be a recognized authority thereon. Contrary to what has been stated by some of our writers, there are no schools or public academies in which these books are taught or explained by masters. Each student selects his own master by whom he is instructed in his own home and at his personal expense.

The number of such private teachers, of course, is great, partly because it would be hard for one master to teach many at a time, owing to the difficulty of handling the Chinese characters, and partly because it is an old custom here for each home to have a private school for its own children. At times it happens that tutors, other than the one regularly employed, may be called in, as it would seem, to prevent the custom of bidding for the position from interfering with the interest of their profession.

In the field of philosophy there are three degrees, conferred upon those who pass the written examinations assigned for each degree. The first degree is awarded in the larger cities and in a public academy, by some prominent scholar, appointed by the emperor for that purpose. In virtue of his office this dignitary is known as Tihio, and the first degree, corresponding to our baccalaureate, is called Lieucai. The Tihio visits the various cities of his province in which the degree is to be conferred and for which a triple examination is required. Upon the arrival of this chancellor, as we would call him, the candidates assemble for the examinations. The preliminary examination is conducted by the local teachers who have attained to the baccalaureate and are preparing for a higher degree, and they are paid from the royal treasury for these particular examinations. Anyone may be admitted to the preliminary examinations, and sometimes four or five thousand from a single district will take them. Those who pass the first test are recommended by the teachers to the four city prefects, who are themselves learned men, otherwise they would not be in office. The prefects then select the candidates who are to be presented to the chancellor. Not more than two hundred may be thus presented, and these are chosen for the excellence of their written composition.

The third examination is conducted by the chancellor, himself, and is far more rigid than those preceding it. Of the two hundred admitted to this examination, the twenty or thirty obtaining the highest grades are granted the degree, depending upon the size of the district from which the candidates are drawn. They are then known as academic bachelors, a distinguished class representing the advanced citizenry of their particular town, and their company is cultivated by all who hope to attain to the same dignity. Their particular insignia is an ankle-long gown, a cap, and leggings, which no class other than their own is permitted to wear. They are given seats of honor at the conventions of the magistrates, and with them they may employ the more intimate rites of address which the common people are never permitted to use. In their home cities they enjoy a great many civil privileges and are looked upon as inferior to none, save the chancellor and the four city prefects, nor is it easy for other magistrates to pass judgment upon the cases they present or on charges made against them.

From *China in the Sixteenth Century: The Journals of Matthew Ricci: 1583–1610.* pp. 33–34. Louis J. Gallagher, S.J., trans. Random House, New York, 1953.

TOWN LIFE UNDER THE TOKUGAWA (Genroku Period, 1688–1703)
G. B. Sansom

The life of the townspeople, especially in the Genroku period, judged if not by European practice at least by European standards, appears to have been extremely dissolute; though it must be remembered that their numbers were few in comparison with the industrious millions of peasants, and also that we learn from books and pictures chiefly of their more extravagant amusements. Further, their morality was not based upon religious emotion, nor was it conditioned by fear of divine retribution. In the history of Japanese thought little part is played by the personal sense of sin, which in Western men has engendered puritanical complexes and driven them to extremes of restless inquiry and despair. The Japanese have cared little for abstract ideas of Good and Evil, but they have always been concerned with problems of behaviour, as questions of a man's duty not so much to himself as to the society of which he is a member. It is therefore not surprising that the most influential moralists of the period, notably Yamaga Soko and Ogyu

(Butsu) Sorai, held utilitarian views which might have been stated by Hobbes in his Leviathan. In general Chinese and Japanese philosophers have tended to the belief that man's disposition is innately good. They have agreed that he needs guidance, and they have set great store by decorum, but they have mostly reprobated only such actions as entail direct evil consequences to society.

One should bear these considerations in mind when studying the life of the Floating World in Yedo, for—the deplorable fact cannot be concealed—its principal figures were the courtesan and the actor, while among its supernumeraries were the disreputable crowd of pandars and procurers who haunted the gay quarters. There had been since the early days of Yedo, at a place on its outskirts called Yoshiwara (Reedy Plain), a pleasure haunt where the citizens gathered to see plays and dancing; and here prostitutes plied their trade until they were suppressed by the Bakufu. In 1617 an enterprising townsman obtained a licence from the authorities, set up the business again, and succeeded in attracting large numbers of citizens to the quarter. Its name, by a change of ideograph, he had altered to mean Happy Fields; but they were soon deserted owing to the competition of a class of female bath-attendants who came into fashion at this time. The bath-houses became gay resorts, whose stylishly dressed clients, both townsmen and the lower orders of samurai, were entertained by the much bedizened bath-girls. One of the most celebrated of these establishments was in front of the mansion of a great daimyo and this open flaunting of illicit prostitution caused the Bakufu to suppress the bath-girls in 1650. After the great fires of 1657–1658 the Yoshiwara was removed to a different district, where the bath-girls and others assembled. By Genroku it was exceedingly flourishing, and is said to have contained some two thousand courtesans. Known as *Fuyajo* or the Nightless City, it was almost self-contained, since it harboured as well as those ladies a numerous population of their attendants, of dancing and singing girls, jesters and other entertainers, together with a most varied collection of trades-people to supply their needs. Hither resorted not only the young townsmen, but also samurai in disguise, and even high officers of the Shogun or his vassals, while rich merchants were known to give costly, fantastic entertainments within its walls. There thus grew up a distinct town, with its own customs, its own standards of behaviour, and even its own language. In this world of licence and disorder, everything was highly regulated. There was a formal etiquette between a house and its clients. There was a strict hierarchy among the courtesans, whose ranks and appellations were solemnly observed. They were treated with forms of great respect, attended by richly-dressed waiting maids and hedged about by an elaborate ritual. From time to time they made public progress through the streets of the quarter, in stately processions which were eagerly witnessed by thousands of spectators from all parts of the city. Everything seems to have been done to make patrons feel that they were sojourning among people of discreet and delicate sentiments. It was, of course, an essentially sordid business, but it does seem to have been invested with glamour and even a certain elegance. The social side of family life was, probably owing to the subordination of women, undeveloped except in its formal aspects, and the townspeople were debarred from public functions: so that it is perhaps not unnatural that they should have flocked to places where they found light and colour and feminine society in luxurious surroundings. However, that may be, the pleasure quarters were a conspicuous feature of city life, not only in Yedo, but in Kyoto, where there was the famous district of Shimabara, in Osaka, which boasted of its Shin-machi, and in many smaller towns, such as the more important stages on the main highways. Many of them were founded in much earlier times, but it was in Genroku, that, to quote from an eighteenth century work, "their splendour was by day like Paradise and by night like the Palace of the Dragon King." Their prosperity encouraged all the crafts of the entertainer, such as instrumental music, dancing and singing, to say nothing of juggling and buffoonery, while their variegated life attracted artists of a Bohemian temperament. The pleasure quarter offered the most tempting models to a painter, in the movement of crowds, the colour of costumes, and the shapes of women who lived by their beauty; the playwright and the novelist could find there all the tragedy and all the comedy they desired; and since the great courtesans and the leading rakes, their patrons, were known by name to all the gossips in the city, books and pictures which depicted their amours or their adventures had a ready sale.

From G. B. Sansom, *Japan: A Short Cultural History*, rev. ed., Appleton-Century, 1929. Reprinted by permission of the publisher.

THE SLAVE TRADE IN AFRICA
J. D. Fage

The buying and selling of slaves on the coast was a complicated business. In the first place, where African political authority extended over Europeans, slaves could usually not be bought or sold without the permission of the African chief. For example, the chiefs of the tribes at the mouths of the Oil Rivers would not allow trade to begin until duties had been paid. At Whydah on the Slave Coast, European factors were required to purchase a trading licence for each visiting ship. They were then required to buy the king's stock of slaves at a price well above the current market price before they were allowed to complete their cargo with slaves bought from private merchants. In addition, the king levied a tax on the purchase price of every slave bought. Even where the Europeans were not subject to African authority, trade was usually impossible unless the European traders gave substantial and frequent presents to the local chiefs and elders.

There was no trading currency in common use throughout the coastal districts. On the Windward Coast, slaves and European imports were commonly valued in relation to bars of iron; on the Ivory Coast, to pieces of cloth; on the Gold Coast, to gold dust; between Accra and Keta, to cowrie shells; on the Slave Coast, to both iron and copper bars; in the Oil Rivers, to brass basins; in the Cameroons, to pieces of cloth. Iron and copper were used by the Africans for making tools and utensils, and were imported from Europe in standard size bars. It was accepted on the Slave Coast that one iron bar was worth four copper bars. Similarly, Europeans imported cloth in standard lengths. Now, except for cowrie shells and gold dust, these media of exchange were all commodities which could be consumed, and their value varied in accordance with the extent of the need for them. As a consequence, the process of bargaining in the slave trade was apt to be unduly complicated and lengthy. An example may help to make this clear. Let us say that on the Slave Coast a European trader who wanted slaves was doing business with an African who wanted guns. They had to agree on the value of a slave and of a gun in terms of bars, and to do this they needed to take into account not only the relative scarcity or abundance of slaves and guns on the coast at the time, but also the relative scarcity or abundance of iron and copper bars. Where the large trading companies were strongly established, possessing depots in which they kept adequate stocks of the imports most in demand, they tried to fix prices, saying, for example, that the price of a certain kind of gun was so many bars. But these prices could easily be upset by the arrival on the coast of an interloper whose trading might result in a temporary glut either of guns or of bars. In addition, the maintenance of stocks was apt to be a chancy business because African tastes for European goods were apt to change. For example, in one year blue cloth might be in great demand on one part of the coast and quite unsaleable on another only a few miles away, while a year later, for no reason apparent to the Europeans, the position might be reversed.

Once acceptable prices had been agreed upon, the slaves on sale were inspected by a surgeon from the ship or factory, and the old and infirm slaves weeded out. In general only about one-third of the slaves taken by Europeans were women. This was partly because less women were offered for sale, partly because the effects of child-bearing meant that the ages between which women could be considered fit for plantation slavery were more narrowly limited than for men. Men were usually taken between the ages of ten and about thirty-five; women usually only up to the age of twenty-five. The selected slaves were then usually branded with the mark of their purchaser and shipped, or confined within forts or factories awaiting shipment. . . .

The goods brought to West Africa by the European traders varied slightly according to the period, the nationality of the traders, and the place where they were trading, but the following commodities found a pretty steady sale: textiles (woollens and linens manufactured in Europe, cottons manufactured mostly in India until the nineteenth century, and silks manufactured either in Europe or in Asia); all kinds of firearms, powder, and shot; knives and cutlasses; many kinds of European-made ironmongery and hardware; iron, copper, brass, and lead in bar form; spirits (rum, brandy, or gin, according to the country of origin of the trader); and many kinds of provisions.

We do not have enough information to be able to state exactly how many African slaves were carried across the Atlantic to America. However, on the basis of the information we do possess, it seems likely that the number of slaves imported into America, from the time the trade began in the sixteenth century until it was eventually brought to an end in the nineteenth century, was at least fifteen million, and unlikely to have been much greater than twenty million. It should be noted that these figures are for the slaves *landed in America*. The number *leaving Africa* must have been considerably greater, since it was rare for a slave ship to complete a voyage without the death from disease of at least a part of its human cargo. It seems reasonable from what we know of the mortality on slaving voyages to assume that *on an average* at least a sixth of the slaves shipped from Africa never lived to see America. On occasions the mortality was very much higher than this. Thus in all probability, somewhere between eighteen and twenty-four million Africans were carried away from West Africa by the European Slave trade.

It has been stated that the number of slaves imported into America in the sixteenth century was at least 900,000. The subsequent growth of the demand for slaves on the plantations, and the intensive competition between European traders to supply this demand, soon made the sixteenth-century trade seem insignificant. In the seventeenth century the number of slaves reaching America was more than three times as great, at least 2,750,000, or an average of 27,500 a year. The eighteenth-century trade was on an even greater scale, at least 7,000,000 slaves reaching America, or 70,000 a year on the average. During the nineteenth century, the demand for slaves continued to increase at first, and it did not finally cease until by the 1880's all the American nations had at length abolished the status of slavery. The efforts made to stop the trade prevented a steady expansion as in the previous centuries; nevertheless, by the time the trade had finally come to an end, a further 4,000,000 slaves had arrived in America.

From J. D. Fage, *An Introduction to the History of West Africa*, 3rd ed., Cambridge University Press, 1962. Reprinted by permission of the publisher.

ANALYSIS AND INTERPRETATION OF THE READINGS

1. Which of the personality traits attributed to Akbar would be most valuable to him as a ruler?
2. What was the connection between education and the social order in China, judging from the journal of the Jesuit Matteo Ricci?
3. What light does the description of the Japanese "Floating World" of pleasure throw on the relations between the feudal classes and the townsmen?
4. Were any limitations imposed upon the Europeans who traded on the slave coast? If so, what kinds of limitations, and why would they have accepted them?

Overseas Exploration in the 15th and 16th Centuries

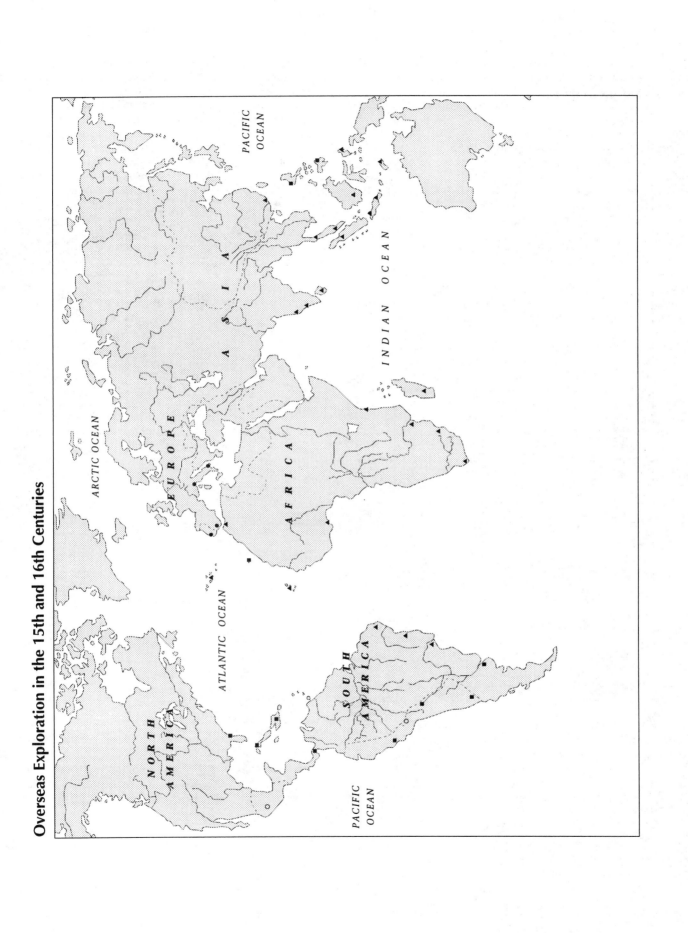

Europe in 1560

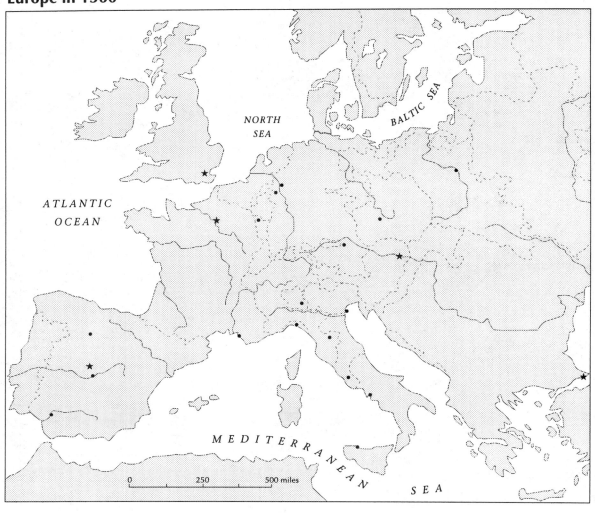

Overseas Exploration in the 15th and 16th Centuries and Europe in 1560

OVERSEAS EXPLORATION IN THE 15TH AND 16TH CENTURIES

1. On the "Exploration" map (see page 129), show the approximate routes followed by these explorers:

Christopher Columbus (first voyage; later voyages)
Bartholomew Diaz
Ferdinand Magellan (and Magellan's ship after his death)
Vasco Da Gama

2. Locate the areas of the Inca, Aztec, Ottoman, *and* Chinese *empires.*

3. Mark the following locations:

Labrador	Gold Coast
Hispaniola	Cape of Good Hope
Philippines	Malay Peninsula
East Indies	West Indies
Canary Islands	Madagascar

4. Label the following locations. Indicate with an S those that were controlled by the Spanish, and with a P those that were controlled by the Portuguese.

Havana	St. Augustine
Lima	Rio de Janeiro
Santiago	Buenos Aires
Panama	Goa
Calicut	Malacca
Macao	Ceuta

EUROPE IN 1560

1. On the "Europe in 1560" map (see page 130 opposite), outline the approximate boundary of the Holy Roman Empire *in the sixteenth century. Indicate the location of* France, Spain, Portugal, England, Poland, Austria, Denmark, *and the* Papal States.

2. Mark the following locations:

Genoa	Venice
Florence	Rome
Madrid	Seville
Bologna	Constantinople
Augsburg	Palermo
Vienna	Prague
Aachen	Worms
London	Geneva

3. Indicate with different shading or colors the areas of strongest influence of the following Christian religions: Anglican, Roman Catholic, Lutheran, Calvinist, Eastern Orthodox.

NOTES